W9-ACG-514

BYRON AND SHELLEY

BY THE SAME AUTHOR

Sir Philip Sidney and the English Renaissance
Elizabethan Taste
A Tradition of Poetry

Poems of Michael Drayton
Poems of Charles Cotton

BYRON AND SHELLEY

THE HISTORY OF A FRIENDSHIP

JOHN BUXTON

HARCOURT, BRACE & WORLD, INC.

NEW YORK

SALEM COLLEGE LIBRARY
WINSTON-SALEM, N. C.

PR
4383
B83
1968b

Copyright © 1968 by John Buxton

All rights reserved. No part of this publication may be reproduced or transmitted in any form or by any means, electronic or mechanical, including photocopy, recording, or any information storage and retrieval system, without permission in writing from the publisher.

First American edition

Library of Congress Catalog Card Number: 68-24385

Printed in the United States of America

Contents

82319

List of Illustrations

(Between pages 148 and 149)

Byron: drawing by G. H. Harlow, 1816
(Probably the drawing from which Shelley asked Ollier to get him a print in March 1817)
Henry E. Huntington Library and Art Gallery

Shelley: painting by Amelia Curran, Rome, May 1819
(Though unfinished, and unsatisfactory to the artist, who wished to destroy it, this is the only known portrait from life of the adult Shelley)
The Trustees of the National Portrait Gallery, London

Mary Shelley, from a miniature given by Trelawny to W. M. Rossetti, in the possession of Mrs Dennis
Mrs Imogen Dennis

Shelley: posthumous drawing by Mary Shelley, 1829
(By that date Mary owned the Curran portrait of Shelley)
The University of Texas at Austin Library

The Villa Diodati, Lake of Geneva: engraving by Edward Finden from a drawing by W. Purser
(Byron's residence June to October 1816)

The Castle of Chillon, Lake of Geneva: painting by Gustave Courbet
Center for Advanced Studies, Wesleyan University, Connecticut

Claire Clairmont: painting by Amelia Curran, Rome, spring 1819
City Librarian, Nottingham

Allegra: miniature by an unknown artist, Venice, 1818
In the possession of Mr John Murray

The approach to Venice, sunset: water-colour by J. M. W. Turner, 1840
British Museum

Teresa Guiccioli: marble bust by Lorenzo Bartolini
(Teresa sat to Bartolini in Pisa, January 1822)

Preface

BYRON and Shelley would have been great poets if they had never met and become friends, but they would not have been the poets whose work we read. Through their friendship each helped the other to know himself more thoroughly and to recognise his own distinctive powers, so that the poetry which they wrote in the six years that passed between their first meeting and Shelley's death has a maturity not attained before. No two men of genius could be more contrasted in personality or have gifts more complementary; because this was so, from the first, their biographers have inclined to favour one at the expense of the other, and so to distort our understanding of both. This was to be expected, for, confronted by our eternal predicament, some will regard the gap between human aspiration and human achievement as tragic, and others will regard it as comic; the idealists will seek to help their fellows to close the gap, the realists will mock them for their failure to do so. In this great division of human temperament Byron and Shelley were generally opposed, though it would be as false to think that the creator of Bonivard or Haidée was incapable of tenderness or pathos as to deny the gifts of humour or of satire to the author of *Peter Bell the Third, The Masque of Anarchy* and the *Letter to Maria Gisborne.*

The friendship between Byron and Shelley was the most important relationship in the experience of either, one which did more than any other to develop the individual qualities of their minds and imaginations. Its course was not very consistent. Three months together in Switzerland were followed by almost two years without seeing each other; then two months together at Venice were succeeded by a separation of almost three years; finally six months together in Pisa gave place to two months in which they saw each other only occasionally.

But true friendship does not require the placidity of regular week-end visiting any more than it needs a correspondence of opinion or belief or capability or ambition. It will survive long absence and will then renew itself with all the more vigour. It is more likely to thrive in natures that are dissimilar and complementary, fulfilling each other, than in those whose similarity must lead, after a time, to the dull insistence of an echo.

Theirs was not a 'literary friendship', if by that is meant something limited to a common interest in discussing together works of literature, whether their own or other men's. It was something far more pervasive and enriching, something which touched on the whole of their experience, without reserve or exclusions. There was nothing they could not talk of together, nothing which such talk did not illuminate for both – all the more so because they were always likely to end up, as they began, on opposite sides. From time to time, when they were apart, there were misunderstandings and recriminations, but these, as soon as they met again, Byron's good nature and common sense and Shelley's generosity dispelled, for the delight they took in being together again left no room for doubts and hesitations. Shelley had much the stronger will, Byron the subtler understanding of human nature. Shelley was born to influence all who knew him, Byron to respond to each different personality. But Shelley's deference to Byron's poetic genius as well as his courteous manners softened the tone of command which might otherwise have sounded domineering, and Byron withstood a temptation to be flippant for the sake of the gaiety which Shelley evoked and shared. Thus their friendship was rewarding, not only to themselves and those about them, most of all to Mary and Teresa, but also to us through its effect upon their finest poetry.

That I have only briefly indicated, preferring not to obstruct the narrative with long critical discourses. Besides, it should be enough, for those who are familiar with their work, to set the poems in the context of their related lives; for the rest, this setting may bring them again, and with more understanding, to the poetry of Byron and Shelley.

Acknowledgments

I WISH to thank those who have allowed me to quote from unpublished letters and other documents in their possession, especially Lord Abinger, who kindly allowed me to check all references to Mary Shelley's journal by the original (which is inadequately represented by the published texts), as well as to quote from unpublished letters; and Mr John Murray, who welcomed me to 50 Albemarle Street on a number of occasions and generously allowed me to quote from unpublished letters and documents which belong to him. The late Sir John Murray also encouraged my interest in the Byron archives. The Curators of the Bodleian Library granted me permission to examine the restricted Shelley MSS. there, and I am deeply indebted to the staffs of the Bodleian Library, the British Museum, and the London Library for all their help. Mrs Leach, of the Music Library in Oxford, helped me to trace performances of opera in the early nineteenth century.

The staff of the Archivio di Stato in Pisa helped me there with topographical and other inquiries, as well as showing me over the Palazzo Lanfranchi which now houses the archives of the city. Others who helped me in Italy were the Marchesa Iris Origo, the Contessa Sandra Tealdi di Gropello, and Professor Gaetano Cozzi: I am most grateful to them for their courtesy.

An invitation to spend four months as a visiting Fellow at the Center for Advanced Studies, Wesleyan University, Connecticut, gave me the longest uninterrupted period for writing that I have enjoyed in twenty years. I am therefore most grateful to the then President of Wesleyan University, Professor Victor L. Butterfield, for extending this invitation to me, and for renewing it when illness suddenly prevented me from taking it up in the previous year; and to Mr Paul Horgan, under whose distinguished Directorship I was privileged to work at the Center. He combined an enthusiastic interest in my work with a tactful readiness to let me get on with it which were alike encouraging. I benefited from the opportunity of reading two of the chapters in an early form to members of the Center. My thanks are also due to the Warden and Fellows of New College for granting me a sabbatical term which enabled me to visit Wesleyan University.

There Mrs Anderson typed out several chapters from my MS. promptly and accurately; in England Mrs Warren has retyped most of the book either from MS. or from much-corrected typescript. I am very much obliged to them both.

Lady Mander, Mrs Imogen Dennis, Miss Sandra James, Fräulein M.-L. Rehder, Professor M. F. M. Meiklejohn and Mr R. Willitts have most kindly helped me to answer a variety of questions of detail; and finally Mr Eric Christiansen and Dr Ian Jack, by their willingness to read through the proofs, have left me much in their debt. To Rache Lovat Dickson, with whom I discussed my first tentative plans for this book and who has continued his friendly interest ever since, and to my wife who has accepted calmly the ups and downs that seem inevitably to precede the publication of any book, I offer, with the book, my deepest gratitude.

CHAPTER ONE

First Meeting

MAY–JUNE 1816: SWITZERLAND

On the afternoon of Monday 27 May 1816 Lord Byron rowed across the Lake of Geneva to Cologny in order to look over the Villa Diodati, which he wished to rent for the summer. He was told that it had already been let to an English family, and he then rowed back to his hotel at Sécheron, where, on stepping ashore, he met Shelley. Byron's personal physician, John Polidori, who had accompanied him on the trip across the lake, withdrew. Shelley had with him Mary Godwin, with whom he had eloped two years before, and Mary's step-sister, Claire Clairmont. Both girls – they were eighteen years old – already knew Byron; but the two men were meeting for the first time. Byron was twenty-eight, Shelley was twenty-three.

Claire was responsible for this meeting of the two poets. Byron signed the deed of separation from his wife on 21 April, and sailed from Dover on the 25th, but before he left London Claire, who had managed to make his acquaintance in March, pestered him with a succession of notes begging him to see her again. Byron found plenty of excuses for avoiding her in those busy hours with his friends, but Claire wrote to tell him that as soon as Shelley's Chancery suit, which concerned the inheritance of his family estates, was settled she would travel with Shelley and Mary on their way to Italy. Her determination to become Byron's mistress if she might not be his friend left her without dignity. Even in London, in order to induce Byron to meet her she had promised to bring Mary with her, for she knew that the beautiful and gifted daughter of William Godwin and

Mary Wollstonecraft would interest him much more than the dumpy and stage-struck daughter of two nonentities. She asked Byron to warn his servants to treat Mary with more courtesy than they treated her, 'for she is accustomed to be surrounded by her own circle, who treat her with the greatest politeness'. And now, in order to persuade Byron to let her see him again in Geneva, she promised not only Mary, who 'is delighted with you, as I knew she would be. . . . She perpetually exclaims, "How mild he is! how gentle! so different from what I expected," ' but she promised also Mary's lover, the poet Shelley, whose good opinion of her disposition and of her literary talent she had already reported to Byron. To confirm this she had sent Byron some of Shelley's letters to her while they were all still in London. Claire was one of those relentless women who are not at all abashed by the knowledge that they bore the man they have decided to engross, and she was as shameless in using her friends as in using her sex to attach him to her. Byron, in spite of himself, had accepted Claire as his mistress the week before he left England, meekly allowing himself to be conveyed on Claire's instructions to some secret rendezvous twelve miles outside London. And he left her as his address 'Poste Restante à Genève'.

Claire, grateful for this minimal encouragement, persuaded Shelley and Mary to give up their previous plan of visiting Scotland and to go instead to the Continent, and especially to Geneva (for Byron forbade her to travel there without protection). Shelley's party, which in addition to himself and the two girls included Mary's baby, William, left England on 3 May. After passport delays in Paris they arrived late in the evening of the 13th at the Hôtel d'Angleterre at Sécheron. It was dark, and it was snowing, but at least the hotel was clean and comfortable, and Mary was relieved that they had escaped the bad inn and dirty beds at Les Rousses, which earlier in the evening seemed inevitable. The Hôtel d'Angleterre had enjoyed an excellent reputation for some years, and M. Jacques Dejean, the proprietor, who had welcomed the Empress Josephine there in 1810, had been host to Queen Hortense earlier in this year.

His establishment enjoyed the great advantage of being outside the walls of the city, so that his guests, untroubled by the curfew, could come and go as they pleased. The extensive private gardens for the exclusive use of visitors ran down to the edge of the lake, where boats were available by arrangement.

At M. Dejean's hotel twelve days later, on the evening of 25 May, Byron, with Polidori and three servants, also arrived. He was tired no doubt, and when he saw that the hotel register in which he entered his name provided a column for the visitor's age – a piece of impertinent formality which would be certain to irritate Byron – he wrote down '100'. Within half an hour M. Dejean fussily sent a note to beg his Lordship to inform him of his correct age; and Claire, who had been looking at the register every day since her own arrival, also sent a note. 'I am sorry you are grown so old. Indeed I suspected you were 200 from the slowness of your journey. I suppose your venerable age could not bear quicker travelling.' And she asked him to write to her under cover to Shelley.

Next afternoon Claire wrote again, scolding Byron because he had not written to her, and asking him to meet her on the top floor that evening, but he must not ask a servant to show him up, 'for they might take you to Shelley which would be very awkward.' Byron, however, was taking his time, and was not ardent to renew Claire's acquaintance. He was in no hurry to meet Shelley – there was all the summer before him – and he was not at home to a distinguished Swiss visitor who called. Besides, there were various practical matters to see to, including a first visit to the Villa Diodati. In the morning he and Polidori walked down through the gardens to the edge of the lake, where they found a boat pulled up on the shore: they pushed off and started rowing, but a waiter appeared at the water's side and called them back – the boat which they had borrowed had been hired, he said, by an English gentleman; in fact, by Shelley. But Shelley had not sent the man to retrieve his boat, for during the heat of the day he and Mary stayed indoors reading and did not go out to sail on the lake until after dinner, usually leaving about six and returning about ten.

Shelley and Mary, escaped from London and Godwin and litigation, were peacefully happy together, and Shelley, always the most modest of men of genius, would not have thrust himself thus discourteously on the notice of the celebrated Lord Byron. True, three years before he had sent Byron a copy of *Queen Mab*, which Byron read and admired, but the memory of this would have increased Shelley's diffidence at meeting the great poet, for he had already far outgrown the crude enthusiasms of that poem. Thus the initiative for their meeting must come, if not from Byron, then from Claire. And Claire, who was anxious that Byron should not meet Shelley before she had spoken with him (presumably because she wished herself to inform Byron of her pregnancy), must so arrange their meeting that it might seem a chance encounter, and she must be in Shelley's company. Fortunately the Shelleys had already made it their routine to walk in the garden of the hotel in the late afternoon, and it cannot have been difficult for Claire, watching out of the corner of her eye for Byron's boat returning from Cologny, to contrive that the three of them should reach the spot where he would come ashore just as his boat ran up on the gravel.

Byron, not wishing to be embarrassed on this occasion by the presence of Polidori, left him in the boat. The doctor had been in a bad temper, he admitted, earlier in the day, and now he lay full length on the bottom of the boat, allowing it to drift on the placid water while his temper improved.

We have no record of the first impression made on each other by the two poets, the one who had already achieved fame such as no other English poet had ever enjoyed, the other still almost unknown. Both were inclined to be shy with strangers, and Byron's practical good sense would make him suspicious of Claire's 'Otaheite philosophers'* – so she had lately described Shelley and Mary to him – just as Shelley's idealism would hinder him from being immediately relaxed with a man who had shown his gift for satire. Neither could have foreseen that from this time on they would influence each other's lives and

* Claire's inverted commas may indicate that she was quoting Byron.

work subtly, intricately, pervasively in ways which they would sometimes recognise and sometimes disregard; but the friendship which began this day was, for both men, the most valuable of their lives. Byron's poetry had already won such acclaim that he could hardly have realised that his best work was still to come. Shelley, who never doubted that Byron was a greater poet than himself, may yet have hoped that he would write better poems than *Queen Mab* or *Alastor*. But paradoxically Shelley's influence on Byron's poetry was more immediate and more important than Byron's on Shelley's.

The two men dined together that evening apart from their mistresses, but with Polidori, who somewhat maliciously noted in his diary that Shelley 'keeps the two daughters of Godwin, who practise his theories', that is, of free love. He also noted that Claire was Byron's mistress. Two men, even two Englishmen of good birth, living in an hotel in a foreign country with their mistresses who happen to be step-sisters are likely, before long, to become on terms of intimate candour, if not necessarily of friendship; and Byron, after a month's travel in the company of servants and of the fatuous Polly-Dolly must have been famished for such conversation as Shelley could provide. We do not know of what they talked on that first evening together, but the complementary nature of their conversation, which later impressed those who listened to its give and take, would already have been apparent.

On the following day Byron went off with Polidori to look at houses which were to let, but found none to his taste. Shelley and Byron walked together in the garden of the hotel and then went out on the lake in Shelley's boat, though a rough wind was blowing. Shelley invited Byron to dine, but he declined as he had a previous engagement. There were, even so soon after his arrival, signs that Byron might become involved in the social life of Geneva. Charles Hentsch, the banker, who at twenty-six was already well known there, and who had a fine house at Mon Repos where he entertained lavishly, came in to apologise for not recognising Byron when he visited the bank on the previous day. He had the tact to say that he had had no idea that he was then speaking to one of the most famous Lords of England. Byron took to him at once (as he would not have done had Hentsch called him one of the most famous poets of England) and saw much of him during his stay in Switzerland, enjoying his company and valuing his advice on matters of business. Marc-Auguste Pictet,* who was editor of *La Revue Universelle* in which notices of Byron's poems had appeared, and who was eager to present the famous poet to some of his friends, had called on the Sunday after Byron arrived, only to be put off with a message that his Lordship was not at home. Byron called on Pictet next day, and received a similar message. Now on the Tuesday, with honour satisfied, Pictet called again to invite Byron to a soirée at the house of Madame Eynard-Châtelain. Madame Eynard, who was related to Pictet, was the wife of the Genevan delegate to the Congress of Vienna, and was an amateur painter of some talent. In her house that evening to meet Byron were the Italian Liberal, Pellegrino Rossi, who had been with Murat at Bologna and had since become naturalised as a citizen of Geneva, and Charles Victor de Bonstetten, Gray's old friend. They all spoke English or Italian, for Byron's French was inadequate for conversation. Rossi, economist and lawyer though he was, could talk, as he did this evening, of poetry, and he expressed a modern romantic preference for Dante rather than Ariosto. Byron must have been especially delighted with Bonstetten, who could talk not only of Gray but also of Voltaire and Rousseau, both of whom he had known; besides, he combined the elegant manners of an eighteenth-century aristocrat with the liberal enthusiasms of the new century, and at seventy retained much of the charm and of the distinguished good looks that once had captivated Gray – 'a fine and very lively old man', Byron thought him. He knew Byron's poetry and indeed had read a paper on the subject the year before at Madame de Staël's house at Coppet; but though he considered Byron the greatest of living poets he was sensitive enough to talk to him not of his own poetry but of Gray's. He admired, as everyone admired, the extraordinary beauty of

* See note 1, p. 269.

Byron's face, but he also noted there traces of his violent and complex character, the mixture of generosity and mistrust, of diffidence and pride.

In spite of this pleasant evening at Madame Eynard's Byron did not continue to take much part in the social life of Geneva. He preferred Shelley's company: they breakfasted together every day and explored by boat along the shores of the lake. Shelley, who had already hired his boat before Byron's arrival, now prevented the boatman charging double to the English milord. For the time being their principal occupation was looking for houses to rent, and their excursions on the lake thus combined business with pleasure. Shelley recounted the story of his life: his youthful novels, his marriage to and separation from Harriet, his relations with Godwin, his previous visit to the Continent with Mary and Claire in 1814. Claire, whose real name was Mary Jane (but whose father was Swiss), had begun to call herself Clara at the end of that year, after Julie's 'constant cousin' in *La Nouvelle Héloïse*, with the implication that she cast Mary for the role of Julie and Shelley for that of St. Preux. (Who but Byron should play the role of Lord B——?) Later she changed Clara, which she found in the English version of Rousseau's romance, to the original Claire (which Byron liked), and by that name she was always afterwards known. Polidori was somewhat confused about the girls' names for, finding that Mary was known as Mrs Shelley, he as it were promoted Claire in her place to be Miss Godwin. Not that it mattered, for they were all clever and charming, and Shelley especially impressed Polidori with his intellectual distinction. Polidori had somehow got hold of a copy of *Queen Mab* – perhaps Byron had brought his copy with him – and he admitted to his diary that, 'the more I read the more beauties I find.' He was a little impatient of Shelley's unworldliness: 'paid Godwin's debts, and seduced his daughter; then wondered that he would not see him.' But this sounds more like an echo of Byron's common sense.

On the 30th, after the usual house-hunting in the morning with Shelley and Mary, Polidori went on the lake in the evening with Mary and Claire and afterwards drank tea, as any guest of the Shelleys was likely to do at any hour, 'and came away at 11 after confabbing'. Next day he read Italian with Mary in the morning, and in the evening again rowed on the lake with her, drank tea and chatted. In the meantime Byron and Shelley were enjoying each other's company alone.

On 1 June they all took tea together after their evening sail on the lake, and Polidori records some characteristic talk of Byron about Samuel Rogers, the poet and wit whose literary breakfasts were a well-known feature of the intellectual life of London. By way of contrast with Rogers' disparagement of the too much praised Lord Lansdowne – 'But how horribly he carves turbot!' – Mary quoted Coleridge's savage lines on Pitt, who 'kissed his country with Iscariot mouth'. Shelley regaled the company with scraps of autobiography: his father's attempt to confine him in a madhouse when he was a schoolboy at Eton, the proposed marriage to his cousin Harriet Grove, Godwin's shabby treatment of him. Next day Polidori read Tasso with Mary, and he took her four-months-old son to be vaccinated. It was Sunday, and during the hours of service the city gates were shut, but Polidori found Dr de Roche, whom he had already consulted, and Shelley rewarded him with a gold chain and seal. After dinner together they all went to look at the house which Shelley had now decided to take, and which was situated on the side of the lake opposite to Sécheron. On their return there was more tea and talk, the subjects again including madness (a favourite topic with the two poets, both of whom had been thought mad by uncomprehending relations), and also the Irish patriot John Philpot Curran, whom Shelley had met, through Godwin's introduction, when he was in Dublin in 1812. Curran had disappointed Shelley by failing to discover the merits of his pamphleteering.

The house which Shelley rented was in a secluded position beside the lake at Montalègre and belonged to Jacob Chappuis: they called it Campagne Chappuis. Probably on 3 June Shelley moved there with Mary and Claire. 'We have exchanged the view of Mont Blanc and her snowy *aiguilles*,' Mary wrote, 'for the dark frowning Jura. . . . The lake is at our feet, and a little harbour contains our boat, in which we still enjoy our evening excursions on the water.' The removal of the Shelleys to Montalègre did not interrupt the routine of walking, reading, sailing and talking which they had established while staying in the same hotel with Byron. Polidori, keeping with conscientious dullness the diary for which Byron's publisher, John Murray, had promised him £500, recorded their daily meetings, the reading of Tasso, the negotiations for the lease to Byron of the Villa Diodati, and a quarrel which he had with Byron and Shelley while sailing. Shelley beat Polidori in a sailing match, and Polidori, affecting the histrionic attitude which so much irritated Byron, sent Shelley a challenge. Shelley laughed at him. Byron told Polidori to recollect that, though Shelley had some scruples about duelling, he had none and would be at all times ready to take his place. Polidori subsided. Unfortunately Polidori was no Boswell, and we can only guess at the conversation in Shelley's boat on the evening of 8 June when they 'talked till the ladies' brains whizzed with giddiness, about idealism'. Shelley, who has made many young ladies' brains whizz since then, must have been in his liveliest mood. On another evening, as Byron returned across the lake from Montalègre, Mary told Thomas Moore, 'the wind, from far across, bore us his voice singing your Tyrolese Song of Liberty'.*

On 10 June Byron moved into the Villa Diodati, 'the prettiest place on all the lake' in his opinion, an early eighteenth-century house with a large balcony, on which Byron would sit and write, with a view over the lake to the Jura. The house belonged to Édouard Diodati, a descendant of Milton's friend, Charles Diodati. Byron would have welcomed this association with one of the triumvirate of English poets whom he opposed to the modern triumvirate of Wordsworth, Coleridge and Southey. It was only a few minutes' walk through a vineyard, where they could listen to the songs of the peasant

* In her novel, *The Last Man*, the hero, Lord Raymond (a portrayal of Byron), gaily sings this song on one occasion.

women, to Shelley's house, so that the daily intercourse between the two friends could continue as easily as when they were together in the Hôtel d'Angleterre. They joined together now in buying for twenty-five louis a small two-masted yacht, built in England, which they kept in Shelley's harbour.

The weather this summer was wet and stormy, but they enjoyed the grandeur of the thunderstorms among the mountains. 'We watch them,' Mary wrote, 'as they approach from the opposite side of the lake, observing the lightning play among the clouds in various parts of the heavens, and dart in jagged figures upon the piny heights of Jura, dark with the shadow of the overhanging cloud, while perhaps the sun is shining cheerily upon us. One night we *enjoyed* a finer storm than I had ever before beheld. The lake was lit up, the pines on Jura made visible, and all the scene illuminated for an instant, when a pitchy blackness succeeded, and the thunder came in frightful bursts over our heads amid the darkness.' This thunderstorm of 13 June is celebrated in *Childe Harold* III, and again in *Frankenstein*. In this romantic scenery, and in this romantic company, Byron acquired a new sensibility to the natural world, which at once appeared in his poem. Some of this was induced by reading Wordsworth, at Shelley's prompting, though more was probably due to Shelley's own talk and to his interpretation of Wordsworth. As Byron later told Medwin, 'Shelley, when I was in Switzerland, used to dose me with Wordsworth physic even to nausea.' And there is at least one passage in *Childe Harold* III which recalls one of these evenings on the lake when the weather was tranquil. Mary described it thus: 'as we approach the shore, we are saluted by the delightful scent of flowers and new-mown grass, and the chirp of the grasshoppers, and the song of the evening birds.' Byron, made newly observant of the same idyllic scene by his companions, recollected it in these Wordsworthian lines:

> There breathes a living fragrance from the shore,
> Of flowers yet fresh with childhood; on the ear,
> Drops the light drip of the suspended oar,
> Or chirps the grasshopper one good-night carol more;

He is an evening reveller, who makes
His life an infancy, and sings his fill;
At intervals, some bird from out the brakes
Starts into voice a moment, then is still.

This was the first evidence of the influence of Shelley on his poetry.

They were secluded here, on the eastern shore of the lake, away from prurient English visitors eager for a glimpse of the sinister and scandalous poet. But even there Byron was watched through glasses supplied by M. Dejean at a small charge to visitors to the Hôtel d'Angleterre, 'and by glasses too that must have had very distorted optics', said Byron. They were said to have 'discerned certain robes and flounces on his Lordship's balcony'. He was accused of corrupting the local *grisettes*, and Lord Glenbervie, more anxious for scandal than for fact, recorded in his diary that Byron was living 'with that woman, who it seems proves to be a Mrs Shelley, wife to the man who keeps the Mount coffee-house.'* A year later Robert Southey visited Geneva and picked up the gossip. On his return to England he lubriciously announced that Byron and Shelley were 'in a league of incest' with Mary and Claire. He did not explain (as Byron pointed out) how the charge of incest was applicable to persons who were in no way related one to another, but his venomous lie was to lead, through public controversy, to Byron's triumphant mockery in *The Vision of Judgment.*

No wonder Byron avoided the English who, in this year after Waterloo, were already flooding back on to the Continent – 'staring boobies', he called them. And Polidori, reflecting his master's contempt, described a party in Geneva where there were 'quantities of English, speaking amongst themselves, arms by their sides, mouths open, and eyes glowing; might as well make a tour of the Isle of Dogs'. Shelley, in spite of being a most gifted linguist, always kept to a small circle of English friends, and even during his years in Italy knew few Italians. Now, fearing that he might never again live in England, he felt

* In *Don Juan* I cxlix Julia claims Lord Mount Coffeehouse, the Irish peer, among her rejected and despairing lovers. So did Byron get his revenge.

SALEM COLLEGE LIBRARY
WINSTON-SALEM, N. C.

a little homesick. Byron indeed never returned to England, and generally continued to express his distaste for English tourists, preferring the company of foreigners, especially of Italians. But now, in Geneva, he much preferred the company of Shelley, with whom he could talk all day and all night on everything under the sun, and of Mary, who was content to sit quietly listening to them. For their sake Claire had to be tolerated, though this was often difficult. She teased Byron with her affectionate sentimentality: 'do you know I cannot talk to you when I see you? I am so awkward and only feel inclined to take a little stool and sit at your feet.' Byron did know, only too well, and was annoyed with himself for so weakly allowing the silly little thing to impose herself on him as his mistress. Once she was tactless enough to say he had a Scotch accent. 'Good God! I hope not!' said Byron. 'I'm sure I haven't. I would rather the whole damned country was sunk in the sea – I, the Scotch accent!' Scots Calvinism was enough to have to endure without being accused of speaking like a Presbyterian. And his letter to his sister, after Claire had returned to England, put the unglamorous affair in its proper light: 'As to all these mistresses, Lord help me, I have had but one. Now don't scold; but what could I do? – a foolish girl, in spite of all I could say or do, would come after me, or rather went before – for I found her here . . . I was not in love, nor have any love left for any, but I could not exactly play the Stoic with a woman who had scrambled eight hundred miles to unphilosophise me.'

If Claire bored Byron, Polidori irritated him with his conceit, his fractious temper, his lack of tact. Not only had he the impertinence to challenge Shelley to a duel, he even thought himself the equal of Byron. Tired perhaps, of hearing Byron's praises, he turned to him on one occasion with 'and, pray, what is there excepting writing poetry that I cannot do better than you?' 'First,' said Byron, 'I can hit with a pistol the keyhole of that door; secondly I can swim across that river* to yonder point; and thirdly I can give you a damned good thrashing.'

* The Rhine.

Polidori, in spite of the demurrer about writing poetry, had literary pretensions, which neither Byron nor Shelley could encourage: 'talked of my play,' he noted on 15 June, 'which all agreed was worth nothing.' But he served Byron as a defence against Claire, since he was too egotistical to suppose that a man might sometimes prefer to be alone with his mistress. Byron in fact did not; but Polidori exasperated Claire. 'Pray if you can,' she wrote to Byron, 'send M. Polidori either to write another dictionary or to the lady he loves. I hope this last may be his pillow and then he will go to sleep for I cannot come at this hour of the night and be seen by him; it is so extremely suspicious.' Probably Byron kept Polidori talking all the longer.

One day, after a shower of rain, Byron was standing on the balcony of Villa Diodati when he saw Mary walking up the path towards the house. He turned to Polidori, who was with him, and said: 'Now you who wish to be gallant ought to jump down this small height and offer your arm.' Polidori promptly did so, slipped, and sprained his ankle. Byron helped to carry him indoors and, after laying him on the sofa, went upstairs to fetch a pillow for him. 'Well, I did not believe you had so much feeling,' was Polidori's comment. In the end Byron could endure him no longer, and dismissed him. Polidori was, as Byron said, 'exactly the kind of person to whom, if he fell overboard, one would hold out a straw, to know if the adage be true that drowning men catch at straws'. A year afterwards Byron still remembered him with distaste. 'I never was much more disgusted with any human production than with the eternal nonsense, and *tracasseries*, and emptiness, and ill humour, and vanity of that young person,' he wrote to Murray. Yet in the same letter, with his usual kindness, he asked Murray to help Polidori to obtain a physician's post in the Admiralty. The letter must be one of the most unlikely testimonials ever written.

Mary, Byron always liked. She was not only handsome and intelligent, but her devotion to Shelley also relieved Byron of any fear that she too, like most women, might hope to become his mistress. (Claire, writing to Byron from Paris on the way out to Switzerland, absurdly suggested that Mary would become his mistress when they met again; so little understanding had she of either.) Mary was one of the very few women who ever wished to be on terms of frank and intimate friendship with him, but no more; she was gentle and kind, had a sharp sense of humour and sound common sense, and she rejoiced in the close friendship that had already grown up between Shelley and Byron. One evening, soon after Byron had gone to the Villa Diodati, he suggested that each of them should write a ghost-story: 'You and I,' he said to Mary, 'will publish ours together.' He outlined the plot of his story a day or two later. Mary thought it 'very dramatic and striking', but he soon dropped it; however, Polidori adopted his ideas and in 1819 published *The Vampyre*, which, because it was thought to be Byron's, enjoyed some success. Shelley began an autobiographical story of which the residue was precipitated not long after in the fifth stanza of the *Hymn to Intellectual Beauty*:

While yet a boy I sought for ghosts, and sped
  Through many a listening chamber, cave and ruin,
  And starlight wood, with fearful steps pursuing
Hopes of high talk with the departed dead.
I called on poisonous names with which our youth is fed.

Mary was determined to accept Byron's challenge and to write her story. She pondered over it for some time, being asked each morning by Shelley if she had thought of a plot. Eventually, after one of these evening conversations between Byron and Shelley, to which, she says, she was 'a devout but nearly silent listener', an idea came to her. They had been talking about the nature of the principle of life, 'and whether there was any probability of its ever being discovered'. 'Perhaps' one of them suggested, 'a corpse would be re-animated: galvanism had given token of such things: perhaps the component parts of a creature might be manufactured, brought together, and endued with vital warmth.' After this conversation Mary could not sleep and then suddenly she realised that she had found her story. 'What terrified me will terrify others; and I need only describe the spectre which had haunted my midnight pillow'. So was she set upon writing the first great work of science-fiction, and next morning she began *Frankenstein, or The Modern Prometheus.*

For several evenings their talk was much of ghosts. They were reading together a collection of German ghost stories in a French translation, *Fantasmagoriana, ou Recueil d'histoires d'apparitions, de spectres, revenans etc.* On the 18th at one of these sessions Byron quoted from Coleridge's *Christabel,** which he had heard Scott recite in 1815 and memorised, the lines about the witch:

Then drawing in her breath aloud,
Like one that shuddered, she unbound
The cincture from beneath her breast:
Her silken robe, and inner vest,
Dropt to her feet, and full in view,
Behold! her bosom and half her side
Are lean and old and foul of hue.

Shelley, 'suddenly shrieking and putting his hands to his head, ran out of the room with a candle'. Byron and Polidori ran after him and, with cold water, brought him to his senses again. Shelley had been looking at Mary while Byron was repeating Coleridge's lines, 'and suddenly thought of a woman he had heard of who had eyes instead of nipples'. Such vivid hallucinations seized Shelley on other occasions; they were very far from Byron's experience, yet he was not inclined to laugh at Shelley as he would have laughed at lesser men. 'I can't tell what seized him,' he told Murray in referring to the incident, 'for he don't want courage.'

But there were times when Byron enjoyed laughing at his new friends for their romantic tastes, all the more because, sharing many of their hopes and ideals, he could thereby laugh at himself too. One evening, Mary told Moore, when they were out sailing on the lake as usual, 'the waves were high and inspiriting – we were all animated by our contest with the

* See note 2, p. 269.

elements. "I will sing you an Albanian song," cried Lord Byron; "now be sentimental and give me all your attention." It was a strange, wild howl that he gave forth, but such as, he declared, was an exact imitation of the savage Albanian mode, – laughing, the while, at our disappointment, who had expected a wild Eastern melody.'

By now, after more than three weeks of daily intercourse, Byron and Shelley were becoming close friends. Utterly different as they were, each had found in the other qualities of mind and temper that he himself lacked. Shelley's lofty idealism did not deprive him of a sense of humour or of an intermittent appreciation of common sense. Byron, always in doubt whether to laugh or weep at the follies of mankind, was stimulated by Shelley's far-ranging, speculative mind. Both were widely read, and both, however much attracted to the world of political action, knew that their destiny was to write poetry, and they were more willing to admit this to each other than to most of their friends. Both had left England to escape from the persecution and embarrassment brought upon them by their estrangement from their wives and were in need of peace and of that refreshment of the spirit that good talk with friends can best provide. Each was ready to accept the other as he found him, without affectation, and without any desire to play a part; with no wish to criticise the other's behaviour, or to care what anyone else thought of it. Thus they were quite natural and at ease with one another. Besides, they enjoyed the same things, poetry and ghost stories, the scenery of lake and mountain and the dramatic storms that moved there, and, best of all, sailing on the lake.

Byron, proud always of the athletic prowess which he had attained in defiance of his congenital lameness, enjoyed sailing as a sport, in which the element of danger gave point to an acquired skill; but Shelley, who from childhood had been fascinated to watch the paper boats which he would launch on any available pool of water, found in sailing his own boat a means of identifying himself with the unseen forces of Nature. Byron with his hand grasping the tiller was taking advantage of the wind to drive his boat where he wished to go – he loved to feel 'the waves bound beneath him as a steed that knows his rider'; Shelley, with a book open in one hand and the other resting on the trembling tiller, felt that he was a part of the waters on which he was borne, and of the winds by which he was impelled. Thus, even in their favourite pastime, Shelley's enthusiasm and Byron's practical ability were complementary.

CHAPTER TWO

The Tour of the Lake

JUNE—AUGUST 1816: SWITZERLAND

On 22 June the two friends set off in their boat on a tour of the lake.* Polidori's sprained ankle provided a sufficient excuse for leaving him behind, and there was no suggestion that they might take Mary or Claire. Their only companions were a servant and their two boatmen. Shelley wrote a long and vivid account of the voyage in a letter to Peacock, which was printed the following year in the *History of a Six Weeks' Tour*. Byron's record of it is to be found in the stanzas of *Childe Harold* which he wrote at the time. The tour was, in some degree, a romantic pilgrimage to sites associated with Rousseau, such as Rousseau himself had recommended to persons of taste and sensibility. Byron quoted the passage from the *Confessions* in a note to *Childe Harold* III, 'Allez à Vevey – visitez le pays, examinez les sites, promenez-vous sur le lac et dites si la Nature n'a pas fait ce beau pays pour une Julie, pour une Claire, et pour un St Preux, mais ne les y cherchez pas.' Shelley told Peacock that, delightful as the voyage had been on every account, it had been especially so for the experience of reading *Julie, ou La Nouvelle Héloïse* in the very landscape which Rousseau there describes. Rousseau had presented his romantic lovers, Julie and St Preux, with such vitality that to those who lived on the shores of the lake memory of them seemed to be of persons who had indeed lived there; but in spite of the universal fame of *Julie*, Shelley had never before read it. Byron, who had read the book so often that he almost knew it by heart,

* See note 3, p. 269.

and suggested to Shelley that he should read it now, was also deeply affected by these reminders of Rousseau. As he walked with Shelley in *le bosquet de Julie* at Clarens – from the window their landlady pointed this out to them, the place where Julie and St Preux first kissed – he suddenly burst out with 'Thank God, Polidori is not here!' At every turn Shelley was stirred to reflections appropriate to a liberal intellectual in the Rousseau country: at Meillerie, where someone told him that the Empress Maria Louisa of Prussia had slept 'in remembrance of St Preux', 'this little incident shows at once how unfit and how impossible it is for the ancient system of opinions, or for any power built upon a conspiracy to revive them, permanently to subsist among man kind'; at Clarens, finding that Julie's little chapel had been pulled down by the monks of St Bernard, 'I knew before that if avarice could harden the hearts of men, a system of prescriptive religion has an influence far more inimical to natural sensibility.' And he regretted to Peacock that 'the cold maxims of the world' had compelled him 'to repress the tears of melancholy transport which it would have been so sweet to indulge' as he walked with Byron at Clarens. But perhaps the presence of Byron also had something to do with inhibiting such Rousseau-like sentimentality.

It was Byron's habit to keep a long poem by him to which he could return from time to time in the intervals of other work, *Childe Harold* and afterwards *Don Juan*. On starting his travels again he resumed *Childe Harold* early in May. A visit to the field of Waterloo prompted him to write the famous stanzas beginning,

> There was a sound of revelry by night;

and he continued to add to the poem as he travelled up the Rhine to Switzerland. During the summer, as his boatman Maurice told Lady Blessington in 1822, Byron would spend hours at a time on the lake, 'absorbed in reflection, and then suddenly writing, with extreme rapidity, in a book he always had with him.' For him, but not for Shelley, poetry could come from an immediate response, without any need for tranquil recollection, so that it is possible to trace the stages of his journey in the stanzas of *Childe Harold* III. Before setting out on the tour of the lake with Shelley he had written some stanzas on 'the self-torturing sophist, wild Rousseau' in which the influence of Shelley is already manifest.

> But his was not the love of living dame,
> Nor of the dead who rise upon our dreams,
> But of ideal Beauty, which became
> In him existence, and o'erflowing teems
> Along his burning page, distempered though it seems.

Such a passage suggests the *Hymn to Intellectual Beauty*, which Shelley conceived during the tour of the lake, rather than the *Confessions.*

Byron recorded the visit to Clarens on 26 June in five more stanzas, which make some use of Rousseau's description of the landscape. But the 'Wordsworth physic' administered by Shelley had begun to do its work, and Byron was finding in the world of Nature a recreative power and solace which was not conveyed by Rousseau's more precise observation. As Byron himself said later, Rousseau 'liked botany: I like flowers, and herbs, and trees, but know nothing of their pedigrees.' Also Rousseau had been setting the scene for characters of fiction; Byron was deriving from the same scene vivid suggestions of Rousseau himself:

> All things are here of *Him*; from the black pines,
> Which are his shade on high, and the loud roar
> Of torrents, where he listeneth, to the vines
> Which slope his green path downward to the shore,
> Where the bowed Waters meet him, and adore,
> Kissing his feet with murmurs; and the Wood,
> The covert of old trees, with trunks all hoar,
> But light leaves, young as joy, stands where it stood,
> Offering to him, and his, a populous solitude.

Such adulation of Rousseau the man is difficult now to accept, but in the presence of the imagined perfection of Julie it was no doubt indelicate to remember the illiterate Thérèse

Levasseur and her five bastards in the Foundling Hospital. Indeed at other times neither Byron nor Shelley was so uncritically devoted to Rousseau's memory. Byron protested, when in 1808 his mother compared him to Rousseau, 'I have no ambition to be like so illustrious a madman.' And in his *Detached Thoughts* he refuted the comparison with some justice, point by point: he did so, as he said, not out of pique, because if it had been true he would have thought it flattering – 'but I have no idea of being pleased with a chimera'. Shelley considered the *Confessions* 'either a disgrace to the confessor or a string of falsehoods, probably the latter'. But for the moment the two poets were on holiday together in country which Rousseau had described with charm and delicacy and had made the setting of a famous love-story; and they were willing to surrender to the power of a great writer without the intrusion of untimely scepticism.

There were other literary associations to be discovered on the tour of the lake. They visited Gibbon's house at Lausanne on the twenty-ninth anniversary of the very day on which he there wrote the final sentences of the *Decline and Fall.* Byron plucked a sprig of acacia from one of the old trees on the terrace where Gibbon tells us that he walked after laying down his pen, and he enclosed it in a letter to Murray. Shelley 'refrained from doing so, fearing to outrage the greater and more sacred name of Rousseau; the contemplation of whose imperishable creations had left no vacancy in my heart for mortal things.' However, a week later Shelley had recovered sufficiently to be able to take a more detached view of *La Nouvelle Héloïse* and to admit that it was, though a work of genius, 'in some respects absurd and prejudiced'.

Byron, less sentimentally affected, wrote a stanza on Gibbon and another on Voltaire, whose village of Ferney was very near Geneva. But besides adding stanzas to his long serial poem Byron seized the opportunity provided by two wet days which kept them ashore at Ouchy to write a new poem. The day before, 26 June, they had visited the Castle of Chillon, where Julie made her last, ill-fated excursion: 'I never saw a monument more terrible of that cold and inhuman tyranny, which it has been the delight of man to exercise over man,' said Shelley; he made no mention of Bonivard. Byron, characteristically moved by the sufferings of one heroic individual rather than led to Shelleyan generalisation, there and then wrote *The Prisoner of Chillon.* He knew the brief account of Bonivard's imprisonment in *La Nouvelle Héloïse*, and the guide told them something of the story. In the poem which he wrote, the best of all his verse tales, Byron succeeds in imagining what long years of imprisonment in the dungeon which he had just visited might mean to an ardent, vigorous man. He differentiates enough between the personalities of the three brothers who were imprisoned together to establish clearly the resolute character of the survivor who is his hero, and his description of Bonivard's mental collapse after the death of the youngest brother is very convincing. So too is the account of his restoration to sanity, begun by a sudden joyful response to the song of a bird, which he heard through the window of his dully familiar prison. This re-awakening of his mind leads at first only to more acute recognition of his wretchedness; but then the bird comes within his sight,

> And it was come to love me when
> None lived to love me so again,
> And cheering from my dungeon's brink,
> Had brought me back to feel and think.

Such awareness of joy and liberty outside the walls of a prison has been conveyed by the song of birds to other prisoners since Bonivard, and Byron's imagination is precise and true.

Byron uses the bird as a link between the world of Nature outside the Castle, which suggests the ideas of liberty and happiness, and the man-made prison within. The guide who had shown them over the Castle 'told us,' says Shelley, 'that there was an opening to the lake, by means of a secret spring, connected with which the whole dungeon might be filled with water before the prisoners could possibly escape!' This story, which Rousseau had mentioned, was untrue, but the suggestion, which appalled Shelley by its further evidence of human brutality, was used by Byron with dramatic force.

> Below the surface of the lake
> The dark vault lies wherein we lay:
> We heard it ripple night and day;
>   Sounding o'er our heads it knocked;
> And I have felt the winter's spray
> Wash through the bars when winds were high
> And wanton in the happy sky;
>   And then the very rock hath rocked,
>   And I have felt it shake, unshocked,
> Because I could have smiled to see
> The death that would have set me free.

For to Bonivard this sinister arrangement provided the one hope of escape, by death, from the misery which he endured.

Shelley was impelled by his visit to Chillon to reflect upon the wickedness of tyrants who used the place as a prison; Byron, to imagine the experience of a man imprisoned there. And the final line, where Bonivard, at last set free, confesses that he 'regained his freedom with a sigh', however paradoxical it may seem, is certainly true, for, to the man who has grown inured to long years of imprisonment, the restoration of liberty brings the prospect of responsibilities and encounters which, at first, he must find difficult to face. A year or two later Byron and Shelley would visit the place where a yet more famous prisoner had been incarcerated, and would both write poems on the subject. But for the moment Shelley was moved to indignation and Byron to a more poetically viable sympathy. The influence of Wordsworth was again apparent, so much so that a writer in *The Critical Review* for December 1816 suggested that among the few books Byron had with him on the tour of the lake were the two volumes of his *Poems* published in the previous year. He recognised in Byron a tardy convert to Wordsworth; he could not know that Shelley had effected the conversion.

The bad weather which provided time for the writing of *The Prisoner of Chillon* nearly brought disaster to them on the 25th while they were sailing from Meillerie to St Gingolph. A squall arose which, in Shelley's words, 'produced waves of a frightful height, and covered the whole surface with a chaos of foam'. They expected the boat to be swamped at any moment. Byron took off his coat and told Shelley to take off his and to grasp an oar. But Shelley, who could not swim, refused to allow Byron to attempt to save his life, 'and seating himself quietly upon a locker, and grasping the rings at each end firmly in his hands, declared his determination to go down in that position, without a struggle'. This is the account which Thomas Moore gives, presumably on Byron's authority. Shelley told Peacock that, knowing Byron would have attempted to save him, 'I was overcome with humiliation, when I thought that his life might have been risked to preserve mine.' Byron, writing immediately afterwards to Murray, said only that he himself 'ran no risk, being so near the rocks, and a good swimmer; but our party were wet, and incommoded a good deal.' But three years later, in another letter to Murray, Byron said that when he offered to save Shelley, 'he answered me with the greatest coolness that "he had no notion of being saved, and that I would have enough to do to save myself, and begged not to trouble me."' Thus were the courtesies between two well-bred Englishmen maintained in the face of danger. The incident must have impressed each of them with the admirable, calm courage of the other. And suitably enough it took place, as Byron pointed out to Shelley, 'precisely in the spot where Julie and her lover were nearly overset and where St Preux was tempted to plunge with her into the lake.' Thus even the Alpine weather seemed in a conspiracy with the spirit of Rousseau.

The holiday ended with two days of pleasant sailing from Ouchy to Montalègre, where they arrived on the evening of Monday 1 July. During this time Shelley may have drafted some passages of the *Hymn to Intellectual Beauty* that are to be found in the note-book which he had with him. Mary says only that the poem 'was conceived during his voyage round the lake with Lord Byron', and Shelley himself, in a letter to Leigh Hunt, says that 'the poem was composed under the influence of feelings which agitated me even to tears'. Whenever the poem was written, the influences that are apparent are of Plato and of Rousseau, not of Lord Byron except in so far as he had directed Shelley's attention at this time to *La Nouvelle Héloïse*. There is a certain diluted Platonism in Rousseau's work, but Shelley had read some Plato at Eton and at Oxford, though Plato was not studied for Greats there until long after. Peacock was chiefly responsible for stimulating Shelley's interest in Plato, as in Greek thought and literature generally, and by this time Platonism was well on the way to ousting Godwinism from Shelley's mind. 'Intellectual Beauty' is Shelley's translation in his version of the *Symposium* of the Greek 'τὸ καλόν', and in this poem Shelley combines with recollection of the visual beauty of the Swiss landscape Platonic speculation such as we find in the *Phaedrus*. There Plato speaks of a kind of madness 'with which a man is inspired whenever, by the sight of beauty in this lower world, the true beauty of the world above is so brought to his remembrance that he begins to recover his plumage, and feeling new wings longs to soar aloft; but, the power failing him, gazes upward like a bird, and becomes heedless of all lower matters, thereby exposing himself to the imputation of being crazed'. The same Platonic theory of recollection Shelley would have found in Wordsworth's *Ode on Intimations of Immortality*. But as usual with Shelley the immediate inspiration of the poem suggests only scraps of detail – the 'summer winds that creep from flower to flower', the 'rainbows o'er yon mountain-river', 'mist o'er mountains driven' – while the contribution of past reading, in Plato and Rousseau, in Thomson and Wordsworth, and of speculations prompted by these and others, is far more important. Here again is the contrast with Byron; in the poems that he wrote, or conceived, during the tour of the lake, most derived from immediate impressions of the scene, or from its human associations. This is the 'journalistic' element in Byron's poetry which it is fashionable now to disparage; but it might, with more justice, be likened to the painter's gift for selecting significant detail in what is before his eyes. As Byron said at the time, most of his poems had been founded on a fact.

Shelley's poetry seldom provides material for illustration: he does not invite his reader, as Byron does, to visualise a scene, but to think about the moral, political, aesthetic or scientific ideas upon which the scene has stimulated him to reflect.

After their return Byron and Shelley resumed for three weeks the previous pattern of their lives at Montalègre. Within four days Byron had put the finishing touches to the third canto of *Childe Harold*, which he then gave to Claire for her to make a fair copy. This she finished by 10 July, and she then turned to copy *The Prisoner of Chillon*, but before she completed the task Byron decided that he could not endure her importunate love for him any longer, and forbade her to come to his villa. In a pathetic note to him she asked: 'Shall I never see you again? Not once again.' He kept the note, as he had kept all the others. Byron may also have decided that her visits to him gave some plausibility to the tiresome scandal that was circulating about him in Geneva, and now that Madame de Staël had returned to Coppet he was enjoying visits there. It was probably Byron's sudden desire for a show of respectability that led to Shelley's regret, in a letter to Peacock, 'that he is a slave to the vilest and most vulgar prejudices'. At least this is the sort of phrase that Shelley would be more likely to use to castigate subservience to social convention than rejection of an unsought mistress. He and Mary knew from past experience how wearisome Claire's presence could become, and Shelley probably agreed with Byron that she lacked either reserve or distinction, though, unlike Byron, he would not have been unkind enough to say so.

Byron paid his first visit to Madame de Staël's château some time about the middle of July. He had met her three years before in London, at Lady Jersey's, and had afterwards seen her frequently during her stay in England that summer. He considered her the cleverest woman he had ever met, and delighted in matching his wits against hers with a candour equal to her own. He especially enjoyed talking to her about her novels, and on one occasion told her that 'her representing all the virtuous characters in *Corinne* as being dull, commonplace, and tedious was a most insidious blow aimed at virtue'. He brushed aside her attempts to interrupt, for it was good fun that he, of all men, should be giving her a lesson on morals. He did not find her very agreeable, however, and summed her up in his usual sharp and succinct manner: 'She *thought* like a man, but, alas! she *felt* like a woman.' The justice of such a judgment may be confirmed by its aptness to certain learned and loquacious ladies of our own day. Byron also remarked, again perhaps not without reason, that she was 'frightful as a precipice', and was rude enough to nickname her 'old Mother Stale'. However, although he often found himself laughing at her, he respected her vigorous independence of mind and her intelligence.

This first visit to Coppet was as melodramatic as any scene in London. On being announced to the assembled guests, 'Byron was surprised to meet a lady carried out fainting.' This was a Mrs Hervey – 'she writes novels', said Byron (she was Beckford's sister Elizabeth) – and the Duchesse de Broglie exlaimed, 'This is *too much* – at *sixty-five* years of age!' No wonder Byron had the impression that the room was 'full of strangers, who had come to stare at me as at some outlandish beast in a raree-show'. But he was used to this by now, and it was something to be able to confront these absurd people – Mrs Hervey soon came back into the room on her own feet – instead of being watched at long range through telescopes. Madame de Staël rather maliciously gave him a marvellous yet vague account of the novel, *Glenarvon*, which Lady Caroline Lamb (the heroine of his most dramatised love-affair) had chosen this moment of his deepest distress to publish. He had not yet seen it himself, he told Murray, 'and I know but one thing a woman can say to the purpose on such occasions, and that she might as well for her own sake keep to herself, which by the way they very rarely can – the old reproach against their admirers of "*Kiss* and *tell*", bad as it is, is surely somewhat less than F—— and publish.' By the end of the month he had read the copy which Madame de Staël lent him:

his only comment was to quote Pope's notorious couplet about Lady Mary Wortley Montagu.

In spite of this discouraging start Byron continued to visit Coppet, and to enjoy the lively talk in this Indian Summer of Madame de Staël's life there. And there were not, as there were in Geneva itself, too many of the sensation-mongering English. The permanent inhabitants of the château this summer, besides Madame de Staël, were M. de Rocca, who would soon be secretly married to her, who looked very ill, but who was capable of being witty at Byron's expense, and whom Byron liked and respected; her daughter by a previous marriage, the Duchesse de Broglie, who was nearly as plain and intelligent as her mother, and her husband, a liberal aristocrat whom Madame de Staël once described as 'the only Englishman in France'; and August Wilhelm von Schlegel, the translator of Shakespeare. Byron did not take to Schlegel, who was small, ugly, and excessively conceited, 'the Dousterswivel of Madame de Staël', he called him. Schlegel in his turn resented Byron's unwillingness, even when prompted by the Duchesse de Broglie, to join the chorus of flattery. Bonstetten, whom Byron liked, was a frequent visitor; and Pellegrino Rossi, whom he had also met at Madame Eynard's, together with Monsignor di Breme, aroused Byron's interest in the Italian patriotic movement through their talk at Coppet.

Madame de Staël rejoiced to have so famous or notorious a man as Byron in her salon, in spite of his tendency to tease her. He could not forgo telling her that she was said to be the heroine of Benjamin Constant's recently published *Adolphe* (which was fair revenge for her comments on *Glenarvon*), and, harking back to that conversation with her three summers before, he told her that *Adolphe* 'ought always to be given to every young woman who had read *Corinne*, as an antidote'. But for all the passionate outbursts which such remarks provoked in her, she 'took a great deal of trouble to bring out the best in Byron' (unsuccessfully in the Duc de Broglie's view), and even attempted to bring about a reconciliation with Lady Byron. This was a predictably disastrous failure; but Byron was grateful for her kindness to him when all the rest of the society in which they had first met was against him, and he said that she had made Coppet 'as agreeable as society and talent can make any place on earth'. He was surely therefore not intending to tease her when, in a sonnet which he wrote some time in July, he linked her name with those others who had brought literary fame to Lac Léman, Voltaire, Rousseau and Gibbon. Madame de Staël professed embarrassment at so extravagant a compliment and gave it as the reason for turning against Byron a little later. But Byron shrugged this off with 'she was always more civil to me in person than during my absence' – a well-known feature of social life.

Byron took Polidori to Coppet with him occasionally, and without mishap. He found Madame de Staël polite and affable as well as talkative, and observed her inclination both to lecture Byron and to treat him as her confidant. But Byron never introduced Shelley to her, either because Shelley was too shy to enter her salon or because Byron himself could hardly envisage his friend in that company. Not that Shelley would have been unable to hold his own with any of them, but he was at his best in an evening's talk with one or two friends, not in a sophisticated cosmopolitan society. He told Hogg that he had 'no great curiosity to see' her or the other literary people then in Geneva; he would not have enjoyed Coppet, and both he and Byron were shrewd enough to realise this. Byron thus returned alone for a time to the sort of society which he had known so well during the years of fame in London, and from which, with feelings of scorn and regret, he had recently exiled himself.

He had been vividly reminded of that life by hearing, at this very time, of the death of Sheridan on 7 July. His old friend Douglas Kinnaird had written to tell him the news and to ask him to write some lines that might be spoken in Sheridan's memory at Drury Lane Theatre. Byron was deeply moved by the news, for he had seen much of Sheridan during those last three years in England and had, as he said, 'always found him very convivial and delightful'. He admired his abilities – he considered that whatever Sheridan had done had been the best of its kind – and he would not condemn him for his weaknesses. Sheridan was the first of the men whom he had known during his own years of fame to die, and his death meant the first final break with those years. Thus his admission to Lady Blessington that every word of his *Monody* came direct from the heart was certainly true, and not in conflict with those romantic scruples about writing at someone else's suggestion which he mentioned in a letter to Murray. He composed his poem on 17 July, which must have been immediately on receipt of Kinnaird's letter. Claire copied it next day, and it was sent off at once to England. Mrs Davison 'discovered leaning on an urn' spoke the lines at Drury Lane on 7 September, two months after Sheridan's death, and the poem was published two days later as a pamphlet, the first of the poems which he had written since leaving England to appear in print. On 22 September Leigh Hunt, who in July had written two papers on Sheridan, reprinted Byron's poem in *The Examiner* with some apt criticism. Byron's talent, he said, 'does not lie so much in appealing to others, as in expressing himself. He does not make you so much a party as a witness.'

A few days after Byron's first visit to Coppet, on 21 July, Shelley set off with Mary and Claire for a tour to Chamonix and Mont Blanc. They left the six-months-old William in the charge of his Swiss nurse Élise, and on arriving at Chamonix next day Shelley immediately sent a short note to Byron in which he asked after his little son. For the rest he suggested that Byron should come to join him at Chamonix: he knew that Byron's response to the magnificent scenery would at once find its expression in poetry, as during their recent tour of the lake. However, Byron, was enjoying his visits to Coppet too much for the moment, and not until later, when Claire was out of the way, did he go to Chamonix.

On the same day, 22 July, Shelley also wrote to Peacock one of those long descriptive letters which, taken together, give so vivid a picture of the Romantic conception of the scenery of southern Europe and are at the same time masterpieces in the Augustan tradition of letter-writing. Byron's letters present the fascinating mobility of his mind with its marvellously alert responsiveness, and as we read we seem to hear the very cadences of his voice. Shelley's letters do not attempt this; there is not the same intimacy of tone; we do not feel that he is in the room with us. Byron never seems to be thinking of any-one except the correspondent whom he is addressing; Shelley writes letters to be handed round. There are no letters of their kind to surpass Shelley's to Peacock; but there are no letters to compare with Byron's. Shelley describes their journey up the valley of the Arve to Sallanches, where they slept the first night, and then on, riding mules, to Chamonix, where they arrived fatigued to death at seven o'clock in the evening. There they stayed at the Hôtel de Londres, where, after signing his name in the register, Shelley added, *δημοκρατικὸς φιλανθρωπότατος καὶ ἄθεος*. He wrote the same four words in other registers on this journey, provoked perhaps by the inscriptions of other visitors, whom the mountains stirred to platitudinous piety. They remained four nights at Chamonix, visiting the source of the Arveyron, the glacier de Bossons, and the Mer de Glace. Characteristically Shelley combines with his poetic description of the scenery scientific theories about the formation of glaciers; but he rejects de Saussure's belief that periods of advance and recession alternate in favour of a conviction that the glaciers must continually augment. Amid such sublime and inspiring scenery it was lamentable to come upon other English visitors: they were best forgotten, and Shelley spares Peacock an account of these 'melancholy exhibitions of tourism'. Nonetheless Shelley's party brought back souvenirs of their visit, 'some specimens of minerals and plants and two or three crystal seals' apparently showing Mont Blanc, and also some seeds of alpines for Shelley's garden in England. Yet the man from whom he bought these things was 'the very vilest specimen of that vile species of quack', which, at Chamonix no less than at Matlock or Keswick or Clifton, subsisted on the tourist trade.

In one of the villages they passed through they were offered a squirrel in a cage, and, in order to rescue it, Shelley bought it.

The frightened little creature, which had been caught only three days before, was given to Mary to carry. It promptly bit her finger so that she dropped it. However, they caught it again somehow, and this time entrusted it to Shelley. 'It appeared at length resigned to its fate,' Mary wrote, 'when we put it on a railing, where it paused an instant, wondering where it was, and then scampered up its native trees.' This charming incident is as typical of Shelley as his reviling of the poor man who was battening on the vulgar tastes of English tourists, or as the Greek inscriptions in hotel registers.

Shelley did not tell Peacock of the squirrel, nor did he mention the poem *Mont Blanc* which he wrote during the visit to Chamonix. He dated the poem 23 July, but it seems more likely that he wrote it on 24 July, when they were driven home early by rain; Shelley's dates in his letter to Peacock are a day in advance. Mary said that the poem was inspired by the view of the mountain 'as he lingered on the Bridge of Arve, on his way through the Valley of Chamouni'. For once Shelley was attempting to make poetry, as Byron habitually did, out of an immediate impression; but the Berkeleyan philosophy which gives it coherence would have found no place in a poem by Byron. Shelley, even when he learnt from Byron to set down in verse his response to something which he had just seen, did not do so in Byron's manner, because his response was mediated through his intellect no less than through his senses, which made the Berkeleyan implications of the poem relevant. Byron under Shelley's influence might proclaim that for him high mountains were a feeling; but Shelley under Byron's influence could not help regarding Mont Blanc as a symbol of that Intellectual Beauty which he had addressed in the recent *Hymn*. For Shelley, therefore,

> the naked countenance of earth
> On which I gaze, even these primaeval mountains
> Teach the adverting mind.

The same scene would lead Byron to impressionistic description, not to nice speculations of philosophy, and when Manfred summons the spirits to his aid all he has to ask of them is self-oblivion, which they are powerless to give.

Phrases which Shelley used in his letter to Peacock recur, naturally enough, in the poem. In the letter he describes the glacier de Bossons which, he says, 'presents the most vivid image of desolation that it is possible to conceive. . . . The pines of the forest which bounds it at one extremity are overthrown and shattered; – there is something inexpressibly dreadful in the aspect of the few branchless trunks which nearest to the ice rifts still stand in the uprooted soil. The meadows perish overwhelmed with sand and stones.' In the poem, pruned of that hypallage, 'the uprooted soil',

> a flood of ruin
> Is there, that from the boundaries of the sky
> Rolls its perpetual stream; vast pines are strewing
> Its destined path, or in the mangled soil
> Branchless and shattered stand; the rocks, drawn down
> From yon remotest waste, have overthrown
> The limits of the dead and living world,
> Never to be reclaimed.

Shelley, believing that the glaciers would continue to advance until they had filled the entire valley, believed also that no plant would ever grow where the ice had once been. Thus for him the inexorable power of the ice at a time when the glaciers were advancing was more terrifying than it is for us who visit these places at a time when the glaciers are rapidly retreating, and who can see for ourselves that the devastation is not perpetual, but that plants will recolonise the moraines. When Shelley was at Chamonix Mont Blanc had been climbed but three times, in 1786 and 1787, so that the mountain was still

> Remote, serene, and inaccessible,

in a way scarcely imaginable now when the view is liable to be interrupted by funicular and cable railways, and the presence of tourist huts has made the ascent merely an exhausting walk. Also Shelley was aware of Buffon's theory that the world would end in a new and universal ice age, which, at least in the presence of Mont Blanc and those sinister advancing glaciers, he found persuasive.

They returned to Montalègre on 27 July and went at once to the Villa Diodati without even calling at Chappuis to see the baby. After three hours' talk with Byron they went down to 'kiss our babe, and go to bed'. Next day Shelley and Byron resumed the familiar pattern of their lives, reading, going on the lake together in the afternoon, talking at the Villa Diodati in the evening. Usually Shelley would go out in the boat alone with Byron; sometimes he would go up to Diodati alone, though at first Mary more often went with him. Once he and Claire went together, leaving Mary behind at Byron's suggestion: no doubt he wished to discuss with Shelley and Claire arrangements for the birth of his child in England, and for its subsequent care. Byron's impatience with Claire seems to have subsided a little: she went up to Diodati sometimes to do more copying for him, but she went always in Shelley's company; and Byron also came down to Chappuis a few times where he must have encountered her. On one of these visits Mary saw the two poets sitting side by side on the garden wall, deep in talk in the bright sunshine. The picture delighted her.

Shelley's twenty-fourth birthday was on 4 August. He and Mary went out together in the boat, and she read the fourth book of the *Aeneid* to him. She had bought him a telescope a few days before in Geneva, and she had also made him a fire-balloon. They had intended to release this from the boat, but the wind was too strong, and when they sent it up from the shore it caught fire almost as soon as it was released, and so was not a success. They also paid a brief visit together to Byron. A few days before Mary noted in her journal that she and Shelley had been together for two years.

On 13 August after recording that they had all gone up to Diodati after dinner, Mary entered in the journal the one word 'War'. After this day she never again went up to Diodati during the remaining fortnight of their stay, although Shelley went almost every day, and even Claire, who had been present on the 13th, went three times. But it is not safe to deduce that there was a state of hostilities between Mary and Byron, for he visited Chappuis half a dozen times after that, and she expresses no resentment or embarrassment in her journal, neither is there any suggestion that Shelley's friendship for him was affected. It seems most likely that Byron, who was expecting visitors from England, did not wish them to meet Mary and Claire and so to suspect that there might be substance to the scandalous gossip which, as he knew, was being circulated about him at home. At this time also Madame de Staël was attempting to bring about a reconciliation with Lady Byron, and it was therefore especially desirable to avoid scandal. One of Byron's visitors, John Cam Hobhouse, went out of his way to give the lie to these rumours in a letter of 8 September to Augusta Leigh, who was then in correspondence with Lady Byron, and in it he says that Scrope Davies, the friend who had come out with him, had probably already given her the same news in person. Hobhouse mentions the recent presence near by of Shelley and the two ladies, without naming them, and admits that both ladies had been 'most liberally assigned' to Byron. His dislike of Shelley may have owed something to his belief that by coming to live on Byron's doorstep with a couple of girls Shelley had given opportunity for fresh scandal about him.

The first of the visitors to arrive at the Villa Diodati, and on the day after Mary's cryptic entry in her journal, was 'Monk' Lewis, so called because of his successful Gothick novel, *Ambrosio, or The Monk*, which he published at the age of twenty in 1795. For its immorality Lewis had been compared to John Cleland, the chronicler of *Fanny Hill*, but Shelley read *The Monk* at the age of twelve. Lewis had recently returned from Jamaica where he had inherited considerable estates, and he was now on his way to Italy. Byron had known him in London, and, though he acknowledged that he was a good man and a clever man, he thought him a 'damned bore'. Lewis disliked Sheridan and, as Byron said, they had words on that subject during this visit. Among Lewis's more tedious qualities were a delight in being contradictory – he sent Byron a sour little epigram on Sheridan as a riposte to the *Monody* – and a propensity never to stop talking. Byron seized the opportunity to set him by the ears with Madame de Staël; there is after all nothing more teasing to a loquacious person than to be confronted with another, and Byron must have enjoyed watching the two of them, each struggling to interrupt the flow of the other's conversation. The subject was slavery, of which Lewis had up-to-date and first-hand knowledge, and on which Madame de Staël was sure to have theories. Besides, this was not the first time they had met; they had encountered one another in London and had squabbled there too, as Byron knew. The opportunity was too good to be missed.

Shelley did not accompany them to Coppet, nor on another jaunt to Ferney, but otherwise he was much in their company during Lewis's stay. While in his teens, in 1792 and 1793, Lewis spent some months at Weimar and there met Goethe; he now translated some passages from *Faust* to Byron and Shelley, neither of whom knew German. Byron was much impressed by this introduction to *Faust*, and for the rest of his life he continued to admire the work of one whom he regarded as the greatest genius of the age. He told Medwin that he 'would give the world to read *Faust* in the original', and that he had been urging Shelley (who by that time, 1821, had learnt German) to do so. And Shelley did then translate some five hundred lines.

But for the present Shelley seems to have been more struck by Monk Lewis's telling of ghost stories, four of which he noted in Mary's journal. He was disconcerted to find that even Lewis, like Byron, refused to believe in ghosts; and he failed to detect that their assertion, that a man who believed in ghosts must also, surely, believe in God, was directed to his own professions of atheism. There was talk also of slavery. The kind-hearted Lewis had done all he could, while on his visit to Jamaica, to improve the lot of the slaves on his plantations, and now, in the company of two liberal-minded friends, he drew up a codicil to his will, dated from the Villa Diodati on 20 August, by which he made it a condition of inheritance that his heirs should visit the estates in Jamaica for at least three months in every third year. He also forbade the sale of any Negro belonging to him at the time of his death. He invited Byron, Shelley and Polidori to witness this document. Next day he continued his journey into Italy, where Byron saw him again some months later.

On 26 August John Cam Hobhouse and Scrope Davies, two of Byron's most loyal and most vivacious friends, arrived at Diodati. Byron managed to prevent them seeing either Mary or Claire, and indeed after the 25th he himself never again saw Claire; but Shelley went up to Diodati on each of the three days that remained before he left for England. Hobhouse, who travelled with Byron during the years when he was writing the first two cantos of *Childe Harold*, did not like the new canto so well – 'there is an air of mystery and metaphysics about it', he said – and, though he later denied Shelley's influence on Byron, at this time he must have observed it, and with some regret. It was hardly likely that the worldly and cynical Hobhouse would approve of the idealistic and (in his eyes) priggish Shelley as a friend for Byron, and he may well have thought that Shelley was diverting Byron from his own natural manner. He even went so far as to deny that Byron and Shelley were ever friends: so much can jealousy pervert truth. The gay and witty Scrope Davies, Fellow of King's, gambler and dandy, was still less likely to admire Shelley, or to take him seriously. It was therefore just as well that Shelley and his party left for England on the morning of 29 August. The presence of these friends from Byron's earlier life at Cambridge and in London, with their lively reminder of what he had forfeited, might very easily have led to a break with Shelley. Shelley could never have had any sympathy with the Byron they had known in England, and the qualities which they brought out in him were in conflict with those which Shelley had discovered. Shelley's departure thus made it possible for Byron to retain and to value this new friendship, and it released him from any need to choose between the two. If he had had to choose there is little doubt that at this time he would have chosen his older friends, not only because they had known him longer, and through his years of fame, but because their company was more light-hearted, less strenuous, than that of the insistently intellectual Shelley. He still regretted his exile, and, as his moves towards a reconciliation with Lady Byron suggest, he had not yet finally severed himself from the old life. Nor was it until he reached Italy that he could discover the new life that he would make for himself, a life in which Shelley would play a far more important part than the old friends whom he had known in England.

CHAPTER THREE

Interlude

SEPTEMBER 1816–MARCH 1818:

BYRON IN ITALY–SHELLEY IN ENGLAND

WHEN Shelley left Geneva for England he agreed to undertake two commissions for Byron: to see to the publication of the poems which Byron had written during the summer, and to make all necessary arrangements for the birth of Claire's child. Byron had formed a most favourable opinion both of Shelley's kindness and tact and also of his business acumen, and in neither was he to be disappointed. He was delighted to be disembarrassed of Claire, who accompanied Shelley and Mary back to England, and he gave Shelley for transmission to John Murray, his publisher, the copies which Claire had made of the third canto of *Childe Harold*, of *The Prisoner of Chillon* and of the other shorter poems that were to be published with it. He knew that a fellow-poet would not attempt to improve his poems in the tiresome way that Hobhouse and Douglas Kinnaird and other friends sometimes presumed to do. Besides, he had discussed these poems with Shelley as soon as they were written, and none could know better than Shelley Byron's intentions for them; he had even given Shelley authority for certain revisions.

On 8 September, the day of his arrival in England, Shelley wrote a short letter to Byron from Portsmouth to give him the earliest news, as he said, of the safe arrival of *Childe Harold*. 'His only adventure since he quitted the paternal roof has been inglorious. He was taken for a smuggler, and turned over and over by a greasy Custom-house officer, to see if lace, etc., were hidden within.' Shelley sent his remembrances to Hobhouse and Scrope Davies, and suppressed the fond messages which Claire asked him to transmit. He promised to write again in three days' time, when he reached London, and this he did. He had immediately taken Byron's poems to Murray, who was eagerly awaiting the new instalment of *Childe Harold*; Murray had already heard from Byron that it was on its way, and he had also been told that Madame de Staël considered it the best thing Byron had yet done. On Byron's instructions he presented Shelley with a copy of Byron's *Poems* bound in blue and gilt. 'Your *favourite* Mary', Claire informed Byron, 'is *impertinent* and *nauseous* enough to think it wonderful you should have remembered your promise.' Shelley was to call on Douglas Kinnaird, Byron's man of business, next day, to discuss with him the terms on which Murray should have *Childe Harold* III. Murray tempered his enthusiasm to propose 1200 guineas, but in the end Shelley and Kinnaird extracted 2000 guineas from him, of which the last 500 were conditional on its success. The Scottish publisher naturally resented the insistence by one poet on a fair price being paid to another, and a year later described Shelley to John Wilson Croker as 'the vilest wretch now living'. Shelley probably expected nothing else. By the 29th, when he wrote again to Byron, Shelley was waiting to receive the first proofs of the poem, and a day or two later he sent Murray his address in Bath, to which he requested him to send the proofs.

Murray however had contrived to misunderstand Byron's instructions about the proofs. In a letter written the day before Shelley left Geneva, and perhaps before he had asked Shelley to undertake the task, Byron had told Murray that he did not know who would be good-natured enough to correct them. He suggested Tom Moore if he was in town, or, if not, then Shelley himself. In the same letter he said that he hoped Gifford would read *Childe Harold*, because he wished to have his comments: within a month he had received these, and found them flattering. Murray thereupon invited Gifford to correct the proofs, which Byron had neither suggested nor authorised. By the middle of October Byron had forgotten exactly what he had written in August, and welcomed Murray's information that Gifford had agreed to correct the proofs. In the meantime Shelley, whose vileness was perhaps already apparent to Murray, had received nothing, not even a letter from him, and was somewhat surprised to read an advertisement at the end of October announcing the publication of *Childe Harold* III and *The Prisoner of Chillon* for 23 November. He wrote a sharp letter to Murray on 30 October reminding him of their conversation in London six weeks before, at which it had been agreed that the proofs should be sent to him. 'I should not do my duty to Lord Byron who entrusted me with the Mss. of his Poems, if I did not remind you, that it was his particular desire that I should revise the proofs before publication. – When I had the pleasure of seeing you in London, I think I stated his Lordship's wishes on this subject to you, remarking at the same time that his wishes did not arise from a persuasion that I should pay more attention to its accuracy than any person whom you might select; but because he communicated it to me immediately after composition; and did me the honour to entrust to my discretion, as to whether certain particular expressions should be retained or changed.' He asked for a reply by return so that he might let Byron know what was happening: he did not wish to be put in a false position with a friend through the ineptitude of his publisher. And in a postscript he pointed out that Murray had not even got the title of a poem right: he was advertising 'The Prisoner*s* of Chillon' – 'Lord Byron wrote it "Prisone*r*".' In the event the third canto of *Childe Harold* was published on 18 November, and the volume containing *The Prisoner of Chillon* on 5 December. Murray sold 7000 copies of each at 5*s* 6*d* in a single day, so that, even if Shelley had secured a reasonable reward for the author, the publisher's profits cannot have been negligible.

In the letter in which Shelley told Byron that he was to receive 2000 guineas for *Childe Harold* he also wrote of the poetry which he expected Byron to write once he had reached Italy and had put behind him the depressing slanders that his enemies such as Caroline Lamb and Henry Brougham* were industriously propagating in England. Shelley knew that while they were at Geneva these allegations had preyed upon Byron's mind so much that, as he told Teresa Guiccioli long afterwards, 'his natural gaiety had almost entirely left him'. Now he sensibly advised Byron to disregard such stuff and to concentrate his gifts on writing the great poems which he confidently believed were within his powers. He knew Byron well enough to understand that he could not help still hankering after the position he had once enjoyed as the fashionable lion of London hostesses; he knew also that Byron was given to disparaging his own gifts as a poet, which somehow seemed unsuited to his rank; and he himself had observed at Ouchy and at Diodati the careless ease with which he composed. He advised him therefore to forget the past and, for the first time, to concentrate all his incomparable gifts as a poet. 'I hope for no more than that you should . . . feel that you are chosen out from all other men to some greater enterprise of thought; and that all your studies should, from that moment, tend towards that enterprise alone: that your affections, that all worldly hopes this world may have left you, should link themselves to this design.' Shelley more than anyone else forced Byron to accept his destiny as a poet instead of allowing himself to be distracted by other ambitions (whose temptation Shelley well understood) or of resting content with the fame he had already won. And when at last Byron found his true métier in *Don Juan* the poem had no more generous or discriminating admirer than Shelley.

On the same day on which Shelley set out for England Byron, with Hobhouse and Scrope Davies, left for Chamonix. They travelled, as Shelley and his party had done a month before, up the valley of the Arve, and like them stayed the night at Sallanches. On signing the hotel register Byron noticed

* A legal broom's a moral chimney-sweeper,
And that's the reason he himself's so dirty.
Don Juan x xv

Shelley's name there, with the defiant Greek inscription after it. He pointed this out to Hobhouse and said, 'Do you not think I shall do Shelley a service by scratching this out?' and he carefully defaced the words. However Shelley had written similar inscriptions at Chamonix and at Montenvers which escaped Byron's notice. (Next year Southey's malicious eye observed one. He copied it for future use.) As always Byron was much more concerned with other people's opinions than was Shelley; it is one reason for his extraordinary success with his public, and for Shelley's lack of it. Like Shelley, Byron was exasperated by the inadequate response of English tourists to the sublime scenery of Mont Blanc. At Chamonix he overheard an Englishwoman exclaim to her party, 'Did you ever see anything more rural?' – 'as if' said Byron, 'it was Highgate, or Hampstead, or Brompton, or Hayes, – "*Rural!*" quotha! – Rocks, pines, torrents, glaciers, clouds, and summits of eternal snow far above them – and "*Rural!*" ' But unlike Shelley he was not thereby provoked to announce his difference from such Philistines by inscribing Greek in hotel registers.

This visit to the mountains, and a longer trip to the Bernese Alps later in the month with Hobhouse – Scrope Davies had gone back to England soon after they returned from Chamonix – provided much of the inspiration for Byron's next long poem, *Manfred.* Already in July he had written seventy lines for what, when he included them in *The Prisoner of Chillon* volume, he called 'an unfinished Witch drama', and it seems very probable that he had discussed with Shelley his plans for this first attempt at dramatic writing. Shelley had read the *Incantation* (as these seventy lines were titled), for it was among the poems he took with him to England, and he knew that it was not intended as an independent lyric. The theme is the ineluctable curse with which he, Manfred or Byron, feels himself to be afflicted, and which compels him to be his own proper Hell. Twice more in the poem Byron recurs to this Miltonic assertion that the mind is its own place. Soon after Byron wrote these lines Monk Lewis came to stay with him and opportunely translated passages from Goethe's *Faust*, which suggested to

Byron's imagination the sort of dramatic poem in which the *Incantation* might be included; and, though Byron quite properly rejected charges of plagiarism from Goethe, he was willing to admit the similarity of the first scene, which the *Incantation* closes, to the first scene of *Faust.* Goethe himself, in a review of the poem, noted the strange uses Byron had made of his own great poetic drama, and especially admired the way in which Byron had turned its motives to his own ends 'so that no one of them remains the same'. Byron's own account of the origins of *Manfred* is candid enough: 'it was the *Staubach* and the *Jungfrau* and something else, much more than *Faustus*, that made me write *Manfred.*' He might have added, in support of this, that he began his poem before Monk Lewis made him acquainted with *Faust.*

The effect of the Alpine scenery, to which, thanks to Shelley's Wordsworthian ministrations, he had lately become much more responsive, hardly needs emphasising; as Byron himself pointed out there are many similarities between passages in the poem and in the journal of his tour with Hobhouse which he sent to Augusta. But there are also recollections from the earlier tour of the lake with Shelley. Thus a reference to 'the sought "Kalon"' must derive from Shelley's philosophising about Plato's τὸ καλόν when, on that tour, he was composing his *Hymn to Intellectual Beauty.* The lines about avalanches which fall

> On the young flourishing forest, or the hut
> And hamlet of the harmless villager,

recall the traces of a fall of rock which he and Shelley had seen on their way to Ouchy. And there is evidence here that Shelley talked to Byron of his visit to Chamonix, which he had encouraged Byron also to undertake. In his letter to Peacock describing the visit, Shelley asked if, in the poem that Peacock was writing at the time (which remains unpublished), he imagined Ahrimanes 'throned among these desolating snows, among these palaces of death and frost'; and Byron so introduces Ahrimanes in the fourth scene of his second act. This passage also suggests the opening scene of *Prometheus Unbound.* In the second scene of the first act Byron describes the fall of the Rossberg, which occurred on 2 September 1806, and in his letter Shelley gives an account of a similar spectacular disaster of which he had heard. But Shelley's influence is so pervasive that more detailed demonstration is scarcely needed.

Byron was proud to acknowledge the influence on *Manfred* of Aeschylus' *Prometheus Vinctus*, which he had learnt to admire as a boy. (As Ruskin said, 'Byron's early power was founded on a course of general reading of the masters in every walk of literature . . . unparalleled in any other young life.') The play's presence in his mind this summer is shown by the poem *Prometheus* which he wrote in July at Diodati. Shelley read *Prometheus Vinctus* this year, and his splendid use of the myth in his lyrical drama owes something to *Manfred* and (we may believe) to the conversations of this summer with Byron. And it is not very likely to be mere coincidence that within a few days of resuming those conversations in Venice after an interval of two years Shelley began work on *Prometheus Unbound.* The interplay of these two poetic minds, so stimulating to both, is too complex to be altogether decipherable by us, who never listened to them talking. They responded differently according to their different temperaments to the books they read and the experiences they shared, and when they were so much together constantly modified each other's responses in various and subtle ways. They themselves would have been more likely to accept these things among the rewards of friendship than to attempt a cool analysis.

More important than Staubbach or Jungfrau for the composition of *Manfred* was that unnamed 'something else'; for the theme of *Manfred* is remorse, and remorse above all for the sin of incest. It is not necessary here to argue once again whether or not the accusation of incest between Byron and his beloved half-sister Augusta can be upheld. But it had been made, and was much in men's mouths this summer, at Coppet and elsewhere:

Rumours strange,
And of unholy nature, are abroad,
And busy with thy name,

as the Abbot of St Maurice tells Manfred. In Shelley's opinion, this was 'the only important calumny that ever was advanced against' Byron; he did not accept it as true. Byron, who could not resist dramatising his own wickedness (for did he not, as a Calvinist, believe that he was predestined to damnation?), was inclined to hint that the charge was true, partly to impress such as Claire with the reckless evil of his nature, partly to intensify his own feelings of guilt. Looking back on the mood of this summer a few months later Byron could laugh at his romantic despair: 'I was half mad,' he told Tom Moore, 'between metaphysics, mountains, lakes, love unextinguishable, thoughts unutterable, and the nightmare of my own delinquencies.' And a fortnight later he told Murray that *Manfred* was 'of a very wild, metaphysical, and inexplicable kind'. Shelley, as for *Childe Harold* III, supplied the metaphysics, which Byron well understood was not his forte; Claire the love unextinguishable; Switzerland the mountains and lakes; and his delinquencies are reflected in Manfred's savage remorse. But nightmares do not interpret experience with humdrum precision; they may arise from an obsessive reaction to repeated accusation, or may be wholly fantastic. When Byron was writing the first two acts of *Manfred* on his tour with Hobhouse the nightmare must have seemed as real as the Staubbach or the Jungfrau; it is only when we wake that we realise that we have been dreaming.

The theme of incest fascinated Shelley no less than Byron. In *Laon and Cythna* and in *Rosalind and Helen*, the two long poems which he wrote during the eighteen months that he spent in England, it is of much significance, though the revisions to *Laon and Cythna* on which his publishers insisted made it less apparent in the re-titled *Revolt of Islam*. In a letter which he wrote to Maria Gisborne after reading Calderón's *Cabellos de Absolon* he made the perhaps rather surprising observation that 'incest is like many other *incorrect* things a very poetical circumstance.' In this opinion he would be confirmed by his admiration for Sophocles no less than for Calderón or Byron. He may have had Byron in mind when in the same letter he said that incest might 'be the excess of love or hate. It may be that defiance of every thing for the sake of another which clothes itself in the glory of the highest heroism, or it may be that cynical rage which confounding the good and bad in existing opinions breaks through them for the purpose of rioting in selfishness and antipathy.' When he wrote those words he had lately seen, and deplored, the cynical rage of Byron's conduct in Venice, and it would be natural enough that he should associate this with the Byron whom he had first known in Switzerland, where the two poets, with Mary and Claire, were to be united by Southey's malevolent imagination in a 'league of incest'.*

Shelley had written little during the months in Switzerland, but he brought home with him the manuscripts of two poems, the *Hymn to Intellectual Beauty* and *Mont Blanc*. As soon as he had completed his business in London, he went to stay with Peacock at Marlow, where Mary joined him on 19 September. He had drawn up a new will in which he named Byron and Peacock as trustees of his estate, and he was now looking for a house near Peacock. Fanny Imlay, Mary's half-sister, warned Shelley that Marlow was not a suitable place for him to live, because of the gossip in the neighbourhood about his desertion of Harriet, who had stayed not far away at Bracknell. Besides Mary judged it wise to keep Claire away from her mother's scrutiny until after her child was born. On the 25th she and Shelley returned to Bath. One of Shelley's first concerns there was to send off the *Hymn* to Leigh Hunt, to be considered for publication in *The Examiner*. Shelley signed the poem 'Elfin Knight', a Spenserian pet name which Mary used of him, and gave no address. Hunt acknowledged its receipt in the only way he could in *The Examiner* for 6 October: 'The Elfin Knight,

* The Contessa Benzon, who introduced Byron to Teresa Guiccioli, was reputed to have borne a son to her half-brother.

the first opportunity.' Shelley was already acquainted with Hunt, but they had met on only a few occasions, and Shelley was too shy and too well-mannered to remind him of this when submitting a poem to him as editor. Hunt had seen some of Shelley's poetry and admired *Alastor*, and in an article in *The Examiner* for 1 December, entitled *Young Poets*, which was mainly devoted to Keats and John Hamilton Reynolds, he found space for some rather tentative praise of Shelley. On the same day on which the article appeared Shelley received an unexpected letter from Hunt which, whatever else it contained, must have made some reference to financial embarrassment, a chronic condition with Hunt as with Godwin. Shelley immediately sent him a large sum of money, and probably in this letter acknowledged his identity with the 'Elfin Knight'. On 5 December he went back to Marlow to visit Peacock and to look again for a house there, where he might be near him. In a letter which Mary began the same day she pictured to herself the home of her dreams: 'a house with a lawn, a river or lake, noble trees, and divine mountains'. But if dreams might not come true, 'give me a garden, and *absentia* Claire, and I will thank my love for many favours.' *Absentia* Claire was to be a recurrent hope for years to come. While he was at Marlow, Shelley received on 7 and 8 December two more letters from Hunt which informed him of the *Examiner* article, which Shelley had missed, and inquired whether he would allow the *Hymn* to be printed over his name. Shelley replied on the 8th and left it to Hunt to decide. He again referred to Hunt's need for a few hundred pounds, and offered to write to Byron on Hunt's behalf, since he felt sure that he would be willing to contribute at least £100 'towards extricating one whom he regards so highly from a state of embarrassment'. They had spoken of Hunt, whom Byron knew well, when they were together at Geneva, and there no doubt Shelley had read *The Story of Rimini*. This came out early in the year with a dedication in the form of a letter to 'My dear Byron'. This tactless familiarity was later to cause trouble. Hunt had shown the manuscript of his poem to Byron, and had asked for, and received, his criticism of it; Byron then generously recommended it to John Murray. Shelley now confessed to Hunt that he had supposed it to be Hunt's only published poetry. From this time on Shelley and Leigh Hunt became devoted friends: Hunt in his old age would recall Shelley as his 'friend of friends', and for Shelley Hunt was

> one of those happy souls
> Which are the salt of the earth, and without whom
> This world would smell like what it is – a tomb.

Within a few days Shelley was to need all the kindness and support that Leigh Hunt could offer.

On 12 December Shelley left Marlow to pay a brief visit to Hunt in his cottage at Hampstead where, for the first time, he met Keats and Horace Smith. On the 14th he returned to Bath. There, next day, he heard from his publisher, Thomas Hookham, news of the death of Harriet, whose body had been recovered from the Serpentine on the 10th. Shelley talked over the news with Mary, and then hurried back to London in order to secure the custody of Harriet's two children, Charles and Ianthe. Next day, 16 December, he wrote to tell Mary how he had fared. 'Leigh Hunt has been with me all day and his delicate and tender attentions to me, his kind speeches of you, have sustained me against the weight of the horror of this event.' Mary too, as always, sustained him with the passionate loyalty of her love, and longed to welcome Charles and Ianthe. 'Then there will be a sweet brother and sister for my William, who will lose his pre-eminence as eldest and be helped third at table – as his Aunt Clare is continually reminding him.' But Claire's petty malice could not detract from Mary's generosity.

For the moment Mary remained in Bath, and Shelley relied greatly on Leigh Hunt both for sympathy and for practical help. Hunt offered to meet Harriet's sister, Eliza Westbrook, at any time convenient to her, and to take charge of Charles and Ianthe on Shelley's behalf; but Shelley's 'libidinous and vindictive' sister-in-law (as he described her to Byron) refused to surrender them. In the meantime Shelley was anxious to make Mary his wife, not, certainly, as a matter of principle, nor even to remove Godwin's natural objection to a daughter's following her father's precepts, but rather for the common-sense reason that if he died then Mary and her children would have a proper legal status. Besides, as the lawyer Longdill had immediately pointed out, if Shelley and Mary were married one at least of the reasons for withholding Harriet's children from their father's care would be removed.

Shelley therefore returned to Bath and brought Mary back to London with him a few days later, where they stayed at first with the Hunts. On the 30th they were married in St Mildred's church, Bread Street, in the presence of Mr and Mrs Godwin. Shelley was amused at the satisfaction which they showed, but had he seen the letter that Godwin wrote to his brother on the occasion, amusement might have given place to disgust. 'I went to church with this tall girl some little time ago to be married. Her husband is the eldest son of Sir Timothy Shelley, of Field Place, in the county of Sussex, Baronet. So that, according to the vulgar ideas of the world, she is well married.' Thus had the principles of the radical thinker and reformer subsided into bourgeois snobbery. When Shelley wrote to Byron soon afterwards to announce the birth of Claire's daughter, Allegra, he did not think it worth mentioning his marriage; but Mary, in her letter on the same occasion, somewhat coyly told him of it. The formality meant little to either of them, but Shelley never allowed the liberal idealism that inspired his passion for reforming society to obscure from his sight the practical necessities of society unreformed. Marriage could make no difference to Shelley's and Mary's love for one another, but it could help others, who did not share their advanced opinions, to be more at ease with them.

Leigh Hunt saw to it that the long-drawn-out anxieties caused by the Chancery suit for the custody of the children did not occupy the whole of Shelley's mind. In *The Examiner* for 19 January he published, over Shelley's name, the *Hymn to Intellectual Beauty*, the first of Shelley's poems to appear in any journal. And he introduced Shelley to a number of his literary friends; so that for the first time in his life Shelley for whom 'social enjoyment was the alpha and omega of existence' found himself a member of a circle of talented men and women. For much of the first two months of the year Shelley was staying in the Hunts' Hampstead cottage, and there too, on 26 January, came Mary, whom Shelley had sorely missed. 'How painful it is to me,' he told her, 'to be deprived of the counsel of your judgement and the consolation of your dear presence.' Mary's journal notes, all too briefly, the company they enjoyed with the Hunts.

Keats, to whom Leigh Hunt had introduced Shelley already during that first brief visit in December, came several times. But, as Hunt said, he was 'a little too sensitive on the score of his origin, and felt inclined to see in every man of birth a sort of natural enemy', so that he was certain to be put off by Shelley's well-bred eccentricities. His memory of Shelley seems to have been principally of his fondness for quoting

> For God's sake, let us sit upon the ground
> And tell sad stories of the death of Kings,

(to which Shelley would have given a Republican twist), and, of Mary, her regrettably upper-class accomplishment of cutting elegant slices of bread and butter. His patronising, 'Poor Shelley, I think he has his Quota of good qualities, in sooth la!!' suggests a personal antipathy which not even the solvent of Leigh Hunt's 'social smile' could remove. Hunt regretted this failure of sympathy between two great poets whom he had introduced to one another, but was wise enough to see that the differences of birth and of education were too stiff an obstacle for Keats to overcome. Keats also resented Shelley's advice to him, based on his own experience with *Queen Mab*, not to be in too great a hurry to publish; and though, when he rejected the advice, he had Shelley's help with the publication of *Poems* 1817, three years later that advice still rankled. The fact that Keats by then recognised its soundness was naturally no alleviation. Shelley's admiration for Keats, though not uncritical, was, as we should expect, more generous and uninhibited; but

Adonais laments the premature death of a poet, not the loss of a friend.

Shelley also met in Hunt's house the third of his trio of Young Poets, John Hamilton Reynolds, whose burlesque *Peter Bell*, published a week before Wordsworth's poem in the spring of 1819 suggested Shelley's *Peter Bell the Third.* But even when sending Hunt the manuscript of this poem Shelley made no mention of Reynolds, and nothing beyond the briefest acquaintance can be recorded.

William Hazlitt was another visitor to Hunt's cottage this year whom Shelley met a few times. On the first occasion, 9 February, they found each other stimulating enough to go on arguing in favour of republicanism against Leigh Hunt and Walter Coulson, who argued for monarchy, but there could be no real sympathy between the passionate and embittered critic and the idealistic poet. Hazlitt had no more appreciation of Shelley's genius as a poet than had Keats, though he had more understanding of the extraordinary range of his mind, perhaps because he had once been the victim of its agility and power. At least Hunt heard from someone that Shelley had 'cut him up at Godwin's table', and attributed to that Hazlitt's vicious attack on Shelley some years later. Hazlitt was disposed to harbour resentment in this way, as Hunt knew; he was also inclined to indulge the pleasures of hating.

At this time the Shelleys met the Lambs at the Godwins', and for Charles and his work Shelley had the greatest admiration. Yet here too, to Shelley's regret, friendship was prevented through the calumny of someone ill-disposed towards him, so that, although he and Mary did visit the Lambs, he was never present at one of those famous evening parties in his rooms in Mitre Court Buildings of which Hazlitt has left so vivid an account.

Of all those whom Shelley now met for the first time only Horace Smith became, and remained, a close friend. Horace Smith is now remembered almost solely for the brilliant parodies that he and his brother James published in 1812 under the title of *Rejected Addresses*, but he was a prolific writer of prose and verse. He was a stockbroker by profession – 'is it not odd,' Shelley once said to Hunt, 'that the only truly generous person I ever knew, who had money to be generous with, should be a stock-broker! And he writes poetry too; he writes poetry and pastoral dramas, and yet knows how to make money, and does make it, and is still generous!' Shelley, himself the most generous of men, did not know, and had no need to know, how to make money, but he knew enough of the world to realise that those who do are often over-anxious to retain it. Horace Smith, on his side, had the perspicacity to see, even at their first meeting, that this 'fair, freckled, blue-eyed, light-haired, delicate-looking person' was no ordinary man, and he left an account of what he saw:

His stature would have been rather tall had he carried himself upright; his earnest voice, though never loud, was somewhat unmusical. Manifest as it was that his pre-occupied mind had no thought to spare for the modish adjustment of his fashionably-made clothes, it was impossible to doubt, even for a moment, that you were gazing upon a *gentleman*; a first impression which subsequent observation never failed to confirm, even in the most exalted acceptation of the term, as indicating one that is gentle, generous, accomplished, brave. . . . Two or three more friends presently arriving, the discourse, under the inspiration of our facetious host, assumed a playful and bantering character, which Shelley by his smiles appeared to enjoy, but in which he took no part. . . . Young as he was, a mind so deeply impressed with the sense of his own wrongs, and sobered by his solemn vow to redress, if possible, the wrongs of his fellow-creatures, was naturally more disposed to seriousness than to levity.

The weather being fine, the whole party sallied forth to stroll upon the Heath, where I attached myself to Shelley, and gradually drawing him apart, enjoyed with him a long and uninterrupted conversation. Well may I say enjoyed, for to talk with a man of extensive reading and undoubted genius, who felt such a devout reverence for what he believed to be the truth, and was so fearless in its assertion that he laid his whole many-thoughted mind bare before you, was indeed a treat. My companion, who, as he became interested in his subjects, talked much and eagerly, seemed to me a psychological curiosity, infinitely more curious than Coleridge's *Kubla Khan*, to which strange vision he made reference. His principal discourse, however, was of Plato, for whose character, writings, and philosophy he expressed an unbounded admiration .... On my confession that I could not manage so subtle a thinker in the original Greek, but that I possessed Dacier's translation, Shelley replied, 'Then you have seen him by moonlight, instead of in the sunshine; the closeness of his logic and the splendour of his diction cannot be transferred into another language.'

When he left England Shelley put his financial affairs in Smith's hands, and continued to correspond with him to within a few days of his death. And when, in his *Letter to Maria Gisborne*, he recalled the friends whom he had left in London, the four whom he most delighted to characterise were Leigh Hunt and Hogg, Peacock and Horace Smith, in whom, he said, were combined

Wit and sense,
Virtue and human knowledge; all that might
Make this dull world a business of delight.

These new friendships with Leigh Hunt and Horace Smith, which were to be so valuable and delightful to Shelley for the rest of his life, did not supplant the older friendships with Hogg and Peacock and with Byron. Of Byron, now in Italy, they thought and spoke much, and had an ever-present reminder in the person of Allegra. On the anniversary of their meeting with Byron at Sécheron Mary for once admitted to her journal something of her personal feelings:

I am melancholy with reading the 3rd canto of *Childe Harold* [she wrote]. Do you not remember, Shelley, when you first read it to me? One evening after returning from Diodati. It was in our little room at Chapuis – the lake was before us, and the mighty Jura.... Dear Lake! I shall ever love thee. How a powerful mind can sanctify past scenes and recollections. His is a powerful mind – one that fills me with melancholy, yet mixed with pleasure, as is always the case when intellectual energy is displayed. To think of our excursions on the lake – how we saw him when he came down to us, or welcomed our arrival with a good-humoured smile. How very vividly does each verse of his poem recall some scene of this kind to my memory.

She indulged her sentimental nostalgia again in June, by reading Rousseau's *Julie* exactly a year after Byron and Shelley had together in their tour of the Lake of Geneva visited the scenes there described. Besides, she had been busy in recent weeks revising and preparing *Frankenstein* for the press, and in putting together material for her *History of a Six Weeks' Tour*, both soon to be published; and these tasks also must have brought Byron very vividly before her memory, reminding her of the carefree happiness of the previous summer. Shelley's recollection was not less delightful to him. Tom Moore guessed the authorship of the *Six Weeks' Tour*, which was published anonymously, and in a letter to him in December, accompanying a copy of *Laon and Cythna*, Shelley told Moore that he and Byron had often talked of him when they were together. The tour of the Lake of Geneva, described in one of the letters in the book, 'was made in the society of Lord Byron, and its memory derives from that circumstance the light of an enchantment which can never be dissolved'.

Mary and Shelley left London for Marlow on 27 February. The house which they had taken, Albion House, was not yet ready for them, and they stayed for nearly three weeks with Peacock, the wise and witty friend to whom Shelley wrote his incomparable letters from Switzerland and later from Italy. They originally met in 1812, and Shelley found him 'an amiable man of great learning, considerable taste, an enemy to every shape of tyranny and superstitious imposture', as he told Leigh Hunt. Peacock had known and liked Harriet, and always spoke up for her; perhaps for that reason he never took to Mary. Neither did Mary for her part like Peacock, and when Hogg came to stay with him in Marlow she did not conceal her distaste for what she called 'the menagerie'. Later in the summer she even told Shelley that Peacock morally disgusted her, apparently in his character of *bon viveur*, which was in strong contrast with the abstemious régime of Shelley's household.

All this was most unfortunate, for Shelley took the house at Marlow in order to be near Peacock, and there he intended to remain – he had the house on a twenty-one years' lease. And there indeed, 'in spite of the Lord Chancellor and the Suspension Act' as Mary said, they were happy. 'We spend our time here,' Shelley wrote to Byron a month after they had moved into their house, 'in that tranquil uniformity which presents much to enjoy, and leaves nothing to record. I have my books, and a garden with a lawn, enclosed by high hedges, and overshadowed with firs and cypresses intermixed with apple trees now in blossom. We have a boat on the river, in which, when the days are sunny and serene, such as we have had of late, we sail.' Shelley had found for Mary the lawn, the river, the noble trees of her dreams; the mountains and *absentia* Claire were beyond his elfin powers. Shelley took long walks about the district with Peacock, and with Hogg and Leigh Hunt when they were visiting Marlow, and often walked up to London, a distance of thirty-two miles to Tyburn turnpike according to Peacock, who added that he never saw Shelley tired with these walks, for all his fragile appearance. Thornton Hunt, Leigh Hunt's eldest son, long afterwards recalled Shelley, after a boating trip on the river, helping the ladies up a steep bank to Albion House. 'While others were content to accomplish the feat for one, he, I think, helped three up the bank, sliding in a half-sitting posture when he returned to fetch a new charge. I well remember his shooting past me in a cloud of chalk-dust, as I was slowly climbing up.' The energy, the unconventional glissade and the courtesy were all characteristic of Shelley.

During this summer Shelley's intellectual energy was equally remarkable. Sometimes in the boat as it floated under the Chiltern beech-woods, or more often on a seat in Bisham Wood high above the river, Shelley wrote the longest of all his poems, *The Revolt of Islam.* In a letter written to Byron soon after his return to England the previous autumn, Shelley had urged him to concentrate his powers, and not to allow any false modesty to prevent him exerting them to their full extent. Shelley had witnessed during those months together in Switzerland the extraordinary impromptu ease with which Byron could compose, and both he and Mary rightly understood that Byron was always ready to allow himself to be distracted by whatever next caught his fancy. To make the most of his gifts, Shelley realised, Byron must undertake, and keep to, some larger, more coherent theme than the travelogue of *Childe Harold* could provide. To this acute insight into Byron's genius and temperament Shelley brought also a persuasive tact:

I would not that you should immediately apply yourself to the composition of an Epic Poem. . . . In a more presumptuous mood, I recommended the Revolution of France as a theme involving pictures of all that is best qualified to interest and to instruct mankind. But it is inconsistent with the spirit in which you ought to devote yourself to so great a destiny, that you should make use of any understanding but your own – much less mine.

The time had not yet come for Byron to accept this advice, and to discover in *Don Juan* (which was to have ended with the French Revolution) the perfect form for his comic genius – a form that allowed digression at the same time as it gave coherence, and that enabled Byron, the incomparable talker, to 'rattle on exactly as he'd talk'. In the meantime Shelley himself adopted part of his advice to Byron, and attempted an epic poem with the ideas and ideals of the French Revolution for its theme. Medwin said that Shelley told him that *The Revolt of Islam* arose from an agreement with Keats that each should write a long poem within six months. But Shelley's poem and Keats's *Endymion* have nothing in common, so that it is more relevant to consider *The Revolt of Islam* in the context of Shelley's letter to Byron. In his preface to the poem Shelley seems to echo some of the phrases in that letter: his poem, he says, 'is a succession of pictures illustrating the growth and progress of individual mind aspiring after excellence, and devoted to the love of mankind'. And, generally, the enthusiastic candour, as well as the modesty, of the letter is reflected in the preface. When Shelley says there that he does 'not presume to enter into competition with our greatest contemporary Poets' we may be certain that he is thinking of Byron, if not only of Byron, and of talk together the previous summer about the great poems they would some day write.

During this summer of 1817, while he was busy with *The Revolt of Islam*, Shelley read the *Iliad* and *The Faerie Queene*, as well as some *Histoire de la Revolution Française*. There was, as usual, much other reading, but these were especially relevant to his epic undertaking. His choice of the Spenserian stanza may owe something to Byron's use of it for *Childe Harold*, though, with his usual diffidence, Shelley said that he had preferred it to blank verse 'because in the latter there is no shelter for mediocrity'. His treatment of the stanza owes more to Spenser himself, whose rhythms he impressed on his memory by frequently reading aloud to Mary from *The Faerie Queene*, than to Byron, but as always his language is entirely his own. 'I have simply clothed my thoughts', he said, 'in what appeared to me the most obvious and appropriate language': no doubt, to a man of genius, it did seem as simple as that. He regarded the poem as his 'first serious appeal to the Public', dismissing with that phrase *Alastor* as well as his juvenilia; but he had no high hopes of a favourable reception for it. When Leigh Hunt reviewed the poem early next year with that unusual perspicacity he always showed when treating contemporary poetry, he pointed out why this must be:

> The book is full of humanity [he wrote]; and yet it certainly does not go the best way to work of appealing to it, because it does not appeal to it through the medium of its common knowledges. . . . The work cannot possibly become popular. It may set others thinking and writing, and we have no doubt will do so; and those who can understand and relish it, will relish it exceedingly; but the author must forget his metaphysics and sea-sides a little more in his future works, and give full effect to that nice knowledge of men and things which he otherwise really possesses to an extraordinary degree.

In the meantime Shelley dedicated his summer task to Mary, who had given birth to a daughter three weeks before, in those impassioned stanzas which are his most concentrated tribute to her, though indeed her character and their love inform the whole of the poem. He finished writing on 23 September and went up to London that same day. Next day he wrote from Leigh Hunt's house to Byron, among much else telling him about the poem. 'It is in the style and for the same object as "Queen Mab", but interwoven with a story of human passion, and composed with more attention to the refinement and accuracy of language, and the connexion of its parts.' Hunt, he told Byron, thought very favourably of it; and he promised to send Byron a copy, 'though I do not tax your patience to read it'. When he was seeking a publisher for it during the autumn he named Byron and Leigh Hunt as poets of established reputation who had a high opinion of his own poetic gifts; and though, when Byron did read it, he found it somewhat bewildering, he was ready to acknowledge that he also found much poetry in it.

More than a year had now passed since Shelley with Mary and Claire left Byron to return to England, and Byron had still made no practical suggestion as to what should be done with Claire's child. Byron had left for Italy with Hobhouse on 5 October 1816, and arrived in Milan a few days later. Soon afterwards he wrote to Shelley and gave an account of the sights of the city and of the *improvvisatori*, one of whom he had heard when visiting the di Breme family, but he had no message for Claire. Shelley showed her the letter, whose indifference to her much distressed her, and when he replied to Byron on 20 November he begged him, if he still refused to write to her himself (as he had promised her before she left Geneva), at least to send some kind message when he next wrote. Claire was then living in Bath where she had gone with Mary straight from Portsmouth, since it was considered preferable to leave Claire's mother and stepfather in ignorance of her pregnancy. The Shelleys were at 5 Abbey Churchyard; Claire had lodgings close by, at 12 New Bond Street. The Shelleys had had previous experience of living in the same house with Claire in England; it had not been a success. On the day Claire left them then

Mary's entry in her terse journal had told more than any exasperated tirade: 'I begin a new journal with our regeneration.' Yet the gentle Shelley was unwilling to believe that Byron could not spare one kind word for the girl who was soon to give birth to his child. She was, after all, a long way away from him.

On 17 January Shelley wrote to inform Byron of the birth of a daughter to Claire five days before. He gave the customary assurances about mother and child, and left more detailed news for Claire's letters to Byron. Mary had written the day after the birth to tell Byron, while Shelley was away on business in London. They called the little girl Alba, after their pet-name for Byron, but, at Byron's wish, she came to be known as Allegra and was christened in that name before the Shelleys left England to take her to her father.

At the end of February Shelley with Mary and Claire and the children moved to Marlow, where Allegra passed for the child of a friend in London who had been sent into the country for her health. The truth was still withheld from the Godwins, but Mary especially found this very difficult now that she was seeing her father again frequently, and even receiving a visit from him at Marlow; however they maintained the deception somehow as long as they remained in England. Shelley, who always delighted in small children, told Byron that his three-months-old daughter was very beautiful, 'her eyes are the most intelligent I ever saw in so young an infant. Her hair is black, her eyes deeply blue, and her mouth exquisitely shaped.' And he asked Byron what were his plans for the little girl. He knew that Byron was thinking of returning to England but that nothing was decided. No letter of this time from Byron to Shelley survives. In a letter to his sister he discusses the problem half seriously, half flippantly: 'I am a little puzzled how to dispose of this new production . . . but shall probably send for and place it in a Venetian convent to become a good Catholic, and (it may be) a *Nun*, being a character somewhat wanted in our family.' He was pleased by Shelley's description of Allegra's prettiness, and looked forward to the time when she would be the comfort of his old age. He told Kinnaird that it was his intention to bring her up himself. In the meantime he took no decision about her, but at least he had the grace to send letters to the Shelleys which could safely be shown to Claire.

In July Shelley wrote again to ask what he intended for Allegra; if Byron were to return to England later in the year, no decision need be taken until then, but her presence in their house did cause some embarrassment, much as he and Mary loved her. There was also the possibility that he might have to leave England precipitately, if any attempt were made to remove William from his custody; if this happened he must know what to do with Allegra. Local gossip, battening on the revelations of the Chancery suit, fathered her on Shelley: it was even alleged that Shelley and Byron had thrown dice for the privilege of begetting her. Southey's 'League of Incest' was proving a fecund myth. Byron replied suggesting that Shelley should send Allegra, but not her mother, out to him in Italy, but without any proposal how this could be arranged. In September, in the letter in which he wrote of *The Revolt of Islam*, Shelley told Byron that he was thinking of coming out to Italy for the winter, 'and in that case I shall be myself the lion to the little Una'.

> The Lyon would not leave her desolate,
> But with her went along, as a strong gard
> Of her chast person, and a faithfull mate
> Of her sad troubles and misfortunes hard:
> Still when she slept, he kept both watch and ward,
> And when she wakt, he waited diligent,
> With humble service to her will prepard:
> From her faire eyes he tooke commaundement,
> And ever by her lookes conceived her intent.

The apt and charming humour of the quotation would appeal to Byron. Mary too had decided that the only sensible course was to take Allegra out to Italy themselves, and the sooner the better. 'It is the labour of several months,' she wrote to Shelley, 'to get any kind of answer from' Byron, and she had no faith in his promises: 'the first object that engaged his attention would put them all out of his head'. Besides, as

Shelley told Mary, it would cost as much to arrange to send Allegra to her father as to accompany her themselves.

Shelley was too busy with his own affairs throughout the autumn to be able to get away, and there seemed no likelihood of Byron's coming to England, so in December Shelley wrote yet again to ask him to suggest some suitable person to bring Allegra out to him in Italy. It is attractive to picture Hobhouse or Scrope Davies or Douglas Kinnaird travelling across Europe with a year-old infant on his behalf, like Spenser's Sir Calepine. But Shelley was full of tenderness for small children, and could not but think that Byron would have similar feelings towards his own child. By now her first dark hair had fallen off, to be replaced by auburn. 'She is grown exquisitely beautiful,' he told Byron, 'and her temper has lost much of its *vivacité*, and has become affectionate, and mild. She is William's playmate, who is so fond of her, that he will be among the many sincere mourners at her departure. They sit on the floor together and amuse themselves for hours in the most sociable way; little William putting more than half the raisins etc. that are given to him into her mouth.' A couple of months earlier Mary had said that William would not go near Allegra, but that he was devoted to his new, month-old sister. William's affections – he was not yet two years old – seem to have been rather capricious, for at first both he and Allegra considered the new baby 'very stupid for not coming to play with them on the floor'. Byron still made no practical suggestion in response to Shelley's letter, but proposed to Hobhouse that a clerk might bring Allegra, along with toothbrush and tooth-powder, magnesia, soda, diachylon plaster, and any good new novels: 'pray desire Shelley to pack it carefully'.

Apart from the anxieties caused by Byron's irresponsibility towards Allegra, which Shelley began to realise could only be ended if he himself took the child out to Italy, there were other reasons for wishing to go there. Shelley's health was not good during this autumn, which is hardly surprising after the strains of the past year. Harriet's suicide had been followed by the long-drawn-out contest over her children, which Shelley had now lost, and he became unreasonably fearful that some attempt might be made to deprive him of the custody of his two children by Mary. Both in *The Revolt of Islam* and in *Rosalind and Helen*, begun in the spring and then laid aside for work on the greater poem, he described parents who had been deprived of their children by an act of tyranny. And the 'agony and bloody sweat of intellectual travail' in the composition of *The Revolt of Islam* must have exhausted him. Albion House was cold and dank, and Shelley was afraid of consumption, so that wintering in Italy seemed desirable for his health's sake. By the beginning of October therefore Shelley decided that they must go to Italy, and, though two months later Mary was still uncertain whether they would go, the decision had been taken.

Before they could leave there was still much to do. Shelley's finances were as confused as ever, and he was even imprisoned for debt for a few days. His optimistic under-estimate of their expenses at Marlow alarmed Mary, who even began to doubt whether they could afford to go to Italy. There were three books to be published, for which Shelley had to make all the arrangements: his own poem; the *History of a Six Weeks' Tour*, which came out in December; and *Frankenstein*, which, after being rejected both by Murray and Ollier, was eventually published in January 1818.* Mary, who had been very much on edge immediately before and after the birth of Clara, fortunately became much more friendly towards Peacock later in the year, and in December she transcribed for him *Rhododaphne*, the best of all his poems, which also had been written this year, during his constant intercourse with Shelley. It was, said Shelley, 'the transfused essence of Lucian, Petronius, and Apuleius'. Shelley somehow found the energy to write another political pamphlet, to begin a translation of Spinoza's *Tractatus Theologico-Politicus*, and to begin translating the Homeric Hymns.

Shelley spent the evening of 4 February, while on a visit to London, with Hunt and Keats, and in friendly rivalry the three

* See note 4, pp. 269–70.

of them sat down to compose each a sonnet on the Nile: it was the last poem Shelley wrote in England. He went back to Marlow next day but left finally on 7 February. Mary followed on the 10th. In the intervals of packing during those three days she found time to read three of Byron's Tales, *The Giaour*, *The Corsair* and *Lara*. They remained in London for a month, seeing much of their friends, Hogg and Peacock, the Hunts, Horace Smith. In February Hunt printed in *The Examiner* Smith's sonnet, *To the Author of the Revolt of Islam*, and during these weeks Hunt's discriminating critique of the poem was also appearing. Shelley wrote a review of *Rhododaphne*, but Hunt did not use it. Besides these literary activities there was plenty of sight-seeing: the Indian Library, the Apollonicon, a Panorama of Rome. They spent a morning at the British Museum looking at the Elgin Marbles, recently placed on exhibition there, whose removal from Athens Byron had scathingly denounced in *Childe Harold* II and in *The Curse of Minerva*.

But their chief pleasure, as always when opportunity allowed, was in the opera. Shelley had a box at the theatre, and there they were regularly to be seen, as Hunt remembered them eighteen months later: Shelley, slim, patrician-looking and eager, dressed in a blue coat and white waistcoat, and by his side Mary, sedate by contrast with him, but strikingly handsome 'with her great tablet of a forehead, and her white shoulders unconscious of a crimson gown'. On the evening of the day they got to London, Shelley and Mary went with Peacock to see *Don Giovanni*. The performance was followed by a ballet, *Acis et Galathée*, in which Mademoiselle Mélanie was prima ballerina. Four days later Shelley saw the same opera and ballet again. On 24 February he and Mary saw *Le Nozze di Figaro*, in which Shelley especially delighted, followed by the ballet *Zéphir*. They had seen the two Mozart operas a year before, but this was the first time Shelley had seen Mademoiselle Mélanie, by whom he was enchanted. They also went to the theatre, a rare event for Shelley, and saw a dramatised version of Byron's *The Bride of Abydos*.

The month drew to a close, and on 9 March Shelley, in accordance with Byron's wishes, arranged for Allegra to be christened. His own two children by Mary, William and Clara, were christened at St Giles in the Fields at the same time. The ceremony had little meaning for Shelley or Mary, but since their atheism was never the intolerant dogma of the modern humanist, they preferred to allow their children the opportunity of making their own eventual choice between belief and disbelief. That same evening Horace Smith, Godwin, Peacock and Hunt all came in to see them. Next day, their last in London, the Hunts spent with them, and Miss Lambe, whose father Dr Lambe was an advocate of vegetarian diet, and who attended Keats, paid a friendly farewell call. In the evening Peacock and the Hunts joined Shelley and Mary at the opera: it was a notable occasion, for they heard the first performance of an opera by Rossini ever given in England, *The Barber of Seville*. Afterwards they all had supper together in Russell Street.

At five o'clock next morning, 11 March 1818, Shelley, Mary and Claire, with their three children and their servants, set off for Dover. On the 12th they had a rough crossing of the Channel and came to Calais 'for the third time' Mary noted. Claire, whose infatuation for Byron had led to Shelley's first meeting with him nearly two years before, was bringing out to him the child whose innocent life was the cause of the renewal of the friendship then begun. They were bound for Italy, where none of them had ever been before; and they were bound for Byron.

CHAPTER FOUR

A Friendship Renewed

1818: ITALY

On leaving England Shelley had expected to see Byron within a few weeks, but more than five months were to pass before they met, months of wearisome negotiation on Claire's behalf which, but for Shelley's dignity and generosity, would have prevented any renewal of friendship. In all this, Shelley exhausted his energies during the summer, and he wrote scarcely any poetry. Even the excitement of coming to Italy for the first time, a pleasure shared with so many generations of English poets, soon lost something of its intensity through his vexation with Claire's uncontrolled silliness – her letters, Byron complained, were like bad German novels – and Byron's chilling suspicion. Perhaps these delays and anxieties made the renewal of friendship, when at last it came, all the more rewarding.

The journey across France took Shelley and his party till the end of the month, moving on each day until they reached Lyons on the night of 21 March. Next day Shelley wrote to Byron, under the vivid recollection of the time they had spent together at Geneva which the distant views of the Jura and Mont Blanc prompted. The letter never reached Byron, and has not been preserved. On the 25th they continued their journey, and next day Shelley made an entry in Mary's journal which characteristically combined political liberalism and admiration for the scenery as they climbed Les Échelles:

The rocks, which cannot be less than 1000 feet in perpendicular height, sometimes overhang the road on each side and almost shut out the sky. The scene is like that described in the 'Prometheus' of Aeschylus; vast rifts and caverns in the granite precipices; wintry mountains, with ice and snow above; the loud sounds of unseen waters within the caverns; and walls of toppling rocks, only to be scaled, as he describes, by the winged chariot of the Ocean Nymphs.

This impression of the road over to Chambéry was to strike deep into Shelley's imagination.

They spent a day in Chambéry to allow Élise Romieux, the Swiss nursemaid who had returned to England with them eighteen months before, to receive a visit from her little daughter, Aimée, whom she had left behind with her mother and father-in-law. From Chambéry their route lay over Mont Cenis, and on 30 March they crossed into Italy. 'The mountains are God's *Corps de ballet*', Shelley declared, and 'the Jungfrau is Mademoiselle Mélanie'; and he celebrated the occasion by gaily singing an improvised revolutionary ditty:

Now Heaven neglected is by Men
And Gods are hung upon every tree
But not the more for loss of them
Shall this fair world unhappy be.

A few days later, Shelley began that famous series of letters from Italy, in which he gave Peacock his first impressions of their arrival in the country. They spent the night at Susa.

No sooner had we arrived at Italy than the loveliness of the earth and the serenity of the sky made the greatest difference in my sensations – I depend on these things for life for in the smoke of cities and the tumult of humankind and the chilling fogs and rain of our own country I can hardly be said to live. With what delight did I hear the woman who conducted us to see the triumphal arch of Augustus at Susa speaking the clear and complete language of Italy, tho' half unintelligible to me, after that nasal and abbreviated cacophony of the French!

Shelley said he was not then in the mood for writing, but promised longer letters when he was rested from the journey. By now they had reached Milan, where they remained for most of April, admiring the Cathedral, going to the opera, delighting in Vigano's ballet of *Othello* (though the prima ballerina could not, in the Shelleys' estimation, compare with Mademoiselle Mélanie whom they had recently seen with Peacock in London), reading much Italian and house-hunting. Shelley wished to escape from the busy town and looked at four houses on Lake Como. They hoped to take the Villa Pliniana, then half in ruins, as Shelley told Peacock: 'It is built upon terraces *raised from* the bottom of the lake, together with its garden at the foot of a semicircular precipice overshadowed by profound forests of chestnut.' On the 13th he wrote a short letter to Byron, inviting him to visit them at the Villa Pliniana, and suggesting that if he would do so Allegra might return with him to Venice. She was 'in excellent health and spirits, with eyes as blue as the sky over our heads'. He inquired whether or not Byron had received his previous letter from Lyons. On the 19th Shelley wrote again to Byron. He was much in their thoughts not only because of Allegra but also because they longed to see him again, and because the fact of being in Italy somehow suggested his presence: 'Albe! Albe everywhere', Mary wrote in her journal.

Byron replied promptly, and, though his letter is lost, its tone may be judged from a letter he wrote at the same time to Hobhouse. 'Shelley has got to Milan with the bastard and its mother; but won't send the child unless I will go and see the mother.' This Byron was determined not to do, and he was suspicious that Shelley might be disposed to take Claire's part. Byron's loathing of Claire was such that he was prepared to use the custody of the child as a kind of blackmail: unless Claire would surrender all right ever to see Allegra, he would not accept responsibility for her. He imputed similar behaviour to Shelley, as if he in turn was attempting blackmail: unless Byron would consent to see Claire, he should not have Allegra.

Byron's letter reached Shelley on 21 April. Next day Shelley replied in a letter which shows the sincerity of his concern for Allegra, and which argues Claire's case with excellent logic. How could Byron expect a mother to surrender all interest in her child, without some assurance that the father would treat it with greater tenderness than he treated her? 'I have esteemed it a duty to leave her to the impulse of her own feelings in a case where, if she has no feeling, she has no claim. But in truth, if she is to be brought to part with her child, she requires reassurance and tenderness. A tie so near the heart should not be rudely snapt. It was in this persuasion that I hoped (I had a thousand other reasons for wishing to see you) that you would have accepted our invitation to the Pliniana.' And Shelley reasonably taxed Byron with cruelty, however he might justify his conduct to himself: 'You know my motives, and therefore I do not fear to ask you again to come to see me at Como; and, for the sake of your child's welfare, to soothe Claire's wounded feelings by some reassurances in the mean while.' Throughout, Allegra's welfare was what most concerned Shelley. He had no intention of pleading for Claire, whose folly he had known too long and too intimately for him to think that Allegra's upbringing should be entrusted to her. On 27 April another letter came from Byron. In the end, against Shelley's advice, Claire decided that she must accept Byron's harsh terms. On 28 April Élise left for Venice with Allegra.

Shelley wrote to Byron the same day, to tell him of Allegra's departure. He had decided that his own children's nursemaid should accompany her rather than the English girl, Milly Shields, who had hitherto looked after her. Nothing was ever too good for Allegra: 'I think she is the most lovely and engaging child I ever beheld. Tell us what you think of her, and whether, or no, she equals your expectations.' And he added that Mary had consented to allow her nursemaid Élise (who had been with them at Geneva) to leave her 'solely that Claire and yourself may be assured that Allegra will be attended almost with a mother's care'. He informed Byron what wages they had been paying Élise. Byron had offered in the letter received a week before to reimburse Shelley for the expenses he had incurred during these fifteen months of Allegra's life, but Shelley, with his normal courtesy, declined. Now he even denied that Allegra had been the cause of his journey out to Italy; it had been undertaken solely in the interests of his own health, and since he had to leave, it was a pleasure to bring the little girl with him. He regretted the misunderstandings that had arisen between them in recent correspondence, generously accepting some part of the blame: 'and I hope that on both sides there is here an end of misunderstandings.' As if to confirm his hope that they might now return to the happy relationship of the summer at Geneva, Shelley sent Byron a copy of *Frankenstein*, with a message from Mary to say that she would regard his approbation as a more flattering testimony of its merit than the success it had won in England. Scott wrote a most favourable review in Blackwood's *Edinburgh Magazine*, and Peacock told them, 'it seems to be universally known and read'.

With the departure of Allegra the need for a secluded house on Lake Como to which Byron could be invited had gone. A few days after Allegra's departure Shelley, with Mary and Claire, left for Pisa, where he asked Byron to write to let them know of the child's safe arrival. They travelled by the classic route of the Via Aemilia to Bologna, and then crossed the Apennines, which stirred Shelley to write a few lines of verse, the first since the sonnet written three months before in the company of Keats and Leigh Hunt. They reached Pisa on 7 May but stayed only long enough to receive the expected letter from Élise, telling of her arrival in Venice. They climbed the Leaning Tower and visited the Cathedral but found the city disagreeable and empty except for the chained gangs of criminals, which depressed them; they did not wait for a letter from Byron. They went on therefore from Pisa to Leghorn, which, although it gave them their first sight of the Mediterranean, was not likely to attract them much more. Indeed Mary decided as soon as they arrived that it was a stupid town, yet they remained there a month. Before they left England Godwin had given them a letter of introduction to a Mrs John Gisborne, who twenty years before, when she was Mrs Reveley, had taken care of the infant Mary. Mary Wollstonecraft died in giving birth to Mary, and when two years later Mrs Reveley lost her husband, Godwin asked her to marry him. (It is strange to think that had she accepted him Mary would have had no connection with Claire, and Shelley and Byron might therefore never have met.) Maria Gisborne and her husband called on the Shelleys on the evening of their arrival. Mary's first impression was that she was 'reserved, yet with easy manners'. Shelley, who found her amiable and accomplished – she had some talent both in music and in painting – told Peacock that she was 'the sole attraction in this most unattractive of cities. We had no idea of spending a month here, but she has made it even agreeable.' They met every evening for a walk, and Mary enjoyed hearing of the famous mother whom she had never known, but who had been Mrs Gisborne's friend.

Henry Reveley, Mrs Gisborne's son by her first marriage, a year or two older than Shelley, was another attraction; he had been trained as an engineer and was busy now with plans for a steamship with which he intended to operate a service between Genoa and Leghorn. No doubt, though of a somewhat taciturn disposition, he talked to Shelley of his hopes, and on 28 May he took the Shelleys with his mother and stepfather to see the engine on which he was working. Shelley's interest in science and technology was at once aroused.

John Gisborne, on the other hand, Shelley found a great bore, 'of the Erymanthian breed' as he told Hogg. Besides, his nose was beyond forgiveness: it 'is something quite Slawkenbergian. It weighs on the imagination to look at it, – it is that sort of nose which transforms all the *g*s its wearer utters into *k*s.' This grim feature, combined with little thin lips and a receding forehead, concealed from Shelley such good qualities as the retired merchant possessed; Peacock, less sensitive to physical ugliness than Shelley, thought these were considerable. It is of little importance now, since John Gisborne has no further claim on our remembrance than as the man who gave his name to Shelley's Maria.

After a month the Shelleys moved to Bagni di Lucca, a village of pretty, painted houses lining both banks of the rock-strewn, noisy Serchio, and at that time a fashionable resort. They rented a small house, Casa Bertini, above the narrow valley.

They engaged a cook and handyman named Paolo Foggi, who was useful but dishonest from the start. For two months and more they lived the quiet, retired life that they most enjoyed, walking or riding by the river and in the chestnut woods that covered the hillsides, reading much more than there had been time for in Leghorn, and planning poems if not yet writing them. The subject which especially engaged Shelley's mind during this first summer in Italy was the life of Tasso. Tasso's poetry was still widely read in England, as we may see from novels of the time, whose heroines are often discovered reading the *Aminta*. Shelley, who had read this and *Gerusalemme Liberata* in 1815, and who much preferred him to Ariosto, now, on arriving in Italy, reread the *Aminta* with Mary, and also read Manso's *Life* of the poet. For their generation this story of Tasso's life – his hopeless love for Leonora d'Este, his cruel imprisonment at the hands of Alfonso, his subsequent madness – made him the very prototype of the Romantic poet, of the man of genius at odds with society. Rousseau himself had been fascinated by the story, and composed what he called a *ballet héroïque* on the subject. This has not been preserved, but it may have contained the first suggestion of *La Nouvelle Héloïse*. Certainly readers of the *Confessions* knew of Rousseau's interest.

For Shelley there was a still more powerful stimulus towards a poem on Tasso. In September 1817 he read Byron's recently published *Lament of Tasso,* by which he was deeply moved. Certain lines, he told Byron, 'have a profound and thrilling pathos which I will confess to you, whenever I turn to them, make my head wild with tears'. The lines are the sixth section of the poem. Shelley probably found them especially applicable to his own experience. As usual with Byron, the immediate inspiration of his poem was factual: 'It was written in consequence of my having been lately at Ferrara,' he told Murray. There he visited the cell in the hospital of Sant' Anna which (for the benefit of tourists) had recently been identified as the place of Tasso's incarceration. (The inscription was set up in 1815.) When Shelley read the poem he must have recalled his visit with Byron to the Castle of Chillon, where the story of the imprisonment of Bonivard had similarly fired Byron's imagination, and he would have recognised Byron's close identification of himself with the imprisoned poet. His own poem on Tasso was to be dramatic, but he wrote no more than a fragmentary song, and a brief scene in which appears a courtier named Maddalo. In Manso's account, Maddalo was a close friend of Tasso who betrayed the secret of his love for Leonora; Tasso challenged Maddalo and wounded him in the duel and was himself wounded; Alfonso then took Tasso into protective custody, to prevent further bloodshed, but Tasso supposed he was being punished for his love for Alfonso's sister. This story is a fabrication by Manso; but Maddalo was a historic character.

Somehow, Shelley was unable to make any progress with the tragedy to which, as he told both Peacock and Hogg in letters written in April, he intended to devote the summer. As it was he wrote less than fifty lines for the play, but at Mary's insistence (perhaps she hoped that thus he would recover his facility) he took up again his 'modern eclogue', *Rosalind and Helen,* begun the year before at Marlow and then thrown aside. This, he admitted, was 'not an attempt in the highest style of poetry', as his tragedy on Tasso would have been, and he must have recognised his current lack of inspiration before returning to a discarded poem. At the end of July he told Peacock, 'I have lately found myself totally incapable of original composition. I employed my mornings, therefore, in translating the *Symposium*, which I accomplished in ten days.' This he undertook 'only as an exercise, or perhaps to give Mary some idea of the manners and feelings of the Athenians'. But before he could write freely again he needed some fresh impulse to his imagination, something more personal and intimate than this first experience of Italy, someone more provocative than the amiable Maria Gisborne.

After sending Allegra to Byron at the end of April, Shelley seems neither to have written to him, nor to have heard from him throughout the summer. He had no longer an obvious excuse for inviting Byron to a visit, for he was too shy and modest to assume that Byron might care to visit him; and Byron would have hesitated to invite Shelley to Venice for fear lest he might propose to bring with him the odious Claire. *Absentia* Claire, which Mary could only hope for, Byron could insist upon. He delighted in Allegra, and a fancied resemblance in her to Lady Byron was much to be preferred to any look of her mother. He was also very much enjoying the process of establishing himself in the Palazzo Mocenigo, on the Grand Canal, which took his mind off the sale of Newstead Abbey. But even he may have felt that the dissipated life he was leading there was not very suitable for the upbringing of a child whom he intended to be the comfort of his old age, and early in August he sent her to the Hoppners. Richard Hoppner, then English Consul in Venice, was the second son of the portrait-painter. Mrs Hoppner was Swiss, and they may have suggested to Byron, with whom they were on friendly terms, that Allegra should come to them.

Claire was much distressed on hearing from Élise that Allegra was no longer in her father's house, and a sudden decision was taken to go to Venice. On 16 August Shelley told Peacock that he intended to leave Bagni di Lucca for Florence on 10 September; the very next day he set off with Claire. They arrived at Venice by gondola (as everyone should) 'in the middle of the night, in a most violent storm of wind, rain and lightning'.The gondolier, without any hint from Shelley or Claire, began talking about Byron: 'he said he was a giovenotto inglese with a nome stravagante who lived very luxuriously and spent great sums of money.' And, as soon as they arrived at the inn where they were to stay the night, the waiter there also started talking of Byron, to leave them in no doubt of the wild reputation he had achieved. In the morning they went round to the Hoppners, who had no idea that they were coming. Claire went in while Shelley waited in the gondola, but he was soon invited to go up too. He took to the Hoppners at once, and asked their advice about approaching Byron; Hoppner told Shelley that Byron often expressed extreme horror at the thought of

Claire's arrival, and said that if she came to Venice he would leave forthwith; her presence must therefore be concealed. Allegra, Shelley reported to Mary, is 'so grown you would hardly know her – she is pale and has lost a good deal of her liveliness, but is as beautiful as ever though more mild.' He found that she recognised him:

She yet seemed to know
On second sight her ancient playfellow,
Less changed than she was by six months or so;
For after her first shyness was worn out
We sate there, rolling billiard balls about.

This gave Shelley the greatest pleasure, for, fond as he was of all small children, Allegra, he confessed, 'was a special favourite'.

At three o'clock on the afternoon of this day, 23 August, he called on Byron. 'He was delighted to see me,' he told Mary, 'and our first conversation of course consisted in the object of my visit.' Byron, talking to Shelley once more after an absence of almost two years, was quite free of the misunderstandings that had troubled their correspondence on the same subject in the spring. He offered to let Allegra go to Claire (whom Shelley said he had left at Padua with Mary) for a week, but was unwilling to part with her for too long, both to prevent the Venetians thinking he had grown tired of the child, and to avoid a repetition of the arguments and miseries that must come with a second parting from Claire. Byron was no doubt eager to talk to Shelley of other matters, as he had so much enjoyed doing in that previous summer by the lake of Geneva, and he would not let Shelley return at once. Instead he took Shelley in his gondola over to the Lido, where he used to keep his horses. It was at that time, as Shelley describes it, 'a bare strand of hillocks, heaped from ever-shifting sand'. 'When we disembarked, we found his horses waiting for us, and we rode along the sands of the sea talking. Our conversation consisted in histories of his wounded feelings, and questions as to my affairs, and great professions of friendship and regard for me.

. . . We talked of literary matters, his fourth Canto which he says is very good, and indeed repeated some stanzas of great energy to me.' It had been published a few months before. And they talked of that summer they had spent together two years ago, 'light memories of remembered hours, none slow enough for sadness'. When they returned from their ride together the gondola was waiting to carry them back to Venice. At Byron's suggestion they paused for a moment to admire the incomparable view of Venice and the Euganean Hills against the sunset. This was one of Byron's especial pleasures. 'My rides would have been nothing without the Venetian sunsets,' he told Medwin. 'Ask Shelley.' Not many days after their ride Shelley recorded the scene in lines which are the counterpart of Turner's vision of Venice:

Half the sky
Was roofed with clouds of rich emblazonry
Dark purple at the zenith, which still grew
Down the steep West into a wondrous hue
Brighter than burning gold, even to the rent
Where the swift sun yet paused in his descent
Among the many-folded hills.

These were the Euganean Hills, the guardians of Petrarch's tomb at Arqua. Near by, at Este, Byron had rented a villa, I Cappucini, from Hoppner. Perhaps he mentioned it now to Shelley:

And then, as if the Earth and Sea had been
Dissolved into one lake of fire, were seen
Those mountains towering, as from waves of flame
Around the vaporous sun, from which there came
The inmost purple spirit of light, and made
Their very peaks transparent.

Byron dragged Shelley away, promising, as one familiar with the lagoon, to pause for an even better view of Venice from the water. As the last of the day's light faded they came back up the Grand Canal to the Palazzo Mocenigo. Still Byron would not let Shelley go; he had been starved of such talk for far too long, and we may be sure that Shelley was in no hurry to leave.

He could not make his excuses to return to Claire, since he had told Byron that he had left her in Padua. Besides, instead of the disintegrating roué of English report, 'slovenly to the extreme, unkempt, with long untied locks that hang down on his shoulders, shabbily dressed,' Shelley found his friend 'the liveliest and happiest looking man I ever met', which must have delighted him. And perhaps, as they talked together through the night, Shelley began to understand that what he had needed to restore him to the writing of poetry was just this, Byron's friendship and Byron's talk.

Eventually Shelley returned in the small hours to the Hoppners', and, after reporting his success to Claire, he sat down at five o'clock to write to Mary. Byron, he told her, had offered them his house at Este; she must pack up and come to join him at once; he gave her detailed instructions for the journey; he enclosed £50 to cover her expenses. 'I have been obliged to decide on all these things without you. — I have done for the best and my own beloved Mary you must soon come and scold me if I have done wrong and kiss me if I have done right – for I am sure I do not know which – and it is only the event that can show.'

Mary received his letter four days later on 28 August. Although her little Clara, now a year old, had been unwell for the past week (which Shelley could not have known) Mary loyally decided to do as he asked. She spent the next two days packing up – 30 August was her twenty-first birthday – and on the 31st set out on her journey with Paolo, Milly the English nursemaid and her two children. After a day's delay in Florence they arrived at Este on 5 September. Clara, exhausted by the long, hot journey seemed now dangerously ill, and Shelley himself was suffering from food-poisoning.

These distresses could not hold back the majestic flood of poetry which meeting Byron again had released in Shelley's mind. Perhaps even before Mary reached Este, Shelley had begun writing *Prometheus Unbound*. She made no entry in her journal for nine days after joining him, but then noted that Shelley was busy with it. By the 22nd he had written twenty-six pages. The suggestion for a play on this theme had its first imprecise origins during that summer with Byron in Geneva, when Byron wrote his *Prometheus*; and the passage of Les Échelles at the end of March this year gave a fresh stimulus to Shelley's imagination. Mary Shelley, returning alone by this route in the summer of 1823, remembered her previous crossing of the pass in Shelley's company: 'the dark high precipices towering above', she told the Hunts, 'gave Shelley the idea of his Prometheus' – or rather the idea for the setting of the first act which he was now writing at I Cappucini. But there can be no doubt that the main inspiration came from Byron, in whose imagination the Aeschylean Prometheus had long played a dominant role. He had followed his poem on the subject in 1816 with *Manfred*, also begun when Shelley was with him, and owing much to his influence. When it was published, Jeffrey, in *The Edinburgh Review*, remarked its Aeschylean qualities. Byron was delighted at his perspicacity: 'Of the *Prometheus* of Aeschylus I was passionately fond as a boy', he wrote. (When he was at Harrow he had translated into verse a passage from the play.) 'The *Prometheus*, if not exactly in my plan, has always been so much in my head, that I can easily conceive its influence over all or any thing that I have written.' The debt which in *Manfred* Byron owed to Shelley was thus most generously repaid.

This renewal of poetic inspiration which followed so quickly on the renewal of friendship with Byron, also showed itself in another poem, begun at this time as a record of that memorable day in Venice. *Julian and Maddalo* is a complex and puzzling poem, but so far as it agrees with Shelley's description of it as 'A Conversation', that is until the introduction of the Maniac, it is factual enough, is indeed a piece of immediate reporting of experience such as Byron wrote in *Childe Harold* while he and Shelley were on their tour of the Lake of Geneva. It is written, as Shelley said, in 'a certain familiar style of language to express the actual way in which people talk with each other', the Horatian plain style of Byron's preference. Shelley's preface to the poem, in which he vividly describes the two protagonists, belongs to his first concept of it. Byron he characterises as Count Maddalo,

a Venetian nobleman of ancient family and of great fortune . . . He is a person of the most consummate genius, and capable, if he would direct his energies to such an end, of becoming the redeemer of his degraded country. But it is his weakness to be proud: he derives, from a comparison of his own extraordinary mind with the dwarfish intellects that surround him, an intense apprehension of the nothingness of human life. His passions and his powers are incomparably greater than those of other men; and, instead of the latter having been employed in curbing the former, they have mutually lent each other strength. His ambition preys upon itself, for want of objects which it can consider worthy of exertion. I say that Maddalo is proud, because I can find no other word to express the concentered and impatient feelings which consume him; but it is on his own hopes and affections only that he seems to trample, for in social life no human being can be more gentle, patient, and unassuming than Maddalo. He is cheerful, frank, and witty. His more serious conversation is a sort of intoxication; men are held by it as by a spell.

This is extraordinarily perceptive, and shows how well Shelley understood Byron. He makes him an Italian, while Julian (Shelley himself) is an Englishman. Byron in Italy avoided the English and consorted with the Italians, whereas Shelley held aloof from the Italians and preferred the company of the Gisbornes and Henry Reveley and the Masons, later of Medwin, Trelawny, Edward and Jane Williams. Byron admitted to becoming very Italianised and even believed, or affected to believe, that he would some day turn to writing his poetry in Italian; and certainly much of his best poetry was written in the tradition of Pulci and Ariosto and in the Italian *ottava rima* stanza. Shelley sensed Byron's intellectual isolation among his crowd of peasant mistresses and squabbling servants, and his discontent; and he observed the contrast between his dissipated way of life and his conduct towards himself, as an old friend with whom he could talk on equal terms. Like everyone who was privileged to hear Byron talk, he was held spellbound by the gaiety and wit, the astonishing range of experience of people and places and books, the rapidity and logic with which he would move from one topic to another, the combination of vivacity and good sense which was the source of his irresistible charm.

Shelley's self-portrait as Julian is in marked contrast. He emphasises his political and moral ideas, not his social qualities, his seriousness and his iconoclasm – the qualities which, to Byron's dismay, he had proclaimed in hotel registers in Switzerland two years before. 'He is a complete infidel, and a scoffer at all things reputed holy; and Maddalo takes a wicked pleasure in drawing out his taunts against religion. What Maddalo thinks on these matters is not exactly known.' This last admission is significant: Shelley never could accept the importance to Byron of his Calvinist upbringing; it was the one failure of sympathy, because it was concerned not with behaviour, which he could forgive, but with intellectual conviction. To Shelley, Calvinism was a degraded superstition, unworthy of any man of intelligence. But, as Byron once said, 'The worst of it is, I do believe.' However incongruous Calvinism may seem with Byron's temperament, he could never entirely free himself from its influence. His behaviour in Venice owed something to his recognition of this incongruity; it was partly the defiant self-assertion of a man who believed (if only intermittently, as most of us retain our beliefs), that he was predestined to damnation and who was convinced of human sinfulness. As Lady Byron observed, in a moment of understanding of her husband's nature which in her was almost unique, Byron's Calvinism was the rock on which all who had to do with him were broken.

This contrast between the two friends came out in their conversation as they returned in Byron's gondola from the Lido that first evening. Byron pointed to the belfry of the Madhouse, whose bell, even as they looked, was calling the inmates to prayer. In fact the belfry must have been that of S. Giorgio Maggiore seen behind the buildings on S. Servolo which since 1725 had been the Madhouse of Venice. Shelley made a sardonic comment:

As much skill as need to pray
In thanks or hope for their dark lot have they
To their stern maker.

Byron laughed at this evidence that Shelley had not changed since they were last together, and he suddenly remembered the occasion when they had been caught in a squall during their tour of the Lake of Geneva. Now he said to Shelley, 'If you can't swim, beware of Providence.' But immediately the mood passed, 'the gay smile had faded in his eye', for his volatile mind at once converted the black and dreary bell of the madhouse tower into a symbol of the human soul in its predicament, which

Hung in a heaven-illumined tower, must toll;
Our thoughts and our desires to meet below
Round the rent heart and pray – as madmen do;
For what? – they know not.

In his poem Shelley says that the conversation here broke off, to be resumed next day. Shelley then remonstrated with Byron for his view of man as a passive thing, subject to the control of Providence; in his own view

it is our will
That thus enchains us to permitted ill.
We might be otherwise – we might be all
We dream of, happy, high, majestical.

Shelley's belief in man's perfectibility necessarily premised a belief in free will. Byron acknowledged Shelley's dialectical skill, yet for him such talk was detached from human experience: 'You talk Utopia.' And with a characteristic preference for example over argument, for actual experience over abstract theory, Maddalo goes on to tell Julian of one like himself who had come to Venice some months ago, and with whom he had also argued. But this man was now an inmate in the madhouse. The account of their visit to him, and of the Maniac's monologue which forms the major part of *Julian and Maddalo* has a different origin, and is no part of the record of that conversation with Byron which meant so much to Shelley.

The stimulus which talking again with Byron gave to Shelley's poetic imagination can scarcely be denied. In the five and a half months since he left England he had written three brief scraps of verse, and to please Mary had finished off a poem which he must have realised he had outgrown. Now, within, at the most, two weeks of seeing Byron, he began a poetic account of their meeting, which can rank with his most mature poetry, and made a large and fluent beginning of *Prometheus Unbound*, which, for most of us, is the greatest of all his poems.

The effect on Byron of talking again with Shelley was hardly less momentous. In the spring he had published the fourth canto of *Childe Harold* and also his first experiment in a new manner, *Beppo*; since then he had written little verse. Already on 10 July he had a new story *à la Beppo* in mind, but he spent the next six weeks on his prose *Memoirs*. On 26 August, three days after Shelley's arrival, he told Murray that he was discontented with these and had given up the plan of publishing them. His mind was already fully engaged, we may believe, in the first canto of *Don Juan*. If he had written any significant part of it by the 23rd he would have quoted those stanzas, not stanzas from *Childe Harold* IV to Shelley, along with the histories of his wounded feelings from the *Memoirs*. But now, reminded by Shelley of his earlier advice to concentrate his powers in some greater enterprise, and aware as he was that the manner of *Beppo* rather than the manner of *Childe Harold* held more promise for him, he began to work hard at *Don Juan*.

There could be no more convincing proof of the impulse to poetry which these two gave each other than the fact that, within a few days of meeting again after a separation of two years, each was at work on his masterpiece, Byron on *Don Juan* and Shelley on *Prometheus Unbound*. If, in the development of the two poems, there is little to define the influence of either one upon the other, this is immaterial; yet Byron's portrayal of Juan in his youthful innocence, in this first canto, owes something at least to his view of Shelley:

Young Juan wandered by the glassy brooks,
Thinking unutterable things; he threw
Himself at length within the leafy nooks
Where the wild branch of the cork-forest grew....

and again:

He thought about himself, and the whole earth,
Of man the wonderful, and of the stars,
And how the deuce they ever could have birth;
And then he thought of earthquakes and of wars,
How many miles the moon might have in girth,
Of air-balloons –

which had been an undergraduate enthusiasm of Shelley's, continued to the releasing of the fire-balloon by the Lake of Geneva on his twenty-fourth birthday. The whole passage is a humorous but kindly portrait of the Shelley who dosed Byron with Wordsworth when they were together before. And Shelley, in the first act of *Prometheus Unbound*, elaborated those arguments against pessimism and despair which he must often have used to Byron and which he had lately put into the mouth of Julian. But the mutual influence of Byron and Shelley was more subtle and more complex than any comparison of texts can suggest, for their qualities of mind and temper, as in most true friendships, were not similar, but complementary; such also were their poetic gifts. Each needed the presence of the other at this moment in their lives in order to bring about that self-knowledge which is prerequisite to all great achievement. Talking together that day in Venice each brought out what was best and most characteristic in the other, and so, fired with an intense excitement of writing poetry, they set out there and then on the chief work of their lives.

CHAPTER FIVE

The Years Apart (I)

1818–1819: ITALY

VERY soon Shelley was to endure deeper despondency than he had ever known, but the power to continue writing which the renewed friendship with Byron had restored to him did not fail. So vigorous was the impulse to poetry which had made him begin *Prometheus Unbound* that it carried him through to the completion of the first act, undiverted by personal distress; and he continued to write his descriptive letters to Peacock with similar detachment. In other poems of this autumn he made a record of his misery and dejection, though for the most part in so esoteric and personal an idiom that precise interpretation is difficult. In particular, the conversion of *Julian and Maddalo* from a happy record of conversation with Byron to the disjointed soliloquy of an unidentified Maniac needs to be examined in the context of Shelley's life.

When Mary reached Este on 5 September, Clara, who was just twelve months old, seemed dangerously ill with dysentery. After a week's rest, and under the care of a doctor whom they had sent for from Padua, she began to recover. On the 13th Shelley wrote to Byron to explain why he had not been able to come back to Venice earlier. But Clara was now better, he told him, 'and I hope to be able to see you at the end of the week'. The improvement in the child's condition was not quite so rapid as he expected, but by the 22nd he felt able to leave for Venice. On the way he wrote to Mary from Padua proposing that she should join him in Venice two days later. He was anxious to get the advice of Aglietti, a man famous alike for his skill and kindness, whom Byron had recommended as the best doctor in Europe. Claire had an appointment with her doctor in Padua at eight-thirty that morning, and if Mary would come with her, he would meet her there. 'You will by this means arrive at Venice very early in the day, and avoid the heat, which might be bad for the babe, and take the time when she would at least sleep great part of the time.' Shelley met Mary as arranged, and they set out for Venice. Clara almost immediately began to show alarming symptoms, and they hurried on as fast as they could. When they got to Fusina they discovered they had forgotten their passport, but the expostulations of the soldiers were swept aside; as Mary recalled twenty years afterward, 'they could not resist Shelley's impetuosity at such a moment.' As soon as they got to Venice, Shelley dashed off to try to find Dr Aglietti, who was out. He returned to the inn where he had left Mary with Clara. Another doctor had been fetched, but he told Shelley he could do nothing for Clara, and within an hour she was dead.

The Hoppners came and took Shelley and Mary back to their house, where they stayed until the 29th. Shelley wrote next day to tell Claire of this disaster: Mary, he said, was reduced to 'a kind of despair'. In her distress Mary made a cruel contrast between Shelley's devotion to Byron's daughter and his indifference to his own. He had sent away Clara's nursemaid Élise, so that she could look after Allegra; he had hurried off from Bagni di Lucca at a moment's notice, when news came of Allegra's removal from her father's house; he had summoned Mary to join him at Este to cover up the fib he had had to tell Byron on Claire's behalf, and the long, hot journey had made Clara seriously ill; now he had gone into Venice to see Byron, no doubt on some business connected with the precious Allegra, and again had sent for Mary to join him; and this latest hurried journey had been too much for poor little Clara, who was now lying in her grave on the Lido. Distraught as she was, Mary forgot that Shelley knew nothing of Clara's illness when he asked her to come from Bagni di Lucca; that he had stayed with her until reassured about Clara's health before returning to Venice; that he had asked her to bring Clara to Venice so that she might have the attention of the most skilful doctor he knew; that he had arranged for them to travel in the cool of the morning, as this would be best for Clara.

For the few days that they remained in Venice the Hoppners were most attentive and kind; so too was Byron, whom they saw every day. Clara died on the Thursday and was buried next day on the Lido. On Saturday Shelley took Mary there to see her grave, and Byron made a point of meeting them. Next day they did some sight-seeing, the Doge's Palace, the Bridge of Sighs – Mary had just been reading the fourth canto of *Childe Harold* – and the Accademia, where Mary admired the pictures. In the evening they called at the Palazzo Mocenigo, and saw Byron's tempestuous mistress Margarita Cogni, La Fornarina as she was called (for her husband was a baker): under that name Mary recorded her in her journal. Perhaps it was on this occasion that Byron read *Don Juan* to them. On the Monday Mrs Hoppner took Mary to visit the Marciana, accompanied by Cavaliere Angelo Mengaldo, a romantic character who had fought in Napoleon's armies in Russia and had a hopeless love for Dr Aglietti's daughter, and who, in pursuance of literary ambitions, had appointed himself to the position of Byron's principal Venetian friend. (Byron had met Mengaldo at the Hoppners' earlier in the year, and hearing of his feat in escaping from the enemy on some occasion by swimming the Danube, challenged him to a swim from the Lido to the Grand Canal. Byron won with some ease.) On Monday afternoon Mary did some shopping, in preparation for their return to Este, and in the evening Byron called again to see them. He gave her two of his poems to copy, *Mazeppa* and the *Ode on Venice*. He hoped this might help to dispel her grief. She returned *Mazeppa* to him on 3 October with a brief note: 'You will see by my copying *Mazeppa* so quickly that there is more of pleasure than labour in my task.' And she asked him to let her have *Don Juan* to copy if La Fornarina would give her consent.

This sounds light-hearted enough, and neither Mary's journal nor Shelley's letters of this autumn – this note to Byron is Mary's only extant letter between Clara's death and mid-December – give any inkling of the despondency which both were enduring. For that it is necessary to turn to the more sensitive and less inhibited register of Shelley's poetry, and especially to the transformation of *Julian and Maddalo*.

This poem, begun as an imaginative record of Shelley's conversation with Byron on 23 August, was continued as a record of Shelley's feeling of helpless despair at the melancholy which had afflicted Mary since Clara's death. Into this are subsumed certain suggestions from the life of Tasso to which Shelley, intending to write a tragedy on this subject, had given so much thought during the previous months. The presence of that theme in his mind from the beginning of the poem is shown by his choice of the name Maddalo for Byron, and though it is futile to speculate how Shelley would have concluded his poem had Clara not then died, it is reasonable to suppose that the change of Shelley's mood from elation to despondency converted what should have been a dramatic portrayal of Tasso in his madhouse to something of a self-portrait. While they were riding on the Lido Shelley would have told Byron of his plans for a play about Tasso which Byron's *Lament of Tasso* had first prompted. In the poem, when Maddalo stops the gondola on the way back, and draws Julian's attention to the tolling bell, he says:

> What we behold
> Shall be the madhouse and its belfry tower.

That is, the tower which we are looking at may stand for the Convent of S. Anna at Ferrara: let us imagine that this is the place of Tasso's imprisonment. (Maddalo does not say, What we behold *is* the madhouse.) Shelley, in his preface to the poem, after characterising first Maddalo and then Julian, adds a note on the third character who, as we have the poem, dominates it. 'Of the Maniac I can give no information. He seems, by his own account, to have been disappointed in love. He was evidently a very cultivated and amiable person when in his right senses. His story, told at length, might be like many other stories of the same kind: the unconnected exclamations of his agony will perhaps be found a sufficient comment for the text of every heart.' And he told Leigh Hunt that the Maniac was 'also in some degree a painting from nature, but, with respect to time and place, ideal'. Such mystification was usual with Shelley when he was writing about his own personal feelings. He was ready enough to speak out in poems of personal happiness such as the first section of *Julian and Maddalo* or the Dedication of *The Revolt of Islam,* but he had a well-bred reserve which made him prefer to keep his griefs to himself. 'I never will be a party in making my private affairs or those of others topics of general discussion,' he told Hunt in a letter of December this year. 'My public character, as a writer of verses . . . is public property.' If, therefore, he wrote verses for publication which concerned his private affairs, it was logical to avoid the perspicuity of Byron's. It was not in Shelley's nature to trail across Europe the pageant of a bleeding heart. He believed too that his emotions ought not to interfere with his intellectual activities, or, as the Maniac declares:

What may tame
My heart, must leave the understanding free,
Or all would sink in this keen agony.

It was this power of intellectual detachment that enabled him to complete the first act of *Prometheus Unbound* undisturbed, while personal emotion was conveyed into the poem which was always personal in conception, *Julian and Maddalo.* Consistently with this creed of his, he kept this poem and the other sad poems of this autumn from Mary; but she knew of *Prometheus Unbound* from the start.

I cannot bear more altered faces,
Than needs must be,

he wrote; and again, presumably at that stage intending that *Julian and Maddalo* should be published only after his death, he addresses Mary:

If this sad writing thou shouldst ever see,

> Thou wouldst weep tears bitter as blood to know
> Thy lost friend's incommunicable woe.

Long afterward, in her note on Shelley's poems of this year, Mary acknowledged the truth of this: 'Though he preserved the appearance of cheerfulness . . . yet many hours were passed when his thoughts, shadowed by illness, became gloomy, – and then he escaped to solitude, and in verses, which he hid from fear of wounding me, poured forth morbid but too natural bursts of discontent and sadness.' And she looked back with remorse to her insensitivity to his feelings at that time, and her failure to dispel them.

Byron knew of Shelley's affliction after the death of Clara, and may have perceived something of its deeper cause. Whether he read *Julian and Maddalo* at this time, we do not know; but it is likely that he would inquire about Shelley's poem on Tasso, for he told him now of his own plans for a drama on Marino Faliero, the Doge of Venice who was executed in 1355.

Shelley gives to Maddalo the summary comment after they have left the Maniac and returned to Maddalo's palace. 'Our argument was quite forgot,' Shelley says, and,

> we talked of him
> And nothing else, till daylight made stars dim:
> And we agreed his was some dreadful ill
> Wrought on him boldly, yet unspeakable,
> By a dear friend; some deadly change in love.

This return to the conversational design with which the poem began concludes thus:

> And I remember one remark which then
> Maddalo made. He said: 'Most wretched men
> Are cradled into poetry by wrong,
> They learn in suffering what they teach in song.'

– a remark which has the authentic pungency of Byron's talk.

Shelley may well have longed, as he says in the final section of the poem, to stay in Venice, which he had come to love for its quiet as well as for its beauty. He could have spent the nights talking to Byron:

I might sit
In Maddalo's great palace, and his wit
And subtle talk would cheer the winter night
And make me know myself.

Talk with Byron always had this effect on Shelley, and he never needed it more than now. But his duty lay with Mary in her melancholy, with his little son William, and with Claire and Allegra. So on the Tuesday after Clara's death he took Mary back to Byron's villa at Este.

I Cappucini was a new house built on the site of a suppressed monastery. It was, Mary remembered, 'cheerful and pleasant; a vine-trellised walk, a *pergola* as it is called in Italian, led from the hall door to a summer-house at the end of the garden, which Shelley made his study.' There were also romantic elements in the scene such as Peacock associated with Scythrop Glowry, and he must have rejoiced to hear from Shelley that, 'At the end of our garden is an extensive Gothic castle, now the habitation of owls and bats.' He had recently finished *Nightmare Abbey* which he mentioned in some of his letters to Shelley that summer. Shelley sent him the quotation from Jonson's *Every Man in His Humour*, which Peacock was delighted to use as a motto for the book. But it was not until the following summer that Shelley was able to read and laugh at his friend's caricature. In the meantime he had a stool to be melancholy upon.

In the letter to Peacock in which Shelley described the Gothic castle at Este, he told him that he had recovered the ability to write which had deserted him during the summer, and that he had just finished the first act of *Prometheus Unbound.* It was 8 October, and, though he mentioned Clara's death, with his usual reticence on such matters he said nothing to Peacock of the despondent personal poems which he had also been writing. These cannot be precisely dated, but it is likely that Shelley completed *Julian and Maddalo* before starting anything else.

A few days later, on 12 October, Shelley and Mary returned to Venice, where Mary remained till the end of the month. They did not stay with the Hoppners, but saw much of them and dined at their house on most days. There they again met Mengaldo, who regaled them with ghost stories (including two that had occurred to himself), and with an account of his experiences during Napoleon's invasion of Russia. Mary's journal, apart from transcriptions of three of Mengaldo's stories, is even more cursory than usual during the first week, and she notes only one occasion when Shelley visited Byron. When she resumes daily entries on the 21st she notes, 'Shelley spends the evening with Albe', and so again on the following day. Probably Shelley went round to the Palazzo Mocenigo on most evenings, for in a note to Byron on the 17th he apologises for not keeping what seems to have been a standing engagement: 'I am so dreadfully sleepy that I cannot come tonight.' In spite of the recurrent arguments about Allegra (now more than ever painful to him) Shelley was always fascinated by Byron's talk, and Byron found in Shelley the perfect foil for his volatile and witty observation of the human comedy. Besides, Byron, who always welcomed Shelley's criticism of his poems, was busy writing the first canto of *Don Juan.* Already in September he had read to Shelley what he had then written: by the 19th, as he told Tom Moore, there were one hundred and eighty stanzas finished. He also read to Shelley the dedication to Southey (written on 16 September), 'more like a mixture of wormwood and verdigrease than satire,' Shelley said; 'the poor wretch will writhe under the lash.' Shelley had no more cause to love Southey than had Byron. He knew, and was the first to tell Byron, that Southey had attacked them jointly for a 'League of Incest' which they were alleged to have formed at Geneva. Southey had also lately referred to Shelley as 'the blackest of villains'. Such things were among the literary matters discussed during that ride together on the Lido.

Allegra was still with Claire, and since the Shelleys were intending soon to leave for Rome and Naples Byron had to decide whether or not she should go with them or return to him. Reasonably enough, he insisted that she should come back to Venice. Apart from his dislike of Claire, he cannot have been much reassured by Clara's death: if the Shelleys could not look after their own daughter better than that, was it wise to entrust his daughter to them, several days' journey away, and far beyond the care, if she became ill, of his good friend Aglietti? So on 24 October Shelley went back to Este, leaving Mary in Venice, and on the 29th he returned with Allegra.

Some time during October, most probably when he was at Este without Mary, Shelley composed his *Lines written among the Euganean Hills*. The poem was written, he said, 'after a day's excursion among those lovely mountains which surround what was once the retreat, and where is now the sepulchre, of Petrarch'. Since Mary's journal contains no reference to such an excursion, we may conclude that it was made in her absence. The long description of Venice in decline owes something to Byron's *Ode*, which Mary had copied at the beginning of the month, something also to the fourth canto of *Childe Harold*, which both had read at the end of September. Then Shelley had been deeply moved by his visit to the dungeons, of which he wrote a vivid description to Peacock. Apparently as an afterthought Shelley added nearly forty lines about Byron, whose fame would be always associated with Venice, as Petrarch's was with the Euganean Hills, or Shakespeare's with the Avon. The poem marks a stage in Shelley's recovery from the despair of the Maniac in *Julian and Maddalo*: there must always be something to hope for, or life could not go on. That *Patavina libertas*, which once had brought men from all over Europe to the University of Padua, might be extinguished there, but would return from elsewhere; Venice in her decay lay helpless now under the occupying Austrian troops, but even so could pride herself on being the refuge of the mighty spirit of Byron. This might seem a little insular to a fellow-citizen of the Bellini and Carpaccio and Giorgione, of Titian, Tintoretto and Veronese, of Tiepolo and Guardi, of Monteverdi and Goldoni, of Marco Polo and Paolo Sarpi. Yet Byron's description in *Childe Harold* IV of Venice's past greatness and present decay revealed the city afresh to painters and connoisseurs whose recent classical tastes had diverted them elsewhere, and largely inspired the vision of Turner.

Other brief scraps of verse, such as the fragment to Mary, ending

> O Mary dear, that you were here;
> The Castle echo whispers 'Here!'

belong to this same time. So too, most probably, does the opening fragment of a sonnet on Byron, 'O mighty mind'. Two completed poems, which are closely related to the passage in *Julian and Maddalo* beginning 'I must remove a veil from my pent mind', were probably written in October: the sonnet, 'Lift not the painted veil which those who live call life,' and the *Invocation to Misery*, addressed to Mary.

As soon as Allegra had been restored to her father's custody Shelley and Mary returned to Este, to get ready for their journey south. The Swiss nursemaid Élise, who had been looking after Allegra since April, returned to their service. Since July, if not before, they had been planning to visit Rome, but had postponed their journey, as Shelley told Peacock, 'partly for the sake of seeing Venice, and partly that little Alba might spend a month or two with Claire before we proceeded to Rome and Naples'. In August Byron had granted Shelley's request on Claire's behalf, and had generously put at his disposal a charming house in a quiet and beautiful part of the country such as he knew Shelley would enjoy. The two months of Allegra's stay were now at an end, and there was therefore no reason to put off any longer the visit to Rome. They spent a few days packing up, and on 5 November set out on their leisurely journey.

Next day they reached Ferrara, where they spent the whole of the 7th sight-seeing. This was the city of Ariosto and Tasso and Guarini which Byron had visited eighteen months before. The vivid impression on Byron of seeing the cell shown as Tasso's prison had led to *The Lament of Tasso* which so moved Shelley; now, on visiting the cell himself, Shelley recalled the phrase which he had used in his letter to Byron on that poem. He used it again in the fragment 'My head is wild with weeping', where he laments that 'a chief among men's spirits should be cold and blind', which clearly relates to Byron. (Claire no doubt had been making scenes.) In his letter to Peacock describing the visit Shelley said nothing of his by now abandoned tragedy on Tasso, nor of Byron's poem; he enclosed a splinter of wood from the door of Tasso's cell.

On 8 November they went on to Bologna where they remained sight-seeing until the 11th, then on again by Faenza, Rimini and into the Apennines. Near Monte Asdrubale Mary noted, 'the scene is fine and Promethean, but not so fine, I think, as Les Échelles.' At last on the 20th they reached Rome, and Shelley, who had written long letters to Peacock from Ferrara and Bologna, now, as soon as they were settled in a comfortable hotel, sat down to write to him again before Rome effaced from his memory the magnificent scenery through which they had come.

He did not write to Peacock again for almost a month. By then he had been in Naples for some time, but he begins his letter with a diatribe against Byron, which nothing could have led Peacock to expect, and which shows a total reversal of the opinions he had expressed when he last wrote to him of Byron a couple of months before. Then Byron had been the liveliest and happiest-looking man he had ever met. Now, he 'hardens himself in a kind of obstinate and self-willed folly. . . . He associates with wretches who seem almost to have lost the gait and physiognomy of man, and who do not scruple to avow practices which are not only not named but I believe seldom even conceived in England. He says he disapproves, but he endures. He is not yet an Italian. . . .' This is the old cry of *inglese italianato, diavolo incarnato* echoing down the centuries. But Shelley discloses what was the source of this extraordinary change in his attitude to Byron. 'You may think how unwillingly I have left my little favourite Alba in a situation where she might fall again under his authority. But I have employed arguments, entreaties, everything in vain, and when these fail you know I have no longer any right. No, I do not doubt, and for his sake I ought to hope, that his present career must end up soon by some violent circumstance which must reduce our situation with respect to Alba into its ancient tie.' To such an insanity of anger against Byron had Shelley been brought that he was even hoping for Byron's murder (in his own best interests, of course), as the only means of restoring Allegra to them!

Extraordinary as this is in so gentle and pacific a man as Shelley, 'a very cultivated and amiable person when in his right senses', it becomes even more so when we remember that during his ten days' stay in Venice in October Shelley apparently enjoyed his frequent visits to the Palazzo Mocenigo – in spite of the risk he must have run of encountering those inhuman wretches who he now hoped might assassinate Byron. He can hardly have wished to spend the whole time arguing about Allegra's future; if he had he would not have been made welcome. This reversal of judgment on Byron's character even affected his judgment on *Childe Harold* IV. In August and October he was admiring its energy and beauty; now he condemns its 'wicked and mischievous insanity'. Even so, he had not become so unbalanced as to deny some good poetry to that canto, or to doubt Byron's greatness as a poet.

Only two or three days later Shelley wrote to Hunt in a much calmer mood. Now 'our poor friend Lord Byron . . . is going on in a way not very worthy of him': no more than that. And so far from wishing for his death, Shelley was commenting on a suggestion that Byron had made when they were together in Venice, that Hunt should join them in Italy, for which he was prepared to lend the necessary funds. Shelley urged Hunt to think seriously about the proposal, and told him that they intended to return to Venice (and therefore to Byron) in the coming spring. About the same time he wrote also to Hogg. Byron, he told him, 'is practising aphrodisiacs at a great rate and I should think must be as tired as Candide was of the mountain where the Deity is worshipped, but he will not own it'.

To cut the Gordian knot of such inconsistency we might conclude that 'mad Shelley', as he had been called when a schoolboy, had indeed temporarily gone out of his mind. And another act of his this December might support such an explanation, for on the 27th he registered a child, whom he called Elena Adelaide Shelley, as his daughter, which she certainly was not, and without any previous consultation with Mary. She was an Italian child whom he adopted, presumably in the hope that her presence would compensate Mary for the loss of Clara, and Claire for the absence of Allegra, a characteristic attempt to assert the claims of intellectual theory to equipollence with human feelings. The two women had been deprived of their infant daughters; let them therefore direct their maternal tenderness to another little girl. Needless to say, both Mary and Claire, with the irredeemable perversity of womankind, declined to conform to the theory; and Elena Adelaide became a source of intense embarrassment until, eighteen months later, she too died.

Easy as it is to deride Shelley, who in these ways was a sort of type-specimen of the left-wing intellectual confronted by life, there is need also to be compassionate towards him. He had undergone great strain in these last few months. There had been the intense excitement of writing poetry again after a summer when he could write nothing, and of writing poetry which he knew was finer than anything he had written before. There had been the difficult negotiations with Byron about Allegra's return to him, about her temporary restoration to Claire, about her final return to Byron – and it is easy to imagine Claire's passionate lack of restraint, which it would be impossible for Shelley to evade. There had been Clara's death, and all its consequences in Mary's despondency. And the Hoppners, whose love of malicious scandal Shelley was after a time to discover to his own cost, had been relaying gosssip from Venice about Byron's debaucheries, adding, for good measure, vaguely disconcerting accounts of Allegra's health. Shelley had invited them to write to him at Naples before he left Venice; it was at Naples that he wrote his savage outburst against Byron. There were minor troubles too. They discovered that Élise had had the effrontery to practise their own theories with Paolo, and was about to bring another bastard into the household; they dismissed the pair of them. And Shelley was feeling ill (which is scarcely to be wondered at) and receiving drastic, painful and ineffectual treatment. Lesser men would have collapsed under the strain, or gone off for a long holiday. Shelley stayed at his post. The lively descriptions of the Italian scene in his letters of this autumn and winter should not lead us to expect a similar detachment when he writes about his personal affairs. In the few paragraphs where he alludes to them, as in the personal poems, we have a record of his sufferings. Among these, not least were disillusion at the reported behaviour of a man whose friendship meant so much to him, and fear that this man might by his folly waste the supreme gift of poetry which Shelley knew he possessed.

They remained for three months in Naples seeing 'absolutely no one', but spending much time in sight-seeing in the city and in the neighbourhood, climbing Vesuvius, visiting the excavations at Pompeii and the Greek temples at Paestum. The evidences of Greek civilisation and the magnificent scenery delighted Shelley, but he resented the grubby intrusion of living Italians. Shelley could see only the present degradation of Italy; Byron hoped for her future freedom. Shelley was particularly offended, as other English visitors have been, by the use of garlic in their cooking. He even made it one of his counts against Byron that he could make love to women whose breath was tainted with the stuff: 'Countesses smell so of garlic that an ordinary Englishman cannot approach them.' How much worse then must the lower orders stink. (Shelley's liberalism never suppressed the fastidious habits of the heir to an English baronetcy. The Hunts and the Gisbornes were to laugh together over this trait when they met in London.) Shelley would have preferred to contemplate the Neapolitan scene swept clean of Neapolitans, 'the filthy modern inhabitants of what ought to be a desert sacred to days whose glory is extinguished'. Byron's tolerant humanity preferred the crowded canals and streets and squares of Venice, vigorous, noisy, garlic-smelling women like La Fornarina – though she indeed was becoming quite impossible this autumn and had to be replaced. Byron was no very ardent sight-seer, and had not come to Italy to live in a museum. His interest in places was always for their human associations.

During this winter in Naples Shelley wrote little. The *Stanzas written in Dejection* were composed in December, and describe his longing for Mary again to respond to his delight in the beauty of the climate and the scene as she once had done. Yet he could still find delight for himself, even if there was no one to intensify the pleasure now by sharing it:

> Yet now despair itself is mild,
> Even as the winds and waters are;
> I could lie down like a tired child,
> And weep away the life of care
> Which I have borne and yet must bear . . .

He began two other poems, but finished neither, *The Woodman and the Nightingale* and *Marenghi.* The latter is based on a story in Sismondi's *Histoire des Républiques Italiennes* which he and Mary were reading in January.* So far as we have the poem it is mainly concerned with Marenghi living the life of a solitary outlaw but finding comfort in the world of nature:

> Yet human hopes and cares and faiths and errors,
> Like billows unawakened by the wind,
> Slept in Marenghi still;

as they slept in Shelley, exiled from Mary's love on the shores of the Bay of Naples.

On the last day of February 1819 they left Naples for Rome where they arrived on 5 March. They took rooms in a palazzo on the Corso. On the way south in November they had spent only one week here, and had intended to return in the spring before going north again to Venice. Shelley again urged Hunt to join him and Byron, but Hunt could not abandon his journalism in London at this time, and Shelley did not go back to Venice, perhaps even avoided going back without some excuse for seeing Byron. Indeed nearly three years were to pass be-

* Mary, publishing this in 1824, placed it among the poems of 1818, but since, in her journal, she makes no mention of Sismondi until January 1819, it seems probable that she antedated its composition by a few weeks. On 23–24 January Shelley wrote to Peacock, 'At present I write little else but poetry, and little of that.' There are no other poems that can be dated to that month.

tween the time when Shelley parted from Byron in October 1818, and the time when they met again, and, throughout, their intercourse, so far as we know, was restricted to the exchange of a few letters. Byron was not one to make much effort to invite his friends to visit him: he expected them to take the initiative, but when they came they were always made welcome. Shelley was too sensitive and too shy to obtrude himself upon anyone; besides, he was always excessively modest about his own genius in comparison with Byron's. Therefore, as in 1818 (when Shelley had been five months in Italy before he saw Byron, and even then sought him out on Claire's business, not as a friend), neither made any approach to the other. In absence, neither understood the other; the difference in temperament which, when they were living in the same place and meeting every day, was so stimulating to both, when they were apart tended to keep them apart.

In the meantime *Prometheus Unbound* had come temporarily to a pause – Mary transcribed Act I in December – but *Don Juan*, of which the first canto was finished on 1 November, was resumed on 13 December and continued with Byron's usual energy to the conclusion of the second canto a month later. The head-wagging with which Byron's friends received *Don Juan* in England early in the New Year would have amused Shelley, who, in spite of his censorious attitude to Byron's behaviour, from the start understood that *Don Juan* was to be the great poem which he had been longing for Byron to write. His judgment of the first canto may well have helped Byron to recognise that this was so, for if their conversations together caused Shelley to realise his powers, Byron felt the same. Soon after he had finished his second canto the Venetian Carnival began, and Byron entered into its spirit with an abandon that shocked even Mengaldo, who was no Puritan; but Byron was no more disposed to be preached at by an Italian than by his friends in England. 'What I get by my brains,' he told one of them with brutal ribaldry, 'I will spend on my b——cks as long as I have a tester or a t—— remaining.' Nevertheless even he realised that he could not continue at the present pace, and in the first canto of *Don Juan*, confessed that, at thirty, he had 'squandered his whole summer while 'twas May'. It is true that this had been his ambition: as he told Tom Moore months before, 'I will work the mine of my youth to the last veins of the ore, and then – good night.' But now when the mine was becoming too quickly exhausted he found that he was not ready to say good night; rather he was willing to accept another, quieter way of life.

One evening early in April Byron went with his friend Alexander Scott to a reception at the Contessa Benzon's, the once famous beauty whose memory still remains in the gondoliers' song of *La biondina in gondoleta.* They took their seat on a sofa opposite the door of the sala, and other guests began coming in from the theatre. Among these was a young woman with large eyes, fair, smooth brow and rosy cheeks, with auburn ringlets falling to sloping shoulders (then so much admired) and full, firm bust; she came on the arm of a husband who, like Julia's in *Don Juan*, was many years her senior. Byron was not in the mood for introductions; besides he had met her a year before. 'You know very well,' he said to his hostess, 'that I do not want to make any new acquaintances with women; if they are ugly, because they are ugly – and if they are beautiful, because they are beautiful.' Eventually, Contessa Benzon, who was an old and loved friend of his, prevailed on him to be introduced. It was her custom to describe her guests when she presented them, and now 'Peer of England and its greatest poet' she added after Byron's name. The girl to whom he was thus presented, even as she entered the room, had been fascinated by the beauty of his face; now, the polite words of introduction brought to his lips one of those wonderful smiles which Coleridge called 'The Gate of Heaven'.* For the first time, as he bent over her hand, she heard in his 'Ne sono profondamente onorato' the tones of that perfectly modulated voice. Contessa Benzon spoke her name: 'La Contessa Teresa Guiccioli.' The new life had begun.

That story has been told with the insight of an exceptional

* See note 5, p. 270.

sympathy by the Marchesa Origo. It concerns us here only so far as it affected Byron's personality, and therefore all his relationships with others. Teresa tamed him perhaps; certainly she made him gentler; but she did not diminish him as a poet or as a man. Shelley came to regard her as Byron's good angel, 'one who has led him from darkness to light, who deserves not only his gratitude, but that of everyone who loves him'. From that generous judgment we have no need to dissent.

Back again in Rome, of which he had had a week's foretaste in November, Shelley revived. In that week he had come to the conclusion that the Romans were much superior to the other Italians whom he had met, and for that reason had been looking forward for some time to his return there. He was not disappointed. In a letter to Peacock a month after his arrival he said: 'We see something of Italian society indeed: the Romans please me much, especially the women: who though totally devoid of any kind of information or culture of the imagination or affections or understanding, and in this respect a kind of gentle savages, yet contrive to be interesting.' And he went on to compare them, in their innocence and naïveté, to children. Among these gentle savages they were most constantly in the company of Signora Marianna Dionigi, a woman of some talent as painter, writer and musician, learned in the antiquities of Rome, and well known for her *conversazioni* to which she invited many foreigners. They called on her four days after reaching Rome, and she must at once have established her authority with them, for she promptly took them off to Mass. A few days later they met the Pope, Pius VII, who had descended from his carriage to walk. He was in his eightieth year, 'a poor old man upon the brink of the grave', in Claire's judgment, but he had four more years to live. During the first two months of the Shelleys' stay in Rome Mary's journal constantly records visits to Signora Dionigi, whom she acidly described as 'very old, very miserly and very mean'; but Shelley afterwards remembered with affection her kindness to them. They went with her to hear sacred music, which delighted

Shelley, and to see collections of paintings. Their introduction to Roman society, which Shelley so much enjoyed – for in spite of his shyness he was a sociable creature – must have been principally due to her. Most probably they were introduced to her by Lord Guilford, a noted philhellene and elegant Greek scholar, who was their first caller in Rome. Byron, who had seen him in Venice in April 1817 (from where he travelled back to England accompanied by Polidori), called him 'the most illustrious humbug of his age and country'. Later on he would have admitted that this was less than just. Perhaps Lord Guilford heard of the Shelleys from Byron.

Shelley's health and Mary's spirits both began to improve in the excitement of seeing Rome in spring: 'now I begin to live,' said Mary. Once the weight of her melancholy had been removed, Shelley resumed *Prometheus Unbound* with intense energy, and by 6 April, only a month after reaching Rome, he had completed the second and third acts. In his preface he says that the poem 'was chiefly written upon the mountainous ruins of the Baths of Caracalla, among the flowery glades, and thickets of odoriferous blossoming trees, which are extended in ever winding labyrinths upon its immense platforms and dizzy arches suspended in the air'. He walked there with Mary on 13 March, and the scene reminded him, so he told Peacock, of an overgrown cliff in Bisham Wood 'where Hogg and I scrambled up and you – to my infinite discontent – would go home'. He was delighted, as he had been at Les Échelles a year before, by the combination of the grandiose works of man with evidence of the power of Nature: there by the old road of 1582 cut through rocky cliffs which reminded him of Aeschylus' *Prometheus*, here by 'the deformity of the vast desolation of the ruins softened down by the undecaying investiture of Nature'. It was, so to say, the scenery of Les Échelles in reverse. Forgetful perhaps that he had written the first act in the less sublime scenery of Este, Shelley in his preface attributed even the inspiration of his drama to the Roman spring; but certainly he found this as exciting and invigorating as he said, feeling his spirits revived by it to a new life.

While Shelley was busy writing Mary took lessons in drawing, and Claire lessons in singing; Mary, with new-found gaiety, told Hunt, 'the *belle arti* take up all our time.' In the same letter Mary mentions Byron: 'It is a long time since we have heard from Venice – but all goes on as badly there with the noble poet as ever I fear – he is a lost man if he does not escape soon.' By an ironic chance she was writing but three days after the meeting with Teresa Guiccioli had provided his means of escape. Three weeks later they were again reminded of Byron when they met at Signora Dionigi's an English eccentric of notable mendacity and plausibility, Robert Finch, who had, as Mary said, 'the dear Corsair expression half savage half soft'. Byron, who first met him with di Breme in 1817, had told them about him in Venice – he called him the Reverend Colonel Finch; but the Shelleys, borrowing from Tom Moore's *The Fudge Family in Paris*, invented their own subtler nickname for him, Colonel Calicot Finch. For indeed, like Biddy Fudge's suitor, 'Colonel' Finch was not what he claimed to be.*

This April Mary had another reminder of the old days with Byron. Maria Gisborne wrote to tell her of the publication in England of a tale called *The Vampyre*, which was attributed to him. From her description of the plot Mary recognised it as the story which Byron sketched out for his contribution to the quartet of ghost stories which, one evening at the Villa Diodati, he proposed they should write, and of which her own *Frankenstein* was the first. She naturally supposed that it was indeed by Byron – in fact Polidori had appropriated it without his leave – and she was curious to see it. 'And I dare say,' she added, 'that we shall like it better than the poetry in which he is engaged at present which is in the Beppo style' – an opinion in which Shelley would never have concurred; and indeed this was not Mary's true judgment of *Don Juan*. When she received *The Vampyre* she would find in the preface the story of Shelley's

* This nickname was the work of genius. Biddy believed that Colonel Calicot was the King of Prussia. In 1829 Colonel Finch and his wife resided in Rome in the Palazzo del Re di Prussia.

seizure after hearing Byron quote *Christabel*; this would have been enough to disprove Byron's authorship.

Shelley did not rest long after completing the third act of *Prometheus Unbound*, which at this time he intended to be the conclusion of the poem, before starting to write another, and very different, drama. A year before, while he and Mary were staying at Leghorn, someone lent him a transcript of the history of the Cenci family, of which Mary made a copy for him. On arriving in Rome Shelley 'found that the story of the Cenci was a subject not to be mentioned in Italian society without awakening a deep and breathless interest; and that the feelings of the company never failed to incline to a romantic pity for the wrongs, and a passionate exculpation of the horrible deed to which they urged her, who has been mingled two centuries with the common dust.' Pity and terror, the Aristotelian requirements for the cathartic effect of tragedy, were to be found in the story of Beatrice Cenci, and now that Shelley had as it were diverted the tragedy on the life of Tasso into the soliloquy of the Maniac in *Julian and Maddalo* he determined to use her story as the plot of a new drama. On 22 April, on one of their sight-seeing expeditions, they saw in the Palazzo Barberini the portrait of Beatrice Cenci, 'the most beautiful creature that you can conceive', and on 11 May they visited the Casa Cenci. Three days later Shelley was already at work on *The Cenci*; by 8 August it was finished.

The family of the Cenci was a Roman family, and the lively interest in their story which Shelley found among those he met at Signora Dionigi's fired his imagination to a sympathetic understanding of human passion which has made of *The Cenci* the one Romantic drama still capable of holding the interest of a theatre audience. He wrote the part of Beatrice with Eliza O'Neill in mind: he (like everyone else) had much admired her performance as Bianca in Milman's *Fazio*, which he saw on 16 February 1818, just before leaving England. And, like the great Renaissance dramatists who were his models, he had 'attended simply to the impartial development of such characters as it is probable the persons represented really were', without any attempt to introduce his own opinions, and in the hope of at last achieving popular success. The theme of incest, which Shelley regarded as 'a very poetical circumstance', he had already treated in *The Revolt of Islam* and *Rosalind and Helen*; and he had recently been trying to persuade Mary to translate Alfieri's *Myrrha*. Here he treated it with such delicacy that he could not believe that it would cause the play's rejection at Covent Garden. It was, after all, a theme which some of the greatest dramatists, Sophocles, Ford, Calderón, had used in drama; but Regency London proved more prudish than seventeenth-century London, or fifth-century Athens. At first he had urged Mary to write the play, for he must have seen at once that it required wholly different treatment from the drama he had just finished, and he may have judged that the success of *Frankenstein* showed that she had the qualities that it needed. Mary demurred, but he consulted with her during his writing of it. *The Cenci*, she said, was 'the only one of his works that he communicated to me during its progress. We talked over the arrangement of the scenes together.' Partly for that reason, partly for a feminine preference for the actual rather than the ideal, she always liked it best of his poems.

It was as well that Mary had this interest to distract her during the summer. They had intended to remain in Rome for three months before going on to Florence, which they had not yet seen; then they thought of returning to Naples; then it was to be Lucca. But all their plans were upset by the illness of their three-year-old William at the end of May. After a fortnight's anxiety, during the last three days of which Shelley watched constantly by his son's bedside, on 7 June William died. They buried him in the Protestant cemetery, which to Shelley, visiting it in the previous November, had seemed 'the most beautiful and solemn cemetery I ever beheld'. He noted then that most of the tombs marked the graves of women and young people.

Three days later the Shelleys left Rome for Leghorn, to be near the Gisbornes. They stayed a week and then moved to a house by the sea, Villa Valsovano, between Leghorn and Montenero within easy reach of their friends. A day or two before William's death Mary's journal breaks off. She took it up again on 4 August, Shelley's twenty-seventh birthday, as she noted. 'We have now lived five years together; and if all the events of the five years were blotted out, I might be happy; but to have won and then cruelly have lost the associations of four years, is not an accident to which the human mind can bend without much suffering.' Shelley resumed *The Cenci* early in July, and he continued to discuss it with Mary, who encouraged him to go on. On 8 August he finished it; he dedicated it to Hunt, whose portrait, to his and Mary's great pleasure, arrived a few days later from England.*

By a strange chance Shelley received his copy of *Nightmare Abbey*, which had been published the previous November, shortly after William's death. He had heard something of it in Peacock's letters of the previous year, and now that it had come he found it, as he told Peacock, though not a cure for melancholy, a welcome palliative. And with serene detachment from personal troubles even at this moment, he revealed that lively appreciation of the more comic aspects of his own personality which Peacock had portrayed in Scythrop: 'I think Scythrop a character admirably conceived and executed and I know not how to praise sufficiently the lightness, chastity and strength of the language of the whole.' For all his passionate idealism, Shelley had both feet firmly on the ground, and delighted to see himself as others saw him. If the picture was hostile, as in the reviews, he was unperturbed. If, as now, it was friendly mockery, he was very ready to laugh. Of Peacock's slighter portrait of Byron as Mr Cypress he said nothing.

They had no news of Byron and little of Allegra all summer. In the middle of September Mary told Amelia Curran (the artist daughter of John Philpot Curran, whom they had got to know well in Rome, where she painted Shelley's portrait in May) that 'the most pressing entreaties on my part as well as Claire's cannot draw a single line from Venice', and she was

* For some reason Shelley dated the dedication 'Rome, May 29, 1819.' In fact he wrote it at Leghorn on 2 September.

afraid Shelley would have to go to investigate. She was very unwilling that he should, both because his health was not good, and because she was expecting the birth of a child in a few weeks. Also their three months' lease of the Villa Valsovano would soon be up, and they must find somewhere to live in Florence. During August and September Mary was writing her novel *Mathilda*, in which she sought to exorcise the melancholy of the year in which she had lost her two children. Here too the theme of incest is important, for it was founded on Alfieri's *Myrrha*: perhaps that is why she never published it. Probably she used the novel as a means of seeking a renewal of Shelley's confidence, which she would be far too inhibited to seek in any way that was more direct. Where others might reveal their inmost feelings in a letter to a friend, and then give it to their spouse to read before posting, Mary chose to disclose herself in fiction which, if she had second thoughts, she could always deny to be self-revelation.

The completion of *The Cenci* by no means exhausted Shelley's imagination. Within a few days he told Peacock that his head was full of all sorts of plans for writing. These included translations from Calderón and from Greek drama: the version of Euripides' *Cyclops* was made some time this year, perhaps in June, but Calderón's *Mágico Prodigioso* was not translated until the last year of his life. Shelley wrote few personal poems in 1819. William's death prompted two brief fragments in June at the head of one of which Shelley wrote:

With what truth may I say –
Roma! Roma! Roma!
Non è più come era prima!

the words of a *ritornello* which Byron quoted in the preface to the fourth canto of *Childe Harold*, and which Shelley too would have heard on the lips of labourers in Rome. Two other scraps of verse were addressed to Mary in her renewed sorrow:

Thou sittest on the hearth of pale despair,
Where
For thine own sake I cannot follow thee.

Shelley hoped that the birth of another child would lift some of her melancholy.

On 5 September news reached him of the Peterloo riots in Manchester. On this famous occasion sixty thousand or more working people gathered in St Peter's Field in Manchester to hear 'Orator' Hunt address them. The Government declared the meeting illegal and the people were forcibly dispersed by troops. Nine were killed and some hundreds wounded or injured. Shelley's indignation boiled over, and he immediately wrote his savage invective *The Masque of Anarchy*, which he sent off to Leigh Hunt on the 23rd, for printing in *The Examiner*. Leigh Hunt was anything but timid, but he decided that the public (indignant as many people were at such high-handed behaviour) were not yet discerning enough 'to do justice to the sincerity and kind-heartedness of the spirit that walked in this flaming robe of verse'. Perhaps he thought that its publication would ruin the chance which Shelley at last seemed to have of achieving something better than notoriety. Eventually he published it in the year of the passing of the Reform Bill.

Shelley wrote other political poems this autumn, including the sonnet *England in 1819* and *A New National Anthem.* In October his mind turned briefly to Spain, prompted by a suggestion that it might be to the benefit of his health to go there for the winter, and he wrote his *Ode, before the Spaniards had recovered their Liberty.* According to Mary he had at this time an intention to write a series of poems ranging himself on the side of the People against their Oppressors. He considered the Peterloo riots as the distant thunders of approaching revolution and, like Milton travelling in Italy in 1639, longed to be home to participate in the great event. But already he had gained self-knowledge enough to realise that the political ambition of his earlier days must give place to poetry:

As I lay asleep in Italy
There came a voice from over the Sea,
And with great power it forth led me
To walk in the visions of Poesy.

The three months' tenancy of the Villa Valsovano terminated

at the end of September, and the Shelleys removed to Florence, where they arrived on 2 October, intending to remain for six months. One motive, Shelley told Hunt, was that Mary might be attended in her confinement by Dr Bell, whom they had got to know in Rome. The child, a boy, was born on 12 November and named Percy Florence. As Shelley had hoped, his birth helped to revive Mary's spirits after five childless months.

In June Shelley had received copies of *The Examiner** containing Leigh Hunt's review of Wordsworth's *Peter Bell: A Tale in Verse* and Keats' review of John Hamilton Reynolds' skit on it (which was published a few days before Wordsworth's poem) called *Peter Bell: A Lyrical Ballad.* These gave him the idea of writing a third poem in the series, and as soon as he got to Florence he set to work on *Peter Bell the Third,* which he had finished by 25 October when Mary copied it. This is a gay and high-spirited poem, with some perceptive sketches of Wordsworth:

> He touched the hem of Nature's shift,
> Felt faint – and never dared uplift
> The closest, all concealing tunic:

and of Coleridge:

> He was a mighty poet – and
> A subtle-souled psychologist;
> All things he seemed to understand,
> Of old or new – of sea or land –
> But his own mind – which was a mist.

But underneath the delightful foolery was serious criticism that Wordsworth by his apostasy from the cause of liberty had brought upon his poetry the unforgivable vice of dullness. There was nothing personal in this attack, as there had been in Byron's dedication of *Don Juan* to Southey. He knew neither Wordsworth nor Coleridge personally, but admired the earlier poetry of both, and hoped for more – not for the absurdities of *Peter Bell,* which he would quote with glee. He sent it off to Hunt on 2 November, but again Hunt withheld it

* For 26 April and 3 May 1819.

from publication, no doubt because he feared that Shelley's desired anonymity could not be preserved, and that it might detract from the more serious work which, as Shelley had told him, he was about to publish.

Even before he finished *Peter Bell the Third* the poetic enthusiasm which in Shelley's present mood was irrepressible led him, when walking one wild autumnal day in the Cascine woods by the Arno, to write his *Ode to the West Wind.* As was frequent with him, he reused in the poem images and phrases which had first come into his mind when describing the Italian scene in letters to Peacock. The poem also very characteristically brings together his delight in the natural world and his passionate hope for the improvement of man's lot upon earth. He also wrote a number of lyrics for music, to please a young English woman, Sophia Stacey (she was the ward of his uncle Robert Parker) who had come to Florence early in November. The most famous of these, the *Indian Serenade*, was written for her to sing to the aria *Ah! perdona* from Mozart's *La Clemenza di Tito*, for she had a beautiful voice, and, as she noted, Shelley was passionately fond of music. He addressed to her the stanzas beginning 'Thou art fair, and few are fairer', and when she left Florence at the end of December he transcribed into a copy of Leigh Hunt's *Literary Pocket-book* for 1814 three other songs, *Love's Philosophy, Time Long Past* and *Good-Night*, and gave it to her, together with a letter of introduction to Signora Dionigi in Rome.

Since his arrival in Rome eight months before Shelley had written two acts of an ideal lyrical drama which he knew was in his best style ('whatever that may amount to'); a tragedy in the Jacobean tradition, intended for the stage; the translation of a play by Euripides; a powerful political invective, and other shorter political poems, all in a direct terse manner; a high-spirited burlesque of Wordsworth; an *Ode* which is recognised as one of the supreme English lyrics; and some charming songs. All this he had done in spite of a month's interruption caused by the illness and death of his beloved little son; in spite of Mary's renewed melancholy just when she was recovering from the loss of Clara; in spite of ever increasing anxiety about Allegra, and Claire's continued presence; in spite of Godwin with his importunate demands for money, and his ready lack of sympathy. Yet it is not the quantity of verse that he wrote in these months, nor even its consistent excellence that is most astonishing; it is the extraordinary variety of manner which he achieved, the virtuosity with which he could turn in a few days from the lofty idealism of *Prometheus Unbound* to the depraved passions of *The Cenci*; from the fierce indignation of *The Masque of Anarchy* to the gay mockery of *Peter Bell the Third*; from a revolutionary parody of the National Anthem to the lyrical exaltation of the *Ode to the West Wind*. Shelley himself recognised this quality of his poetry. 'I do not know if it be wise to affect variety in compositions, or whether the attempt to excel in many ways does not debar from excellence in one particular kind.' Such versatility is without parallel in the history of literature.

The continuing lack of news from Venice became more and more upsetting to the Shelleys and Claire, especially as they were quite unaware of any reason for it. On 18 October Shelley, who had somehow heard that the uncommunicative Hoppners were on leave in Switzerland, wrote to the English Vice-Consul there to ask for news of Allegra and of Byron. It was almost a year since he had last seen them. By the time the letter reached Venice the Hoppners had returned, and no doubt it was handed over to them. Mrs Hoppner deigned to write, to tell them that Allegra was with Byron at La Mira on the Brenta, where he had taken a six months' lease of the Villa Foscarini, and that His Lordship was hoping to take the child to England with him in the coming spring.

For a time Shelley 'deserted the odorous gardens of literature to journey across the great sandy desert of Politics'. He wrote a long letter for *The Examiner* in defence of Richard Carlile, who had just been sentenced to three years' imprisonment and severely fined for publishing some of Paine's works, and he began *A Philosophical View of Reform*. But the poetry could not be held back, and in late November and early December he wrote the fourth act to *Prometheus Unbound*, which since May he had regarded as complete in three acts. He needed a *Paradiso* to balance the sombre *Inferno* of the first act, and he poured forth this marvellous sequence of lyrics with the facility which hardly deserted him this year. Even so he could write to the Gisbornes, while Mary was actually transcribing this last act, 'if the faculties of my mind were not imprisoned within a mind whose bars are daily cares and vulgar difficulties I might yet do something'. With such modest estimation of what he had done, with such diffident hope for the future, did Shelley close this *annus mirabilis*.

CHAPTER SIX

The Years Apart (II)

1820–1821: ITALY

WINTER in Florence, even in a mild season, is not very agreeable, and the winter of 1819–20 was anything but mild: 'an epic of rain, with an episode of frost, and a few similes concerning fine weather,' Shelley called it (he had lately been reading Calderón). On 26 January therefore he took the opportunity of a spell of better weather to escape, with Mary and the baby and the new Swiss nursemaid and Claire, to Pisa. They had disliked Pisa when they first visited it in May 1818, but now Shelley wished to consult Dr Vaccà, a distinguished physician who had the further attraction that as a young student in Paris he had taken part in the storming of the Bastille. The Gisbornes knew him, and so did the Masons whose acquaintance the Shelleys had made when passing through Pisa the previous September. They too were a recommendation to Pisa, and so was the nearness of Maria Gisborne at Leghorn.

'Mr and Mrs Mason' was the accepted designation of George William Tighe, the son of an Irish member of Parliament, and the Countess of Mountcashell, who had been living together in Pisa for eight or nine years. Mrs Mason, a tall, gangling woman of handsome features and liberal opinions, had when a child been a pupil of Mary Wollstonecraft;* later she corresponded with Godwin. She had therefore been delighted to

* Mary Wollstonecraft portrayed herself under the name of 'Mrs Mason' in her *Original Stories from Real Life*. Her pupil, the future Lady Mountcashell, is there named Mary; and she expresses a wish 'to be like Mrs Mason'. When she left her husband and seven children in 1805 she therefore became 'Mrs Mason'.

meet the daughter of Mary; and now she made the Shelleys most welcome in Pisa. Mr Mason (or Tighe) was a retiring, well-read man whose company, unlike John Gisborne's, could be enjoyed for his own sake. He was known as Tatty, from his devotion to the potato: in the hope of finding something suitable for the climate of Tuscany he experimented with different varieties which he had sent to him from Ireland. He grew some of them in pots, to the surprise of his neighbours. Mrs Mason added to her other good qualities sound, practical common sense and a lively sense of humour. During their first months in Pisa the Shelleys and the Masons met almost every day, more often than not at the Masons' Casa Silva which was on the south side of the river. There were other English in Pisa, whose company the Masons and the Shelleys avoided; a lady 'who mounts her Chastity and rides over us all', Mrs Mason warned them; an old Mr Dolby who went about with his pockets stuffed with books, his spectacles hung on a gold chain about his neck, singing to himself; and there was one distinguished Englishman, Walter Savage Landor, who (having rashly accepted Southey's opinions) refused to meet Shelley. This was a loss to them both, as Landor afterwards admitted. 'I blush in anguish at my prejudice and injustice', he wrote in one of the *Imaginary Conversations*, and he sought then to make amends with generous praise of one who 'possessed all the delicate feelings of a gentleman, all the discrimination of a scholar, and united, in just degrees, the ardour of the poet with the patience and forbearance of the philosopher'. Shelley, who already admired *Gebir* when he was at Oxford, retained his liking for Landor's writing as long as he lived.

They had not been long in Pisa when another Englishman of their acquaintance made a characteristic appearance. Mary described the occasion to Maria Gisborne:

The other day as Claire and Shelley were walking out they beheld a little dirty blacksmith's boy running away from a tall long-legged man running with an umbrella under his arm after him, crying 'Fermatelo, fermatelo!' The boy got into a house and cried 'Son nella mia botega! Non toccami! Son nella mia botega!' Shelley approached and asked 'Cosa c'è?' For the tall umbrella gentleman had seized the boy by the collar. He (the tall man) cried, 'Cercate il governatore – subito cercate il governatore!' 'Ma perche? Che cosa è?' 'Signor, non fa niente che cosa sia – cercate il governatore, subito cercatelo!' and this with the greatest vehemence. A crowd collected. Claire twitched Shelley and remonstrated. Don Quixote did not like to leave the boy in thrall, but deafened by the tall strider's vociferations, and overcome by Claire's importunities, he departed; and then Claire, out of breath with terror, as you may well suppose, said 'For mercy's sake have nothing to do with those people: it's the Reverend Colonel Calicot Finch'.

Shelley's rushing to the assistance of a small boy, and his subsequent escape from the ravages of another Erymanthian bore are equally typical of him.

During their first few weeks in Pisa the Shelleys lived in rooms in a house called Casa Frassi on the Lung' Arno near S. Nicola. There was nowhere for Shelley to use as a study, so that he wrote little or nothing, for it was still too cold for him to write out of doors, as he preferred, 'under a tree, in a garden or on the bank of a river'. On 14 March they moved to the top floor in the same house; here they were not so cramped, and Shelley at once started writing again. The revolution in Spain, which began on New Year's Day, inspired his *Ode to Liberty*, published later in the year in the same volume with *Prometheus Unbound.* In the previous October Shelley, in another ode, had called on the Spaniards to rise against their oppressors; now that they had done so he welcomed their courage with passionate enthusiasm, and even, as he told Hunt, entertained the idea of going there. At the head of the poem, for a motto, Shelley printed two famous lines from *Childe Harold* IV:

> Yet, Freedom, yet, thy banner, torn but flying,
> Streams like a thunder-storm against the wind.

The poem continues the argument which Julian had used to Maddalo, that 'it is our will that thus enchains us,' and which he had pursued in the first act of *Prometheus Unbound*: how vain has been all man's achievement,

> If on his own high will, a willing slave,
> He has enthroned the oppression and the oppressor.

Such had recently been the disastrous outcome of the high hopes of the French Revolution, in the military tyranny of Napoleon. Byron's lines opened the stanza which follows his description of that same fatal Saturnalia, and in the ode, whether or not deliberately, Shelley echoes the noble rhetoric on behalf of Liberty of *Childe Harold.* But the Spanish revolution concerned Byron only in so far as it 'set the Italians in a ferment'. He himself was becoming involved in the revolutionary movement of the Carboneria and had no time for happenings in Spain. As usual, his interest was not in the ideal and remote, but in the practical and immediate.

In the opening stanza of his ode Shelley referred to his dismay at what was happening elsewhere, and especially in England, where the Cato Street Conspiracy of February, a plot to assassinate the Ministry, seemed to Shelley to place another obstacle in the way of political reform. Earlier in the year he had told Medwin, after a reference to the political situation in England, 'These are not times in which one has much spirit for writing poetry'; but now the exciting news from Spain stirred him from this mood, and

> My soul spurned the chains of its dismay,
> And in the rapid plumes of song
> Clothed itself, sublime and strong.

So he put into his ode some of the thoughts which during the winter he had been developing in *A Philosophical View of Reform*, by this time almost finished.

Shelley wrote other poems this spring, as soon as he had somewhere to write. *The Sensitive Plant*, which derived from his friendship with Mrs Mason, was written in March; *A Vision of the Sea*, a kind of Coleridgean extravaganza, perhaps prompted by the storm scene in *Don Juan* II, followed in April, so did *An Exhortation*, and perhaps the dramatic fragment *Orpheus*. These poems further explore the despondent mood of the personal poems written in the winter of 1818–19, and with the same reticence and mystification. Mary was much happier since the birth of her child, as Shelley had hoped, but he had his own anxieties over the adopted child in Naples. The Gisbornes were in his confidence about this, and helped him to get the services of a lawyer, Federico del Rosso, to deal with some problem that had arisen; but from Shelley's instructions to them to address letters on this subject to 'Mr Jones' it seems likely that Mary deeply resented this foolish affair. There was thus still something less than the old mutual trust between Shelley and Mary, even if this was no longer due to her melancholy but to his well-intentioned folly.

Besides, there was always Claire, squabbling with Mary, badgering Shelley about Allegra, writing foolish letters to Byron; Claire with her amusing but often barbed comments on people they knew; Claire, certainly to walk or ride with (but she had a propensity to falling off her horse), and Claire of the sweet singing voice to accompany them to the opera – on 8 February they saw Rossini's *La Cenerentola* together. But still, must *praesentia* Claire be a permanent condition of their lives? Mary often wondered about this, though Shelley's charitable and innocent nature, which had once prompted him to suggest that Harriet should come to live with him and Mary, would never have allowed him to think of Claire as a source of irritation. Mrs Mason saw the danger clearly enough, and eventually she persuaded Claire to go away; but the time had not yet come.

In the early months of the year Claire had occasional letters from Mrs Hoppner with news of Allegra. This was not altogether reassuring – Mrs Hoppner was not a very reassuring kind of woman – and at the end of April she reported that Byron, thinking how best to educate Allegra, was inclined to place her in a convent. This suggestion, it is scarcely necessary to observe, caused consternation in the devoutly atheistical household of the Shelleys. If Byron's decision also implied a decision not to return her to the Shelleys he had some sound reasons. 'I so totally disapprove of the mode of Children's treatment in their family, that I should look upon the Child as going into a hospital. Is it not so?' he wrote to Hoppner. 'Have they *reared* one? Her health here has hitherto been *excellent*, and her temper not bad. . . . But the Child shall not quit me again to perish of starvation and green fruit, or be taught to believe that there is no Deity.' Mrs Hoppner with her usual tact relayed this to Claire, who noted in her diary for 30 April: 'A letter from Mad. Hoppner concerning green fruit and God.' Byron's reference to the loss of Mary's three children may seem cruel, but it was not intended for their eyes; and it was true.* Clearly he would have been much to blame if he had allowed Allegra to return to that household. 'There is no comparison of her situation now,' he said, 'and that under Élise or with them. She has grown considerably, is very clean and lively.' And in the same letter he by no means refused Claire permission to see Allegra. 'Whenever there is convenience of vicinity and access, her Mother can always have her with her; otherwise no. It was so stipulated from the beginning.' Byron's letter was, indeed, full of his usual common sense. His concern for Allegra's well-being was that of any responsible father; he simply insisted on being in a position to exercise that responsibility and to see that the child was properly looked after. If Claire was really eager to see Allegra, let her come over to Ravenna, where he had gone to be with Teresa.

Claire saw the matter in a different light and the day after receiving Mrs Hoppner's letter wrote to Byron, 'my damned Brute' as she called him in the privacy of her diary. (Byron returned the compliment a little later by referring to her as 'a damned Bitch'. So far as we know, these courtesies were not exchanged.) She thought of going at once to Ravenna with Shelley; but in two days heard from Byron himself, to say that he had no intention of sending Allegra away yet. In his letter to Hoppner Byron said that he might put her in a convent to be educated 'in a year or two'. Mrs Hoppner maliciously suppressed the last phrase, so that Claire imagined Allegra's

* Mary's first child, a girl, born prematurely 22 February 1815, died 6 March 1815; William, born 24 January 1816, died 7 June 1819; Clara, born 2 September 1817, died 24 September 1818.

removal to a convent to be imminent, and with her normal impetuosity wrote off a doubtless foolish letter to Byron, based not on what he had said, but on what Mrs Hoppner had reported. It is not surprising that Byron was angry. Mary told the Gisbornes a few days later 'the Hoppners have behaved shamefully.'

As it was, a further exchange of letters between the Bitch and the Brute took place, and on 19 May Claire recorded the receipt of 'A brutal letter from Albe'. However, Shelley went off to Casciano three days later, returning on the 25th.* In his absence another letter came from Byron, this time addressed to Shelley, and a day after his return Shelley replied:

Claire tells me that she has already answered what relates to the differences of opinion between you and her about Allegra; so I am spared the pain of being an interlocutor in a matter over which, I believe, I have no influence either as it regards her or you. I wish you had not expressed yourself so harshly in your letter about Claire – because of necessity she was obliged to read it; and I am persuaded that you are mistaken in thinking she has any desire of thwarting your plans about Allegra – even the requests that annoy you spring from an amiable and affectionate disposition. She has consented to give up this journey to Ravenna – which would indeed have been a material inconvenience, and annoyance to me, as well as you – but which, for such a purpose, I hardly felt that I could refuse. When we meet, I can explain to you some circumstances of misrepresentation respecting Allegra which, I think, will lead you to find an excuse for Claire's anxiety.

It is easy to recognise that, if only Shelley had gone off then to see Byron at Ravenna, he could at once have removed this latest misunderstanding; he would also have discovered earlier, and less painfully, the extent of the Hoppners' duplicity, and would have put Byron on his guard against it too. But, since he did not go, the 'circumstances of misrepresentation' were left unexplained, and ill-feeling was allowed to continue. Yet there could be no finer example of Shelley's charitable, forgiving nature than in the last part of his letter, which shows that he had read Byron's strictures, in the letter on 'Green fruit and

* See note 6, p. 270.

God', on his and Mary's upbringing of their own children. Byron, he mildly remarked, was 'misinformed as to our system of physical education'; and though admitting his own denial of Christian faith, he was, he said, 'as little inclined to teach a child disbelief, as belief, as a formal creed'. He had only smiled at Byron's protest at his supposed creed. And this to a man who had harshly reminded him of his failure to keep alive any of his and Mary's three children. To no man could the charge that he was *anima naturaliter christiana* be laid with more certainty.

Shelley took the occasion of this letter to Byron to comment on the first two cantos of *Don Juan* which had been published the previous July. Byron had read some of the first canto to him even before it was finished, and also the Dedication to Southey; and Mary noted that they were reading the published poem at the beginning of this year. Shelley remarked the omission of the Dedication but without regret. He especially admired the account of the storm in the second canto: he himself had just been attempting something of the sort in *A Vision of the Sea*, though he said nothing of this to Byron. Most of all he admired the love-letter written by Julia after the discovery of her liaison with Juan. 'The love letter, and the account of its being written, is altogether a masterpiece of portraiture; of human nature laid with the eternal colours of the feelings of humanity. Where did you learn all these secrets? I should like to go to school there.' Byron's answer, if he made one, has not been preserved: it would probably have been flippant – a recommendation to La Fornarina, perhaps. But Mary would have approved of Shelley's wish to learn Byron's secrets of portraying human nature, whatever reservations she might have about the method. Shelley's attempt at such portraiture in *The Cenci* was more to her liking than *Prometheus Unbound*. In his letter Shelley referred to *The Cenci*. 'You will find it,' he told Byron, 'less horrible than you had reason to expect. At all events it is matter-of-fact.' And, with that modest deference to Byron's greatness as a poet which he never lost, Shelley added, 'If I had known you would have liked to have seen it, I could have sent you a copy.' When he did see it, months later, Byron told Shelley he thought it 'a work of power and poetry', though he considered the subject undramatic, and disapproved of Jacobean drama as a model. In this same letter Shelley took Byron to task for his 'bitter mockery of our common nature' in *Don Juan*, which he thought unworthy of his genius. 'The power and the beauty and the wit, indeed, redeem all this – chiefly because they belie and refute it.' He apparently had no liking for the vivid contrast of Julia's love-letter with her tirade against Alfonso a few stanzas earlier, and no appreciation of the masterly way in which Byron makes us accept both as true to Julia's character. However much Shelley admired Byron's insight into human behaviour, he could not accept his comic (and therefore, at times, satiric) presentation of it. To Shelley the gap between human aspiration and human achievement was always tragic; it was his mission, as a poet, to help to close that gap. Byron was well aware of the tragic aspect of life, but also, like Shakespeare, of how closely it verges on the comic. As he said in *Don Juan*,

> If I laugh at any mortal thing,
> 'Tis that I may not weep.

For the most part, he preferred to laugh.

On the same day on which he wrote to Byron, Shelley also wrote to Leigh Hunt and to the Gisbornes, who were now in London. He said nothing of his concern for Claire and Allegra, but to the Gisbornes he admitted something of the weariness he must have felt: 'I ought to have peace of mind – leisure, tranquillity; this I expect soon.' A fortnight later his hope was at least briefly realised. Mary wrote in her journal: 'A better day than most days and good reason for it, though Shelley is not well. Claire away at Pugnano.' But the relief was only temporary, and a plan to find a post for Claire in Paris came to nothing. A month later Claire was writing in her journal:

> Heigho the Claire and the Maie*
> Find something to fight about every day.

* Mary spelt her pet-name Maie; Claire here spelt it Ma.

But the irritations caused by her presence were to continue for some time yet. Shelley added a postscript to a letter which Mary wrote to Maria Gisborne on 19 July: 'Mary who, you know, is always wise, has been lately very good. I wish she were as wise now as she will be at 45, or as misfortune has made me. She would then live on very good terms with Claire.' And he referred to Mrs Mason's continuing effort to find some post for Claire.

For once this summer Shelley was provoked by a hostile review to resentment. Normally he disdained reply, but the attack on his personal character made in *The Quarterly Review* of April 1819, under the guise of a review of *The Revolt of Islam*, was more than even he could bear without protest. Shelley had been led to believe that it was by Southey, and at the end of June he wrote a firm and dignified letter to invite him to deny authorship. Southey replied, and said that he was not the author. (The review was in fact written by John Taylor Coleridge.) He took the opportunity of a letter to preach to Shelley from the Christian security of a man who had informed his friends of a 'League of Incest' established by Byron and Shelley in 1816. He even had the effrontery to claim that Shelley would certainly acquit him of personal ill-will. Southey's letter is a masterpiece of hypocritical pomposity: he claimed to be, Byron said, 'a good Christian, and vindictive'. Shelley retorted Southey's vaunted Christianity upon him, by referring him to Christ's reply to the Pharisees when they brought him the woman taken in adultery. The self-righteous complacency of Southey's reply to this letter need not be quoted: it has an echo in the criticism of Matthew Arnold and of T. S. Eliot. Shelley ignored it, and so may we.

There were other distresses this summer: the inevitable demands for money from Godwin, whom Shelley had come to detest; attempts at blackmail by Shelley's former servant, Paolo Foggi, who was spreading among the local English the libel that Elena Adelaide was the daughter of Shelley and Claire; and then the death in Naples of this little girl. No wonder Shelley felt, 'as if the destruction that is consuming me were as an atmosphere which wrapt and infected everything connected with me'. (This image perhaps gave Mary the idea for her novel *The Last Man.*) But with the help of his lawyer, Federico del Rosso, whom Shelley had previously consulted about Elena, Paolo was for the time being silenced. In spite of all this Shelley's resilient spirit revealed its natural gaiety, at this very time, in his verse *Letter to Maria Gisborne.* He wrote it in their house at Leghorn, to which he moved, with Mary and Claire and the baby, on 15 June in order to be in close touch with del Rosso, and to challenge by his presence the libellous English residents. They remained there until 4 August, Shelley's birthday. The letter is written in the familiar style in which Shelley began *Julian and Maddalo.* He had intended to write three similar poems, the scenes of which should be Rome, Florence and Naples; but that plan never came to anything. Now his mind broke out of its prison of vulgar difficulties, as he thought of his friends in England, as he contemplated himself sitting in Henry Reveley's study surrounded by pieces of the mechanism for his projected steam-boat,

> Great screws, and cones, and wheels, and grooved blocks,
> The elements of what will stand the shocks
> Of wave and wind and time.

He catches sight of a pretty wooden bowl, filled not with wine but with quicksilver; and his mind races away to a myth about this being the drink of gnomes. Then he makes a paper boat to float there, as he had made hundreds of similar paper boats from his childhood, to float on Warham pond, on puddles in the road, on the Serpentine – anywhere:

> And in this bowl of quicksilver – for I
> Yield to the impulse of an infancy
> Outlasting manhood – I have made to float
> A rude idealism of a paper boat . . .

This is the Shelley in whom every child delighted, as Allegra had done in *Julian and Maddalo*; a very different being from the creature of Southey's dingy imagination. He looks about him and sees other objects, strange and familiar, among these a broken tea-cup:

> A thing from which sweet lips were wont to drink
> The liquor doctors rail at – and which I
> Will quaff in spite of them – and when we die
> We'll toss up who died first of drinking tea,
> And cry out, – 'Heads or tails?' where'er we be.

Amidst this chaotic mess of Henry's, Shelley sits like Spenser's Archimago,

> Plotting dark spells, and devilish enginery,
> The self-impelling steam-wheels of the mind
> Which pump up oaths from clergymen, and grind
> The gentle spirit of our meek reviews
> Into a powdery foam of salt abuse . . .

Then his imagination turns to Maria Gisborne, far away now from her home, her furniture, her possessions, which recall her so vividly and all the happy hours they had spent together in Italy, walking, talking, Shelley learning Spanish from Maria, or reading to her his latest poems, even before they were finished, 'some interrupted flow of visionary rhyme'.

In imagination he follows her to London, and thinks of those whom she will see there; first Godwin, or rather

> That which was Godwin, – greater none than he
> Though fallen – and fallen on evil times . . .

The Miltonic quotation shows Shelley's unaltered estimate of Godwin's greatness, though personally (as he told the Gisbornes in the very letter which accompanied his verse epistle) he now accounted him his 'bitterest enemy'. She would see Coleridge and Leigh Hunt and Hogg and Peacock and Horace Smith, all of them characterised with penetrating wit and sympathy: Coleridge, 'a hooded eagle among blinking owls', Peacock 'a strain too learnèd for a shallow age, too wise for selfish bigots'.

He recalls his thoughts from his friends in London, to invite Maria to look upon the night with all its starlit beauty, but with all the human squalor which it hides. Finally, he invites her to spend the coming winter, when she is back in Italy, with him; he will have got rid of all his despondency and low-thoughted care by then. He looks forward to the time:

> . . . we'll have tea and toast;
> Custards for supper, and an endless host
> Of syllabubs and jellies and mince-pies,
> And other such lady-like luxuries . . .

And talk – oh! so much to talk about when she is back in her own house, Casa Ricci, where he is writing to her.

The *Letter* is a delightfully high-spirited poem, and shows Shelley using the Horatian manner of Byron's preference with skill to match his. Byron had quoted Horace's 'Difficile est proprie communia dicere' at the head of *Don Juan*, whether as a challenge to himself or to his readers: he had succeeded wonderfully, turning from subject to subject, from mood to contrasting mood, with astonishing ease. Now Shelley (who had once said that he would 'rather err with Plato than be right with Horace') emulated on a far smaller scale Byron's versatility, packing into his poem everything from tea and toast to plans for a steam-boat, from London vice to Italian weather, from learning to read Calderón to a penchant for paper boats. It has all the charm of Shelley in his gayest, most vivacious mood, the Shelley with whom his friends could never think of anyone to compare. Yet the letter in which he enclosed it told the Gisbornes of Godwin's angry demands which had so upset Mary; of Paolo Foggi's slanders; of Elena's dangerous illness. When the mood for writing poetry was on him, nothing could repress it: he entered the enchanted world of his imagination and he was happy.

The same high spirits led Shelley, while at Leghorn, to write his still more famous poem, *To a Skylark*. 'It was on a beautiful summer evening,' Mary recalled, 'while wandering among the lanes whose myrtle-hedges were the bowers of the fire-flies, that we heard the carolling of the skylark which inspired one of the most beautiful of his poems.' He must have heard skylarks many times before, at home in England, in Switzerland, in Italy; but now his own happy mood responded so closely to the sustained joyousness of a skylark's song that his stanza even imitated its pattern of clear ringing notes followed by rapid trilling. Of all the countless poems written out of man's delight in the song of birds, none comes closer to the gay, untroubled innocence of the bird itself. The mystery of what the singing bird is feeling remains:

> What objects are the fountains
>   Of thy happy strain?
> What fields, or waves, or mountains?
>   What shapes of sky or plain?
> What love of thine own kind? what ignorance of pain?

There was an extraordinary propriety in Shelley's being inspired to write to a Skylark, as there was in Keats' writing to a Nightingale. The gaiety of the skylark's song, the melancholy of the nightingale's; the energetic soaring flight of the skylark toward the sky till the bird itself is unseen, the motionless nightingale among 'verdurous glooms, and winding mossy ways'; the infrequency of poetry about the skylark, the long literary tradition of praise for the nightingale, matched by Shelley's invention of a new stanza to suggest the song, and Keats' adaptation of the sonnet to fashion his stanza – all these things point the contrast between the two poets. So too does Shelley's detached interest in the skylark for its own sake, compared with Keats' concern with his personal experience. Shelley was responding to the song of one particular skylark which he heard on a certain summer evening; Keats was responding to a literary tradition whose antiquity moved him – he could have written his poem without ever listening to a nightingale's song. Besides, the skylark, the most vigorously active of all European birds while it is singing, was especially suited to the treatment of Shelley's natural style, with its emphasis on verbs rather than on adjectives; but the nightingale, inactive and hidden among the leaves as it sings, invited Keats' rich and crowded epithets.

At the end of his poem Shelley turns back from the bird's carefree existence to man's predicament:

> We look before and after,
>   And pine for what is not:
> Our sincerest laughter
>   With some pain is fraught;
> Our sweetest songs are those that tell of saddest thought.

In doing so he turns back, perhaps unconsciously, to Byron's comment that men 'learn in suffering what they teach in song' – a bitter destiny unknown to creatures unburdened by man's moral sense. Yet even if we could free ourselves from this sense of guilt, Shelley says, how could we ever approach the joy which the skylark knows?

Not long after he wrote this poem Shelley heard from the Gisbornes that Keats had had a haemorrhage, on the very day after they had visited him, and that Leigh Hunt with his usual kindness had brought him to his house. Shelley at once wrote a most generous letter inviting Keats to come to Italy, and to stay with them. Keats replied, a little distantly (for he was always self-conscious with Shelley) and declined the invitation. It was in this letter that Keats gave Shelley, by means of a phrase from Spenser, the often quoted advice to 'load every rift of his subject with ore'. Such advice shows that Keats had no understanding of Shelley's poetry: he modestly supposed that Shelley would have been a better poet if he had tried to write like Keats. But whereas Keats in his poetry attempts to bind to himself a joy (in Blake's words), to make for ever static some moment of realised beauty – 'for ever wilt thou love and she be fair' – and crams and clogs his verse with rich, descriptive epithets, Shelley seeks always through a preference for verbs to suggest movement and action, to catch the joy as it flies and so to live in eternity's sunrise.

Nowhere is Shelley's method shown more clearly than in another poem written this spring or early summer, *The Cloud.* When Keats wrote about clouds, as he did on several occasions, he described what they looked like: his lines may be compared to Constable's sketches of clouds, which he dated and timed. Shelley never pauses to describe his Cloud, but he tells you what it is doing, and how it is formed, and characteristically makes poetry out of the scientific account of cloud formation and precipitation. In such writing the verbs must do almost all the work, and where epithets are admitted they must not delay movement, but must be either light touches of colour, 'green plains', 'purple sea', 'blue smile', 'golden wings', or they must be verbal adjectives, 'thirsting flowers', 'lashing hail', 'sailing rack', which add to the general sense of activity. Statistics are not often a helpful adjunct of criticism, but they may be used to point out this feature of Shelley's style. In *The Cloud* there are more than seventy verbs, and less than fifty epithets, of which about one in three are verbal forms. If Shelley learnt from the Greeks to use verbs as he does he could do so because of some temperamental affinity. He needed to use verbs like this because of the nature of his imagination. Intuitively he drew upon his experience of the Greek language and of Greek poetry, just as in *Prometheus Unbound* he had to some degree followed Aeschylus, and the Greek use of lyric in drama. He had there drawn also on Byron's lyrics in *Manfred*, and he did so again in *The Cloud*. And he made use of knowledge gained at Adam Walker's scientific lectures. So do the imaginations of great poets invade the work of others and ruthlessly seize whatever is valuable to them; but in the process they transform it to something new and rich and strange.

In July, during an interval in original composition, Shelley returned, as often on such occasions, to translation. 'I have been translating the hymns of Homer,' he told the Gisbornes, 'for want of spirit to invent.' On the 14th he finished his version of the Homeric *Hymn to Mercury* in *ottava rima*. His only previous use of the metre was in a short poem *The Question* written early in the year. Now he had been reading Forti-guerra's comic epic *Ricciardetto* aloud to Mary in the evenings, and the lively stanza appealed to him for rendering the Hymn about the mischievous and light-fingered Hermes into English, as an ideal method of conveying the mock-heroic quality of the Greek. Probably the translation occupied only a few days, and indeed he never truly finished it, for he left three or four stanzas incomplete. Though *Ricciardetto* gave the immediate impulse to Shelley's use of *ottava rima*, he had clearly also learnt much from Byron's English use of the stanza in *Don Juan*.

A month later the same swift rhythm was still running in his head, and in three days only he wrote *The Witch of Atlas*. The Shelleys left Leghorn on 5 August and took a house, Casa Prini, at the Baths of Pisa. It was one of a row of picturesque little houses with tiny gardens backing on to the canal. On the 12th and 13th, while Mary and Claire were sight-seeing in Lucca, Shelley went off on his own to climb Monte San Pellegrino. He returned tired but happy and next day began his poem; on the 16th he had finished it. The mood of these last weeks continued here, gay, fantastic, mythopoeic. As Bagehot was to say, Shelley's imagination had in it more of the power by which the forces of nature were first made into myth than that of any other modern poet. In this too he revealed his affinity to the Greeks. Mary did not much like the poem, and Shelley dedicated it to her in some playful stanzas: surely, he says, his Witch can compare favourably with *Peter Bell*, at least, which took Wordsworth nineteen years. Mary's objection, that the poem lacked human interest (as Dr Johnson said of *Paradise Lost*) derived from her realisation that Shelley needed the encouragement of some popular success. He had shown in *The Cenci* that he could write in a manner more likely to command it, and yet here he was writing again in a manner which could never be popular. She was right, in that *The Cenci* was the only one of his poems, apart from the unauthorised reprinting of *Queen Mab*, to reach a second edition in his lifetime; and she must have known that Shelley was finding the lack of success of his poems discouraging. In April he acknowledged that he had sought success, and missed it, in contrast with Byron and Moore; in May, writing to Leigh Hunt, he said that if his poems never acquired popularity, he was ready to believe this was because they did not deserve it. Yet he wished his poems to be the trumpet of a prophecy; he had, as he confessed, a passion for reforming mankind, and he knew that poetry must be his means to that end. But if his poetry remained unread, and if the few who read it could not understand him, what hope was there? Byron, in his man-of-the-world manner, had said much the same of *Don Juan*: 'The poem will please, if it is lively; if it is stupid, it will fail.' As Mary truly said, 'Shelley did not expect sympathy and appreciation from the public; but the want of it took away a portion of the ardour that ought to have sustained him while writing.' In her unrelaxed way she could not accept *The Witch of Atlas* as a *jeu d'esprit*, but thought of it only as a diversion from Shelley's true vocation.

Shelley was incorrigible. He had been reading news from England about the trial of Queen Caroline, George IV's estranged wife, who, having been excluded from the Coronation, returned to England only to be put on trial for infidelity. The case aroused passionate partisanship, as her cause was taken up by all who hated George IV, among these being Shelley and Mary. Shelley was disgusted by the whole degrading business. 'What silly stuff is this to employ a great nation about,' he wrote to his cousin Thomas Medwin; 'I wish the King and Queen, like Punch and his wife, would fight out their disputes in person.' But squalid as the whole affair was, it might yet lead to the fall of the Tory Ministry, or so Shelley hoped. On 24 August Mrs Mason came over for the day to visit them, and Shelley read aloud his *Ode to Liberty*.* It was market day, and as he was reading, he 'was riotously accompanied by the grunting of a quantity of pigs brought for sale to the fair'. If the traditional view of Shelley as an egocentric and humourless romantic were correct, he should at this point have clapped his hand to his forehead and fled screaming from the room. In fact, he compared the grunting of the pigs which had so rudely interrupted the reading of his impassioned ode 'to the chorus of

* So Mary says in her notes written nearly twenty years later. But it would have been more likely that Shelley read his *Ode to Naples* (which is also an Ode to Liberty) completed that very day, and inspired by the insurrection there.

frogs in the satiric drama of Aristophanes; and, it being an hour of merriment, and one ludicrous association suggesting another, he imagined a political-satirical drama on the circumstances of the day, to which the pigs would serve as a chorus.' Such was the inspiration of his Aristophanic comedy, *Oedipus Tyrannus, or Swellfoot the Tyrant*. He finished it within a week, and at once sent it off to Horace Smith, who had it printed as a pamphlet. But the Society for the Suppression of Vice forced it to be immediately withdrawn, and only seven copies were sold. It was, as Mary said, 'a mere plaything of the imagination', but it was concerned with an actual situation, in which Mary was a vigorous partisan. Besides, 24 August was in other ways a happy day for her, since Mrs Mason took Claire back with her to Pisa for a few days. That would reconcile Mary to Shelley's levity.

Claire, who had perhaps heard that Allegra was not well, had been writing her usual foolish complaints to Byron, who was at last provoked to write to Shelley, to say that he would be glad to hear from him, though he refused to correspond with Claire. Byron wrote on 25 August. Shelley wrote to him on 17 September, to say that he had not seen any of Claire's recent letters, though having seen others (which he had asked her not to send) he could well believe that they were childish and absurd. He understood Byron's sense of responsibility towards Allegra in refusing to allow her to visit Claire so far away from him. He refused to act as intermediary for Claire, though he would be glad to convey messages from Byron to her: 'Of course I should be happy to hear from you on any subject.' And at the end of the letter he repeated this with more warmth. 'It would give me great pleasure to hear from you, and to receive news of more cantos of *Don Juan*, or something else. You have starved us lately.'

At this time Hoppner, who like so many who knew Byron had a possessiveness towards him, was attempting to undermine his friendship for Shelley. No doubt he realised that their friendship was far profounder in sympathy and far more stimulating than anything he could ever hope for with Byron;

in his jealousy therefore he sought to destroy it. And there was means to hand. Shelley had dealt with the blackmailing Paolo Foggi in July; thanks to Federico del Rosso he was given four hours to leave Leghorn. A month or so later the Shelleys' former nursemaid, Élise, now Foggi's wife, was in Venice. She saw Mrs Hoppner – they were both Swiss, and Élise, who had brought Allegra to Venice in 1818, knew her well. She repeated the story which Paolo had attempted to circulate in Leghorn: that the child Elena Adelaide whom Shelley adopted in Naples (just before dismissing Élise and Paolo from his service) was the daughter of Shelley and Claire. Hoppner was a skilful slanderer, and at first he did no more than hint to Byron of some misdeed by Shelley. Byron wrote to Hoppner in defence of Shelley: 'I regret that you have such a bad opinion of Shiloh; you used to have a good one. Surely he has talent and honour, but is crazy against religion and morality.' Hoppner sensed here an inconsistency – how could a man be 'crazy against morality' and have honour? – and also a chance of working on Byron's dislike of Claire – this was the letter in which Byron referred to her as 'a damned Bitch'. He therefore elaborated the story: 'It will fortify you,' he wrote to Byron, 'in the good resolution you have already taken never to trust Allegra again to her mother's care.' His letter continues:

You must know then that at the time the Shelleys were here [that is in the autumn of 1818], Claire was with child by Shelley: you may remember to have heard that she was constantly unwell, and under the care of a physician, and I am uncharitable enough to believe that the quantity of medicine she then took was not for the mere purpose of restoring her health. I perceive too why she preferred remaining alone at Este, notwithstanding her fear of ghosts and robbers, to being here with the Shelleys. Be this as it may, they proceeded from here to Naples, where one night Shelley was called up to see Claire who was very ill. His wife, naturally, thought it very strange that he should be sent for; but although she was not aware of the nature of the connexion between them, she had sufficient proof of Shelley's indifference, and of Claire's hatred for her: besides as Shelley desired her to remain quiet she did not dare to interfere. A mid-wife was sent for, and the worthy pair, who had made no preparation for the reception of the unfortunate being she was bringing into the world, bribed the woman to carry it to the Pietà, where the child was taken half an hour after its birth, being obliged likewise to purchase the physician's silence with a considerable sum. During all the time of her confinement Mrs Shelley, who expressed great anxiety on her account, was not allowed to approach her, and these beasts, instead of requiting her uneasinesss on Claire's account by at least a few expressions of kindness, have since increased in their hatred to her, behaving to her in the most brutal manner, and Claire doing everything she can to engage her husband to abandon her. . . . This account we had from Élise, who passed here this summer with an English lady who spoke very highly of her.

This Iago-like fabric of lies was carefully based on Byron's detestation of Claire, and his wish to have nothing more to do with her. Hoppner shrewdly prefaced it with the suggestion that, once he had read the account, Byron would refuse ever to allow Claire to see Allegra again.

Byron replied in a casual note a fortnight later. 'The Shiloh story is true no doubt, though Élise is but a sort of Queen's evidence.* You remember how eager she was to return to them, and then she goes away and abuses them. Of the facts, however, there can be little doubt. It is just like them.' And he enclosed Shelley's recent letter to him. Byron's scepticism about Élise's reliability did not, unfortunately, overcome his readiness to believe the worst of Claire. That this might imply for some a defamation of Shelley's character caused him little concern. He himself had weakly yielded to Claire's importunities and allowed himself to be seduced by her: why should not the same fate befall Shelley, especially as Shelley never pretended to believe in monogamy and apparently could endure Claire's proximity better than himself? He had little reason to believe in the chastity of either. He was the last person to condemn Shelley for taking Claire for his mistress (if he had done so), though he may have thought as little of his taste in such

* Referring to the trial of Queen Caroline, with its sordid details.

matters as Shelley had thought of Byron's when they were last together. As his letter shows, Byron was not much interested in Hoppner's revelations: they could hardly make him think worse than he already did of Claire; they made no difference to his friendship for Shelley. So little did he regard them, indeed, that he scarcely thought about the matter again until he saw Shelley the following August. Byron has often, in these latter times, been condemned for not loyally rejecting these charges against his friend. But this is to assume that both Byron and Shelley accepted standards of morality available to the middle classes a century or more later. If Byron is to be criticised at all for his attitude, it must be for treating too lightly something which he should have realised Shelley would treat more seriously. Besides, there was something piquant in scandal, 'it is a sort of cayenne to the mind,' he once remarked, 'I confess I like it, particularly if the objects are one's particular friends.' If he had passed on Hoppner's letter to Shelley at once he would have given him a chance to refute the charges, and to clear up the misunderstanding. But Shelley did not know of Hoppner's slander, and so far as Byron was concerned it was not worth bothering about.

Shelley's wish to hear news of more cantos of *Don Juan* may or may not have been gratified: there is no surviving letter to him from Byron for some months. In fact Byron had sent off the third and fourth cantos to Murray on 19 February. He originally intended them for the third canto, but finding this too long, he divided it into two. In the spring he sent Murray three Italian pieces: his translation into *terza rima* – 'of which your British Blackguard reader as yet understands nothing' – of the episode of Paolo and Francesca from the fifth canto of Dante's *Inferno*, his translation of the first canto of Pulci's *Morgante Maggiore*, and *The Prophecy of Dante*. Since then he had been involved in the scenes and arguments that led to the Pope granting Teresa, on her father's petition, a separation from her husband. (The Pope, when Bishop of Imola, had officiated at the wedding of Teresa's parents.) Teresa left Palazzo Guiccioli on 15 July, but Byron with ironic pleasure at so un-English an anomaly, continued to occupy the top floor of the palace to which Count Alessandro had invited him at the beginning of the year. The Count now gave notice to Byron to leave his apartments, but Byron disregarded this request, and he was still there a year later.

During the summer he had been writing his historical tragedy *Marino Faliero*, and he sent off the last act on 17 August. This was the first of a series of historical tragedies which he intended to write, and in which he preferred the model of Alfieri to the Jacobean models which Shelley had, in his view, been ill-advised to use for *The Cenci*. It was produced at Drury Lane, in spite of efforts by Byron to prevent this, in the following April and May. For some weeks he wrote nothing, and he even felt doubtful about going on with *Don Juan*. He thought the third and fourth cantos had not got the spirit of the first two: 'the outcry has not frightened but it has *hurt* me, and I have not written *con amore* this time.' Soon after he began the third canto he had challenged Kinnaird to deny the excellence of the first two: 'It may be profligate but is it not *life*, is it not *the thing*?' And then, 'I had such projects for the Don, but Cant is so much stronger than C—— now-a-days, that the benefit of experience in a man who had well weighed the worth of both monosyllables must be lost to despairing posterity.' Now that the new cantos were finished he told Kinnaird that they were 'very *decent*, but dull – damned dull.' Even Teresa was discouraging. She associated *Don Juan* with Mozart's *Don Giovanni* and was dismayed by the implication. 'I don't feel inclined to care further about *Don Juan*,' Byron wrote to Murray on 12 October. 'What do you think a very pretty Italian lady said to me the other day? She had read it in the French, and paid me some compliments, with due DRAWBACKS, upon it. I answered that what she said was true, but that I suspected it would live longer than *Childe Harold*. "Ah but" (said she) "*I would rather have the fame of Childe Harold for* THREE YEARS *than an* IMMORTALITY *of Don Juan!*" ' Four days later he began the fifth canto. Once started he wrote steadily, and completed it in six weeks.

In the New Year Byron began a journal, not being for the moment in the mood for writing poetry, but on 13 January he noted, 'Sketched the outline and Drams. Pers. of an intended tragedy of Sardanapalus, which I have for some time meditated.' Next day he wrote the opening lines; he completed it by the end of May. Within two months more he had written another historical tragedy *The Two Foscari*. In the letter informing Murray about this Byron said that he had promised Teresa not to continue *Don Juan*: he must therefore consider the three cantos which he was about to publish as the last. Byron saw that Teresa's objection arose 'from the wish of all women to exalt the *sentiment* of the passions, and to keep up the illusion which is their empire. Now *Don Juan* strips off this illusion, and laughs at that and most other things.' He kept his promise for the rest of the year.

Byron continued living at Ravenna, but as the year went on he became more and more concerned about Allegra's future. In February it seemed possible that the revolutionary movement in Naples, which Shelley celebrated in an ode the previous August, and to which Byron offered his services, might spread to the Romagna. Had it done so Byron and the Gambas would have been dangerously involved. Byron therefore decided to place Allegra in the girls' school run by the Capuchin nuns of the convent of S. Giovanni Battista at Bagnacavallo, some twelve miles away, where she would be well cared for if anything happened to him. He wrote in April to inform Shelley about this. Shelley in his reply, after his now normal disclaimer about anything Claire might have written or might yet write, said, 'Mary, no less than myself, is perfectly convinced of your conduct towards Allegra having been most irreproachable, and we entirely agree in the necessity, under existing circumstances, of the placing her in a convent near to yourself.' This is perhaps disingenuous. Not many days later Mary was writing to tell Claire that she agreed with her that 'as soon as possible Allegra ought to be taken out of the hands of one as remorseless as he is unprincipled'. She may have said this to discourage Claire from a mad plan of abducting Allegra, for she assured her that

Allegra was well looked after and in a healthy place. Byron was pleased to have Shelley's approval, and to know that he would do his best to protect him from Claire's recrimination.

In the same letter Shelley writes, all too briefly, about Byron's poetry. 'I see by the papers that you have published a tragedy on the subject of which you spoke when I saw you in Venice.' This was *Marino Faliero*, which in fact had not yet been published when Shelley wrote. Byron had then told Shelley of his plans for a play on an Italian subject, in response to Shelley's mention of his intended tragedy on the life of Tasso. Shelley told Byron that he was eager to see 'this new phasis of his power', and then made a muddled reference to other works of Byron which can only have led Byron to think he had not read them with much attention. Once again, as in 1817, he urged Byron 'to subdue himself to the great task of building up a poem containing within itself the germs of a permanent relation to the present, and to all succeeding ages'. In view of his admiration for *Don Juan* again expressed here, it seems odd if Shelley did not yet see that that was the poem which would fulfil his hope. If he had urged Byron to continue *Don Juan*, of which he had seen only the first two cantos, he might have helped him to resist Teresa's objections.

Shelley told Byron of Keats' death in Rome, of which he had only just heard, some seven weeks after the event. In his reply a few days later Byron regretted the death of Keats, but with his usual good sense questioned Shelley's attribution of its cause to *The Quarterly Review*: 'Is it *actually* true? I did not think criticism had been so killing.' He was to return to this in *Don Juan*,

> 'Tis strange the mind, that very fiery particle,
> Should let itself be snuffed out by an article.

The effect on himself of a hostile review was, as he truly said, 'rage, and resistance, and redress – but not despondency nor despair'. Indeed Shelley's suggestion, so far from arousing Byron's greater sympathy, confirmed him in his contempt for Keats. But he excised from his letter to Murray on Bowles's strictures on Pope* the passage in which he derides Keats, who had been foolish enough to attack Pope in *Sleep and Poetry*. In his reply Shelley said, quite truly, that Pope had 'been selected as the pivot of a dispute in taste', in which he professed himself to be neutral. He must have been prompted by Byron's letter to read Pope again, aware that he had not read him for some time, for at the end of May Mary noted that he read to her *The Rape of the Lock* and *The Essay on Criticism*. Shelley did not much admire Keats' poetry except for *Hyperion*, and though he gave his opinions in a very different manner from Byron, he objected to what he called 'system and mannerism'. Byron attacked Hunt and his followers, Keats among them, on the same grounds: 'When a man talks of his *system*, it is like a woman's talking of her *virtue*. I let them talk on.'

As for himself, Byron told Shelley, he had neither the inclination nor the power to undertake a great poem. But he would like to see Shelley again: 'Could not you and I contrive to meet this summer? Could not you take a run here *alone*?' He said nothing about Hoppner's slanderous allegations, not because he had forgotten them, but because they in no way affected his friendship for Shelley. Shelley replied on 4 May, suggesting that Byron might join them at Pisa for the summer. Claire was not there, and was likely to be away all summer and perhaps even longer. She had been living away from the Shelleys much of the time since the previous October, thanks to Mrs Mason's tactful insistence. 'If you come, bring whom you please, and make what arrangements are convenient to you.' To reply to an invitation with a counter-invitation can be very irritating, though Shelley's motive seems to have been the hope of seeing more of Byron if he would come to Pisa than would be possible if he himself went to Ravenna, where his visit would have to be short. But the weeks passed, and Byron made no answer. He was indeed under considerable suspicion for his association with Italian Liberals, among them Teresa's father and brother. His servant Tita was arrested and imprisoned; then Conte Pietro Gamba, Teresa's brother and Byron's very good friend,

* This was not published until 1835.

was arrested and sent into exile; and soon afterwards her father Conte Ruggero was ordered to leave within twenty-four hours. Byron knew that he too must soon leave if he was to keep out of trouble. But he could not decide what provision to make for Allegra. He thought of going to Switzerland with the Gambas, and wrote to ask Hentsch, the Geneva banker, to find him a house. If he went there, he would take Allegra with him. At this crisis in his affairs another letter came from Shelley, disappointed at not having received a visit from Byron, and suggesting that he himself should come over to Ravenna for a week or so in the autumn: 'Are you sure a visit would not annoy you?' Byron must have written immediately, asking him to come at once, so that they could discuss what was best to be done for Allegra. Shelley was in Florence when the letter came, but saw it on his return to Pisa on 2 August. Next day he left for Ravenna. On 5 August Byron added a postscript to a letter from his secretary, Lega Zambelli, to Pietro, to say that he was expecting a visit any moment from Shelley – he described him, to avoid a lengthy explanation, as 'a relation of Allegra's' – in order to decide about the child's future. So, once again, Allegra brought together Shelley and Byron.

CHAPTER SEVEN

Preparations for Pisa

AUGUST–OCTOBER 1821: ITALY

SHELLEY left Pisa on 3 August. He stopped for the night at Leghorn to see Claire, with whom he spent the next morning, his twenty-ninth birthday, rowing in the harbour and sailing on the sea; but he did not tell her that he was going to see Byron, for fear that she might try to accompany him. He warned Mary not to let her know: 'She would misinterpret everything.' He left at two o'clock, and went on by Florence and Bologna, on the way having a carriage accident. 'The old horse stumbled and threw me and the fat vetturino into a slope of meadow over the hedge. My angular figure stuck where it was pitched, but my vetturino's spherical form rolled fairly to the bottom of the hill.' No damage was done, so on they went, and Shelley reached Ravenna at ten o'clock in the evening of 6 August. He went at once to see Byron and they stayed talking till five in the morning.

There was much to talk about: what to do with Allegra; what to decide about Teresa; poetry; politics, and so forth. For once there was no dispute about Allegra. If Byron left Italy for Switzerland, he would take her with him. Teresa, he told Shelley, was very fond of her, and there seemed no reason why she should not look after the child when Byron moved from Ravenna. Teresa herself, whom Shelley had not met, was causing Byron more anxiety. He had managed, in spite of tearful scenes, and last-minute delays, and pleas to be allowed to return, to get Teresa out of Ravenna, where, if she remained after her father left, she was in danger of being shut up in a convent. She was now in Florence with her father and brother, who were planning to leave at once for Switzerland. Byron had written to Hentsch to ask him to find a house for them, as well as for himself, but as the days passed he began to realise that such panic measures were not necessary. Besides, Geneva was full of those scandal-loving English; it was expensive; he disliked the deceitful and money-grubbing Swiss; the Gambas were no longer in any danger; he had only recommended Switzerland in the first place as preferable to a political prison. . . . Let them all calm down, and he would join them before long in Tuscany.

Byron told Shelley about these problems as soon as he saw him. He even showed him some of Teresa's letters, which gave Shelley a good impression of her. He consulted him about places to live in Tuscany: where could he find a suitable house? Where would he be free of English tourists? Shelley had been living in Tuscany for some time; he must know what would suit him. Would Shelley write to Teresa to try to persuade her to give up this silly plan of going to Switzerland? Shelley, a little surprised by such a request, complied. 'An odd thing enough for an utter stranger to write on subjects of the utmost delicacy to his friend's mistress,' he wrote to Mary, 'but it seems destined that I am always to have some active part in everybody's affairs whom I approach.' And he saw that if he could help to persuade La Guiccioli to remain in Tuscany, then he would at last have Byron near him again. Nothing could please him more than that, and he would be very glad to accept such a result as the fee for writing on his behalf to Teresa.

In his first letter to Mary, written on the morning of 7 August, Shelley also recounted the slander which the Hoppners had derived from Élise a year before, and had then passed on to Byron. Only now did Byron tell Shelley of it, and show him Hoppner's letter of the previous September. Shelley was deeply shocked, not at the allegation that Claire was his mistress, which was nothing new – 'all the world has heard so much and people may believe or not believe as they think good' – but at the suggestion that he could ever abandon or destroy a child. That was what most hurt him, as it was so utterly contrary to his character: how could anyone who knew him believe him capable of such an act of cruelty? And he asked Mary to write to the Hoppners to rebut the charges as only she could, that is, 'in case you believe and know and can prove that it is false'. The depth of Shelley's shock at the accusation is shown by the intrusion of some slight doubt about Mary's reception of the story, '*in case* you believe . . . that it is false'. He need not have doubted, as Mary's passionate rebuttal, written on 10 August as soon as she received Shelley's letter, shows in its almost incoherent haste: 'my thoughts far outrun my pen, so that I can hardly form the letters.' Through this wonderful letter Mary's devotion to Shelley shines with a pure radiance. How could anyone who knew Shelley, who had even seen his face, believe such calumnies? 'Shelley is as incapable of cruelty as the softest woman. To those who know him his humanity is almost as a proverb.' And she declared her love for him with a sincerity which surely shamed the jealous and malicious liar whom she addressed. 'Love caused our first imprudence, love which improved by esteem, a perfect trust one in the other, a confidence and affection which . . . has increased daily, and knows no bounds.' The supposedly cold and inhibited Mary never spoke more certainly from her heart.

In a postscript Mary added that she was sending this letter to Ravenna so that both Shelley and Byron could see it. In the course of the letter she said that Byron's 'generosity and knowledge of the world had made him reject the slander with the ridicule it deserved,' but she wished him to read her letter now, 'to see how entirely fabulous' the story had been.* Mary was being over-generous to Byron, who had not so much disbelieved the allegations as considered them of no account.

* In Shelley's letter, as it is preserved, there is no mention of Byron's attitude to this slander, but the letter is incomplete, and four lines have been heavily deleted. Mary may have made the deletions, for when she printed the letter in *Essays, Letters from Abroad, Translations and Fragments by Percy B. Shelley,* 1840, she indicated omissions by asterisks, but did not indicate these deletions. If the deleted lines referred to Byron's rejection of the slander she may well have realised, by that time, that this was not the whole truth.

No doubt when he showed Shelley Hoppner's letter he prefaced it with some dismissive phrase; and when he observed Shelley's reaction to it, he would have tried to calm him by ridiculing the whole story.

Shelley received Mary's letter on the 16th. By now he was quite indifferent to the slander, he told Mary. Indeed, even when he first told her of it he did so only in the final paragraph of a letter most of which was taken up with Byron: Byron's health, Byron's writing, Byron's concern for Teresa and Allegra; and he had slept for six hours before writing to Mary about it. This does not suggest extreme agitation such as Mary suffered on receipt of his letter. He was nonetheless as determined to suppress the calumny as he had been when Paolo Foggi attempted blackmail a year before, even if it came to prosecuting Élise. Shelley gave Mary's letter to Byron for forwarding to Mrs Hoppner with his own comments. He explained to Mary that Byron had promised Hoppner not to show his letter to Shelley. 'Lord Byron is not a man to keep a secret good or bad – but in openly confessing that he has not done so he must observe a certain delicacy – and therefore he wished to send the letter himself.' As soon as he saw Shelley that first evening Byron must have realised that he had been wrong to accept Hoppner's request to keep his slander secret from its victim, and, valuing Shelley's friendship and respecting his character far beyond Hoppner's, he showed the letter to Shelley. This placed him in an embarrassing position, as Shelley understood; but the fact that Mary's letter was found among his papers after his death does not mean that he never forwarded it. On the contrary, it seems clear that Byron did forward it, but with a request that it should be returned to him.* Certainly Hoppner was aware of the gist of it, and of Byron's rejection of the story which he had told him. Hoppner attempted some form of justification, but Byron disdained to reply. He never again referred to the matter, and Shelley too regarded it as closed. His final words on it to Mary were 'So much for nothing.'

* See note 7, p. 270.

But Mary's distress was not so soon calmed, for in the following April she received a letter from Claire whose help she had sought: 'I wish you would write back what you wish Élise to say to you and what she is to say to Madame Hoppner. I have tried in vain to compose it.' Mary and Claire must have decided that the only way to bring the matter to an end was to persuade Élise to acknowledge that she had been lying.

As always Shelley had found it far easier than Byron to preserve his dignity, but this did not injure their friendship. He remained as Byron's guest in the Palazzo Guiccioli for ten days, where he naturally had to adapt his habits to those of his host. He got up at twelve, had breakfast, and then 'we sit talking till six. From six till eight we gallop through the pine forests which divide Ravenna from the sea.' (One of Teresa's anxieties at leaving Byron behind in Ravenna was lest he should be assassinated on one of his daily rides. His membership of the Carbonari, of which he spoke to Shelley, made her fears not unreasonable.) After the ride, 'We then come home and dine and sit up gossiping till six in the morning.' Such was their daily routine. 'I don't suppose this will kill me in a week or fortnight, but I shall not try it longer,' Shelley told Peacock. And he cheerfully catalogued the livestock with which Byron filled the Palazzo Guiccioli. Apart from servants, Byron had 'ten horses, eight enormous dogs, three monkeys, five cats, an eagle, a crow, and a falcon; and all these, except the horses, walk about the house, which every now and then resounds with their unarbitrated quarrels, as if they were the masters of it.' Even this collection was not all, for in a postscript Shelley added, 'I find that my enumeration of the animals in this Circean Palace was defective, and that in a material point. I have just met on the grand staircase five peacocks, two guinea hens, and an Egyptian crane. I wonder who all these animals were before they were changed into these shapes.' The elderly Conte Alessandro, gloomily ensconced on the ground floor of his own house, may well have found this menagerie as hard to bear as cuckoldry. It was more unexpected.

Shelley took the opportunity while he was in Ravenna, which

he had never visited before, to go sight-seeing. He shared Gibbon's belief that Christianity was the source of all the ills that afflicted the Roman world, and he therefore had no taste for Byzantine architecture. He visited Dante's tomb, and saw some of the early printed books in the Library. On 15 August he went to the Duomo but was refused admittance, apparently as a friend of Byron. Immediately Byron wrote to Conte Alborghetti, the Secretary General of the Province, whom he knew, demanding the punishment of the Campanaio, and threatening to take the law into his own hands if this were not done. Shelley does not refer to the incident.

On the previous day he went over to Bagnacavallo to see Allegra.

At first she was very shy, but after a little caressing and especially after I had given her a gold chain which I had bought at Ravenna for her she grew more familiar, and led me all over the garden and all over the convent running and skipping so fast that I could hardly keep up with her. She shewed me her little bed, and the chair where she sate at dinner and the carozzina in which she and her favourite companion drew each other along a covered walk in the garden. – I had brought her a basket of sweetmeats, and before eating any of them she gave her companion and all the nuns a portion. – This is not much like the old Allegra. I asked her what I should say from her to her mamma and she said – 'Che mi manda un bacio e un bel vestitino' – 'E come vuoi il vestitino sia fatto?' 'Tutto di seta e d'oro' was her reply. . . . I then asked – what shall I say to papa – 'Che venga farmi un visitino, e che porta seco la mammina' a message which you may conjecture that I was too discreet to deliver.* Before I went away she made me run all over the convent like a mad thing – the nuns who were half in bed were ordered to hide themselves, and on returning Allegra began ringing the bell which calls the nuns to assemble, the tocsin of the convent sounded, and it required all the efforts of the prioress to prevent the spouses of God to render themselves

* Shelley probably misunderstood Allegra, who is more likely to have meant Teresa (whom she had often seen in Byron's company) than Claire whom she would hardly remember, for she had not seen her since October 1818, when she was less than two years old.

dressed or undressed to the accustomed signal. – Nobody scolded her for these scappature.

These three happy hours that he spent with Allegra were reassuring to Shelley. When Byron in the end decided to leave her at Bagnacavallo on removing from Ravenna, Shelley did not disapprove of the decision, for he knew that she was well cared for. He never saw her again.

Byron needed Shelley's advice about where to live in Tuscany, once he had given up the plan of going to Switzerland. He needed his assistance in finding a suitable house there. He needed his help in persuading Teresa to accept his change of plan. This Shelley seems to have achieved very easily by the letter which he wrote to her two or three days after reaching Ravenna. He himself had spent a summer with Byron at Geneva, and he told Teresa, out of his own experience, of the kind of annoyance to which she and Byron were likely to be subjected if they went there: accustomed as she was to Italian manners she could hardly be expected to imagine the savagery of the English. 'The inhabitants on the banks of the lake opposite Lord Byron's house used telescopes to spy upon his movements. One English lady fainted from horror (or pretended to!) on seeing him enter a drawing-room. The most outrageous caricatures of him and his friends were daily spread about.' Having thus sufficiently scared the timorous Teresa, who would not relish the prospect of being examined in Byron's arms through a telescope, Shelley appealed to her regard for Byron. 'The effect of all this on Lord Byron's spirits was very unfortunate. His natural gaiety had almost entirely left him.' Shelley's skilful advocacy was successful. On 15 August Teresa's reply reached him at Ravenna, agreeing to abandon the plan of going to Switzerland. But victory was not conceded without typically feminine conditions. 'Signore – la vostra bontà mi fa ardita di chiedervi un favore – me lo accorderete voi? Non partite da Ravenna senza Milord.' Shelley, after transmitting Teresa's words in his letter to Mary, said: 'Of course being now, by all the laws of knighthood, captive to a lady's request, I shall only be at liberty on *my parole* until Lord Byron is settled at

Pisa. I shall reply of course that the *boon* is granted, and that if her lover is reluctant to quit Ravenna after I have made arrangements for receiving him at Pisa, I am bound to place myself in the same situation as now, to assail him with importunities to rejoin her.' Shelley's gay acceptance of the laws of antique courtesy shows his pleasure at his success. The fee for writing to his friend's mistress which he had said he would be pleased to accept was about to be paid.

Before Teresa's letter came Shelley had asked Mary's opinion about where would be the best place for Byron to look for a house in Tuscany. Florence was open to the same objection as Geneva: too many staring English. There would not be a suitable house in Prato, or Pistoia. Lucca, perhaps, or Siena? Or Pisa, but then there was the problem of Claire's visits to them there: 'Gunpowder and fire ought to be kept at a respectable distance from each other.' That was in his letter of 10 August. Next day he began his letter to Mary with 'You will be surprised to hear that Albe has decided upon coming to *Pisa.*' She must on no account tell Claire of this. She must make inquiries if any of the large palaces were to be let. Shelley was delighted, for even if they kept to their plan of spending the winter in Florence they could look forward to enjoying Byron's company in the spring. Besides, of two ways of life which Shelley proposed as now acceptable to them, the first, to retire with Mary and their child to some remote island, to 'read no reviews and talk with no authors', was rejected as soon as stated. The second, 'to form for ourselves a society of our own class, as much as possible, in intellect or in feelings; and to connect ourselves with the interests of that society', seemed more feasible. And if this way were to be adopted, Pisa was the place, for 'our roots were never struck so deeply as at Pisa.' Therefore, Pisa let it be, and Pisa with Byron, whose presence would help to protect them there from the slanders and persecutions of English gossip-mongers to which they would be subject in Florence. At once Shelley began to imagine the society of like-minded friends in Pisa: Byron and Teresa and the Gambas, the Masons, the Williamses (new friends who would stay if the Shelleys did); Horace Smith was already on his way from England; perhaps the Hunts could be persuaded to come out too. What an exciting and delightful prospect!

Next day Shelley left to rejoin Mary, with Byron's promise to come as soon as Shelley had found him a house. On the way Shelley had to pass through Florence. He called on Teresa, whom he now met for the first time; he thought her beautiful and sentimental – a damsel in distress needing his knightly succour. (Years before he had seen himself as a Spenserian 'Elfin Knight'.) He brought her a brief letter from Byron. He reassured her about Byron's safety: his rides in the lonelier parts of the pine-forest had been given up. He promised her that she would soon be reunited with him. Before going on to the Baths of Pisa he paid her a second visit; was he not on parole to her? She took to him at once, though she was alarmed at his fragile appearance. 'How is it possible,' she wrote to Byron, 'to be so thin, so worn out?'

Teresa must have written to Shelley almost as soon as he left her, to thank him for his kindness, and to express her complete confidence in him. In his hurried reply on 22 August he told her he had already fixed on a house for Byron – he might even be able to tell her the contract was signed before posting his letter. Mary must have been busy in his absence for the agreement about a house, the Palazzo Lanfranchi on the Lung' Arno, to be so quickly concluded. Shelley told Teresa of his gratitude to her for all she had done for Byron. She was his good Angel, leading him from darkness to light. He did not tell her that he thought it most important to get Byron away as soon as possible from Ravenna, to prevent him falling back into the old dissipations of Venice. Byron recognised this, and indeed used it as a threat to detain Shelley with him in Ravenna, for his respect for Shelley's character, like his love for Teresa, would keep him to a decent way of living. However, Shelley could not simultaneously protect Byron's morals in Ravenna and find a house for him and his mistress in Pisa. And no doubt he believed Byron's promise to come immediately the house was taken. Byron believed it himself.

Byron: drawing by G. H. Harlow, 1816

Shelley: painting by Amelia Curran, Rome, May 1819

Mary Shelley, from a miniature given by Trelawny to W. M. Rossetti, in the possession of Mrs Dennis

Shelley: posthumous drawing by Mary Shelley, 1829

The Villa Diodati, Lake of Geneva: engraving by Edward Finden from a drawing by W. Purser

The Castle of Chillon, Lake of Geneva: painting by Gustave Courbet

Claire Clairmont: painting by Amelia Curran, Rome, spring 1819

Allegra: miniature by an unknown artist, Venice, 1818

The approach to Venice, sunset: water-colour by J. M. W. Turner, 1840

Teresa Guiccioli: marble bust by Lorenzo Bartolini

Pisa: engraving by Fambrini

This view, looking down the Arno, with the Ponte alla Fortezza in the foreground, shows, the first house on the left, Tre Palazzi di Chiesa, where the Shelleys and the Williamses lived 1821–2, and on the right, the house with arches above the windows on the first and second floor, the Palazzo Lanfranchi, where Byron lived October 1821 to May 1822. The Porta alle Piagge was just out of the picture on the right, near the end of the bridge.

Edward Ellerker Williams: painting by George Clint

Jane Williams: painting by George Clint

Thomas Medwin:
from an oil painting

Leigh Hunt: painting by
B. R. Haydon

Edward John Trelawny: drawing by Joseph Severn, 1835

Byron after his daily ride at Pisa: silhouette cut in paper by Marianne Hunt, 1822

Casa Magni, San Terenzo: engraving from a drawing by Captain Daniel Roberts R.N., 1822

The Bolivar *(below) and the* Don Juan*: rawing by E. E. Williams, 1822*

The shore near Viareggio

Shelley writing Prometheus Unbound *amid the ruins of the baths of Caracalla, Rome: posthumous painting by Joseph Severn, 1845*

Byron: drawing by Count Alfred D'Orsay, Genoa, spring 1823

As soon as the contract was signed Shelley wrote to tell Byron. The Gambas, and especially Teresa, were delighted with the house. Shelley was looking for additional stables for those ten horses, and he asked for instructions about furnishings and so forth. The Palazzo Lanfranchi is a large house, 'large enough for a garrison', said Byron when he saw it, with more than fifty rooms, some of these very large and recently decorated with frescoes by the eighteenth-century owners, the Toscanelli. It was no perfunctory office of friendship that Shelley undertook, but in his delight at the thought of having Byron with him in Pisa he made light of these practical matters. He also arranged transport for Byron's possessions. Confident that Byron would at once set out for Pisa, he told him how he could avoid Florence by a detour through Barberino.

Byron always hated moving. It was such a bother with all his furniture and dogs and books and monkeys and servants and peacocks and guinea-fowl and everything else. He was quite comfortable in the Palazzo Guiccioli: what was the hurry? Excuses came easily to his practised pen. 'We are getting ready,' he told Teresa on 26 August, 'if there is any delay it will be that blessed Lega's – whom I abandon to your reproaches.' On 4 September: 'That man Lega has not gone on with the preparations – so scold him well.' Next day: 'The only reason that is keeping me here now is Lega's slowness.' On 15 September: 'We are only waiting for the carriers to get the things off.' But when they did arrive they had not brought enough carts. On the 23rd, when the carts left, Byron said that he would leave towards the first of October. On 5 October: 'We should have left this week. . . .' A week later, bad weather was the excuse, but anyhow 'a few days more or less can make no difference'; he was thinking of leaving on the 22nd. After another week, he had decided to leave about the 25th; on the 23rd he said it would be the 27th; on the 26th that it would be the 28th; on the 28th that he was leaving in three hours more, 'I have just made them take off my bed-clothes – blankets inclusive – in case of temptation from the apparel of sheets to my eyelids.' At last he left on the 30th.

Teresa's exasperated impatience at these delays, which were hardly flattering to her charms or to her affection, were communicated to Shelley. She visited the Shelleys at the Baths of Pisa. She moved with her father and brother into the Casa Parra, five minutes' walk from the Palazzo Lanfranchi, where the Shelleys visited her. She thought of taking lessons in English from Shelley, but Byron advised against this, because of his and Shelley's reputation for immorality. 'If you are not careful the English in Florence and Pisa will say that, being tired of you, I handed you on to him.' No doubt they would. (With all those postponements of his journey to her, may not Teresa have wondered if he was indeed tired of her?) On 21 October Shelley, who since the beginning of the month had been daily expecting Byron's arrival, wrote to him: 'When may we expect you? The Countess G. is very patient, though sometimes she seems apprehensive that you will *never* leave Ravenna. . . . Your house is ready and all the furniture arranged.' He began to feel sorry for Teresa and to fear that she would 'have plenty of leisure and the opportunity to repent of her rashness' in attaching herself to Lord Byron, whose constancy he doubted.

With so many practical matters to discuss and to arrange while they were together in Ravenna, Byron and Shelley still found time to talk of poetry. Early in the year, at the time of his romantic concern for Emilia Viviani, the daughter of the Governor of Pisa, who was incarcerated by a cruel mother in a convent school, Shelley wrote *Epipsychidion*, a poem whose remote Platonic idealism was hardly likely to appeal to Byron. Nevertheless, perhaps prompted by Byron's anxiety lest a similar fate should have befallen Teresa, Shelley talked to him of his relationship with Emilia. In a letter of 14 September he told Byron of Emilia's recent marriage, and asked for his discretion when he got to Pisa. 'They have made a great fuss at Pisa about my intimacy with this lady. Pray do not mention anything of what I told you; as the whole truth is not known and Mary might be very much annoyed at it.' (He had forgotten his scepticism about Byron's ability to keep a secret.) Shelley is not likely to have shown *Epipsychidion* to Byron, whom he would hardly have classed among the *συνέτοι* for whom it was intended, even if Byron's stanza on Platonic love in the first canto of *Don Juan* did not irreverently obtrude upon his memory.

O Plato! Plato! you have paved the way,
  With your confounded fantasies, to more
Immoral conduct by the fancied sway
  Your system feigns o'er the controlless core
Of human hearts, than all the long array
  Of poets and romancers: – You're a bore,
A charlatan, a coxcomb – and have been,
At best, no better than a go-between.

Mary, provoked to some jealousy perhaps (for Emilia, unlike Jane Williams, was well educated as well as beautiful) and hurt by Shelley's reference to her coldness, felt much the same about the poem: 'Shelley's Italian Platonics,' she called it; alone of all his major poems she wrote no notes about it. Besides, how could he ever hope to achieve the measure of popular success which he needed, if he would write poetry so abstruse that a mere one hundred copies, by his own estimation, would satisfy the demand?

Byron was not likely to be much more in sympathy with the subject of *Adonais* which Shelley wrote early in June, even though Shelley had persuaded him of the high quality of *Hyperion*. He refused to believe that Keats' death was due to unfavourable reviews, and Shelley, knowing this, apologised, when he sent Byron a copy, for referring to it in the poem. At Ravenna in August Byron made no comment on *Adonais*. Shelley ironically suggested that this was due to modesty induced by his high praise in the poem as

The Pilgrim of Eternity, whose fame
Over his living head like Heaven is bent,
An early but enduring monument.

More probably it was due to embarrassment at finding himself thus paraded among the mourners of that 'tadpole of the Lakes.' Or perhaps, like his friend Tom Moore (whom Shelley had also recruited to mourn Keats) he simply did not understand who the Pilgrim of Eternity was. Shelley in *Adonais* mourned the loss of a poet whose bad taste he deplored as much as did Byron, but whose wonderful powers and promise he recognised in the unfinished *Hyperion.* From Theocritus on poets had mourned the premature death of young poets in pastoral elegy, and Shelley was following a tradition which in English both Spenser and Milton had adorned. That Byron would have approved.

Apart from these two poems Shelley had written little, and his letters show his increasing despondency at the failure even of *The Cenci* to achieve any success. In February he admitted to Peacock, 'Nothing is so difficult and unwelcome as to write without a confidence of finding readers; and if my play of *The Cenci* found none or few, I despair of ever producing anything that shall merit them.' Yet the very next day he was sending *Epipsychidion* to his publisher, with the request that he should print only a hundred copies. Perhaps the quotation from Dante, with which he began the poem,

> My Song, I fear that thou wilt find but few
> Who fitly shall conceive thy reasoning,
> Of such hard matter dost thou entertain,

helped to reconcile this inconsistency. If Dante could write poems of an unpopular, metaphysical nature, why should he trouble about the reception of his own? But all through the spring and summer, apart from the brief rush of inspiration early in June when he wrote *Adonais*, he was conscious of an inability to write poetry. He wrote of his despondency to Byron. Indifference to praise or blame, he said, 'deprives me of an incitement to do what now I never shall do, i.e. write anything worth calling a poem'. But with truth he could add that his lack of success had not turned him into an unfeeling and malignant critic. That was before he wrote *Adonais*; and afterwards in another letter to Byron he said, 'Heaven knows what makes me persevere (after the severe reproof of public neglect) in writing verses.' It was what Byron called 'the lava of the imagination' which could not be stemmed. At the same time a London bookseller pirated *Queen Mab*. Shelley protested in a formal letter to the Editor of *The Examiner* in order to avoid implication in the reissue, but in fact he was amused by so ironic a comment on the indifference of the public to his far finer, mature poetry.

Even his visit to Byron failed to encourage him. Byron admired *Prometheus Unbound*, whose myth played so great a part in his own poetry; and he was interested in Shelley's attempt at the same species of lyrical drama as he had composed in *Manfred*. But he did not like *The Cenci*; he said not a word of *Adonais*; and it would have been absurd even to show him *Epipsychidion*. Besides, Shelley could not fail to compare his own lack of success with Byron's fame. He did so without a trace of jealousy; but yet it was saddening. 'I despair of rivalling Lord Byron,' he wrote to Mary from Ravenna, 'as well I may; and there is no other with whom it is worth contending.' This at least shows his awareness of his own powers as a poet, but how could he go on writing what no one cared to read? He had plans enough for poetry: for a tragedy on Charles the First, for a play on Troilus and Cressida, and for another on Timon of Athens in which he intended to treat current political and social evils, and for much else. Yet, 'It offends me to see my name classed among those who have no name.'

Byron, obedient to Teresa's interdict, had written no more of *Don Juan* this year. He read the fifth canto to Shelley while he was his guest in the Palazzo Guiccioli. 'It sets him not above but far above all the poets of the day:' Shelley told Mary, 'every word has the stamp of immortality. . . . It fulfils, in a certain degree, what I have long preached of producing – something wholly new and relative to the age, and yet surpassingly beautiful. It may be vanity, but I think I see the trace of my earnest exhortations to him to create something wholly new.' Cantos III, IV and V were published in London while Shelley was in Ravenna. As soon as Byron received copies he sent one to Shelley in Pisa. In thanking him Shelley again expressed his admiration:

It is a poem totally of its own species, and my wonder and delight at the grace of the composition no less than the free and grand vigour of the conception of it perpetually increase. The few passages which anyone might desire to be cancelled in the 1st and 2nd Cantos are here reduced almost to nothing. The poem carries with it at once the stamp of originality and a defiance of imitation. Nothing has ever been written like it in English – nor if I may venture to prophesy, will there be, without carrying upon it the mark of a secondary and borrowed light. You unveil and present in its true deformity what is worst in human nature, and this is what the witlings of the age murmur at, conscious of their want of power to endure the scrutiny of such a light. We are damned to the knowledge of good and evil, and it is well for us to know what we should avoid no less than what we should seek. – The character of Lambro – his return – the merriment of his daughter's guests made as it were in celebration of his funeral – the meeting with the lovers – and the death of Haidée, – are circumstances combined and developed in a manner that I seek elsewhere in vain. The fifth canto, which some of your pet Zoili in Albemarle Street said was *dull*, gathers instead of loses splendour and energy – the language in which the whole is clothed – a sort of chameleon under the changing sky of the spirit that kindles it – is such as these lisping days could not have expected, – and are, believe me, in spite of the approbation which you wrest from them – little pleased to hear. One can hardly judge from recitation and it was not until I read it in print that I have been able to do it justice.

Shelley saw in *Don Juan* as it was developing the splendid fulfilment of Byron's genius in that work on a grand scale which he had urged on him when they first met five years before, and to which he had returned in April of this year, and once more in the letter in which he proposed his visit to Ravenna. 'This sort of writing only on a great plan and perhaps in a more compact form is what I wished you to do when I made my vows for an epic. – But I am content. – You are building up a drama, such as England has not yet seen, and the task is sufficiently noble and worthy of you.' How gratified Byron must have been to receive such enthusiastic but discriminating praise from the friend whose judgment of his poetry he most valued, and often invited.

Shelley knew that Byron had plans for more cantos, and that he was already regretting his rash promise to Teresa not to continue. In September he wrote to Byron of this: '*Don Juan* is your great victory over the alleged inflexibility of your powers; and interest must be made to take an embargo off such precious merchandise.' If anyone could persuade Teresa, Shelley could. He had persuaded her to abandon her intention of going to Switzerland, on Byron's behalf; now he must induce her to raise the embargo on *Don Juan*. It was not very difficult, for Teresa liked and respected Shelley; and so when Byron came to Pisa, and was living in almost daily intercourse with Shelley, Teresa after a time permitted him to take up *Don Juan* once more.

Shelley never doubted that *Don Juan* was Byron's best work. He was not much taken with *Marino Faliero*, which Byron read to him at Ravenna, and of which he had spoken to Shelley as a possible theme for a tragedy when they were together in Venice three years before. Shelley preferred his own *Cenci* because he believed that Byron was wrong to reject the freer English or Spanish models for the false classicism of the French tragedians and Alfieri. Yet Byron's power was such that he might well triumph over these obstacles which he had placed in the way of his genius. 'He will shake off his shackles as he finds they cramp him. I believe he will produce something very great; and that familiarity with the dramatic power of human nature, will soon enable him to soften down the severe and unharmonising traits of his *Marino Faliero*.' The two other historical plays which Byron had written this year, but which were not published until December, *Sardanapalus* and *The Two Foscari*, he did not read or show to Shelley.

Another subject which must have come up in conversation while Shelley was with Byron in Ravenna was Robert Southey. The Dedication of *Don Juan*, which Byron had read to Shelley in September 1818, he suppressed when the first two cantos were published the following summer. They were anonymous, and his friends Hobhouse and Frere had advised against its inclusion in the circumstances. Byron agreed: 'I won't attack the dog in the dark. Such things are for scoundrels and renegadoes like himself.' The Dedication was prompted by Southey's reference to the 'League of Incest' in which he alleged Byron and Shelley joined when they were at Geneva, and though it was not published Southey was told of it. Besides, he can hardly have been pleased to find Byron quoting, in the final stanza of the first canto, four lines from his *Epilogue to the Lay of the Laureate*, only to follow them with an insulting disclaimer:

> The four first rhymes are Southey's every line:
> For God's sake, reader! take them not for mine.

A hostile review of *Don Juan* I and II in Blackwood's *Edinburgh Magazine* provided Byron with the occasion for another attack on Southey, this time directly referring to the 'League of Incest' slander, though without mentioning Shelley by name. He wrote this in the spring of 1820, but it too remained unpublished. But he included in *Don Juan* III three scornful stanzas on Southey:

> He lied with such a fervour of intention,
> There was no doubt he earned his laureate pension.

In the meantime, on 29 January 1820, George III died, and Southey, as poet laureate, conceived it to be his duty to celebrate the virtues of the old, mad, blind, despised and now dead King in a poem, *A Vision of Judgment*, which was published on 11 April 1821. In his Preface Southey made an attack on what he called the Satanic school of poetry, especially directed against *Don Juan*, which he regarded as 'an act of high treason in English poetry'. To this Byron replied with some dignity in a note appended to *The Two Foscari*, which was published in December. He referred to an allegation that he had written the notes to *Queen Mab*,* whose recent pirated edition

* This shows Southey's extraordinary complacency, for in 1817 he had been refused damages against the piratical printers of his youthful, republican poem *Wat Tyler*. Shelley knew this, and quoted it as the precedent which would deny him any redress for the republication of *Queen Mab*.

had been the excuse for further attacks on Shelley. This absurd charge Byron dismissed, but at the same time he expressed his admiration for Shelley's poems. 'No one knows better than the real author [of the notes to *Queen Mab*] that his opinions and mine differ materially upon the metaphysical portion of that work; though in common with all who are not blinded by baseness and bigotry, I highly admire the poetry of that and his other publications.' Only a few weeks before they met, Shelley had been writing to deny responsibility for the republication of *Queen Mab*, but he knew that it was certain to occasion fresh attacks on him. Byron again referred to the old calumnies against himself and Shelley which Southey 'scattered abroad on his return from Switzerland. . . . They have done him no good in this world; and, if his creed be the right one, they will do him less in the next.' And he derided Southey's boasted friendship with Landor, from whose preface to a collection of Latin poems he had quoted in a note to the Preface to *A Vision of Judgment*. Byron would have heard from Shelley of Landor's refusal to meet him in Pisa, which Shelley rightly attributed to Southey's influence, and he may reasonably have supposed that his own friendship with Shelley was more valuable and more enlivening than any friendship between Southey and Landor could ever be.

To this attack Southey promptly replied in a letter to the Editor of *The Courier* dated 6 January 1822. He denied having scattered any calumnies against Byron or Shelley on his return from Switzerland. It was true that he had copied into his notebook Shelley's Greek inscription from the hotel album at Montenvers, and had spoken of this on his return to England. 'If I had published it, the gentleman in question would not have thought himself slandered by having that recorded of him which he has so often recorded of himself.' There was a malicious shrewdness in including this in a reply to Byron; for Byron had himself erased Shelley's *δημοκρατικὸς φιλανθρωπότατος καὶ ἄθεος* from one album where he wrote it. Such were the embarrassments which friendship with Shelley might bring upon him. Southey concluded his letter to *The Courier* with invective against Byron as the founder and leader of the Satanic School; and with a final piece of advice: 'When he attacks me again let it be in rhyme. For one who has so little command of himself, it will be a great advantage that his temper should be obliged to *keep tune.*'

The advice was superfluous. As soon as Byron read the 'spavined dactyls' of Southey's *Vision of Judgment* he began his own incomparable parody. This was on 7 May 1821. But he set it aside while he finished *Sardanapalus* and wrote *The Two Foscari*, and only in September, while he was packing up in preparation for his removal to Pisa did he take it up again and complete it. Shelley's visit, when their minds went back to that summer of 1816 about which Southey (or so they believed) had scattered his calumnies against them both, and to their last meeting, when Byron had read to Shelley his Dedication to Bob Southey of *Don Juan*, must have restored the mood in which Byron first imagined his poem. When Byron read Shelley the fifth canto of *Don Juan* at his house Shelley inquired about its further continuation, only to be told of Teresa's interdict. It is likely that Byron knowing as he did Shelley's personal concern in the theme would then make some mention of the new poem in the same manner which he had begun on Southey. Shelley had recognised more quickly than anyone else that Byron's natural genius was for comedy and satire, that *Don Juan*, more than any of his other poems, allowed the varied qualities of his mind their fullest scope. If he could not yet persuade Byron to resume *Don Juan*, he would surely encourage him to complete another poem in a similar manner, rather than to diverge again into neo-classical drama, which he thought a waste of Byron's powers. But Shelley's mere presence, and his acknowledged admiration for *Don Juan* would be enough, even if, against all probability, Byron and he never spoke of Southey this August, to help him to recapture the mood in which three months before he had begun *The Vision of Judgment.*

Byron sent off the finished poem to Murray on 4 October – 'in my finest, ferocious, Caravaggio style', he told Hobhouse – and, though a year passed before it was published (and then not by Murray), it proved to be the decisive conclusion of the long-drawn-out conflict with Southey. Satirical attacks on Southey for changing his political allegiance might be damaging, but must also arouse sympathy among those who had experienced a similar conversion from youthful liberalism. Wordsworth would have been among these. After reading *Don Juan* I and II he chided *The Quarterly Review* for not attacking it. 'What avails it to hunt down Shelley and leave Byron untouched?' he inquired with his customary charity. Attacks on Southey's poetical manner must also be only partially effective, since some readers (Wordsworth no doubt among these too) preferred his manner to that of *Don Juan*. But the good-humoured ridicule of Byron's *Vision of Judgment* showed up Southey for the fool that he had become, so that it has never since been possible to take him seriously as a poet.

While Byron, dallying in Ravenna to Teresa's distress, was thus cheerfully occupied in the destruction of his and Shelley's common enemy, Shelley's idealising imagination turned to a very different theme of common interest. On 1 April he and Mary heard the news of the opening of the Greek War of Independence, brought to them that day by the young Greek prince, Alexander Mavrocordato. He had been introduced to them four months before, and since then they had seen him frequently. Mary especially liked Mavrocordato. She had lessons in Greek from him; she taught him some English and found him a very quick pupil, though when he wrote to her he preferred to use French. Shelley regretfully found him less attractive. 'I reproach my own savage disposition that so agreeable, accomplished and amiable a person is not more agreeable to me,' he confessed to Claire. However, news of the Greek revolt was very exciting, whatever Shelley's reservations about Mavrocordato as a modern representative of the nation which Aeschylus and Sophocles and Plato once made splendid.

Shelley had been hoping to visit Greece in 1821, and in the previous September asked Byron for his assistance if the visit should take place. Now, because of the war, as well as for other reasons, it must be postponed, but, as Mary exclaimed in her letter giving Claire the news, 'What a delight it will be to visit Greece free!' Mary's journal briefly records the ups and downs of the revolt as she heard of it from Mavrocordato; she followed the news with the liveliest interest, for after the recent defeat of the revolution in Naples this gave new hope for a liberal success. Besides, Greece had for the Shelleys, as for so many of their contemporaries, far greater power to evoke romantic enthusiasm than any other country; for was not Greece the birthplace of political liberty? It was certain therefore that Shelley, who had celebrated the cause of liberty in Spain and in Italy with two odes, would wish to write of it in this new manifestation. But during the spring and summer it was the news of the death of Keats with his achievement decried and his promise unfulfilled, which came close to Shelley's disappointment at the neglect of his own poetry, that inspired him to write, while as yet the less personal concern for the success of the Greeks could not. Indeed, even his letters of this summer are curiously silent on the Greek War, and from the time when Prince Mavrocordato first brought the news until early in June, when a ship came to take him and his suite to join the Greek army in the Morea, Shelley never refers to it. Even then his only comment on Mavrocordato's departure to fight in the cause of Greek liberty scarcely reached a tepidity of admiration. 'He is a great loss to Mary,' he told Claire, 'and *therefore* to me – but not otherwise.'

Shelley well knew Byron's interest in Greece and his hope for Greek independence, declared in *Childe Harold* I and II, yet in the three surviving letters to him of this summer, he never mentioned the revolt, not even when a regretful reference to the failure of the Neapolitan revolution might have suggested it. Byron seems not to have received the news until May, and then his native scepticism, reinforced by the recent disaster to the cause in which he had been engaged in Italy, restrained his enthusiasm. He first referred to the affair in a letter of 4 June to Tom Moore: 'The Greeks! what think you? They are my old acquaintances – but what to think I know not. Let us hope howsomever.'

Byron's and Shelley's caution did not imply a lack of interest in the cause of Greek liberty, so much as a reluctance to commit themselves to further disappointments which might indeed be still more intensely felt. They talked together in Ravenna of the news from Greece, which seemed to be good, though Shelley thought Russian intervention undesirable. In fact Hypsilantes, whose proclamation of 7 March, in which he announced that he had Russian support, was the start of the revolution, had been ignominiously defeated at Dragashan in June and was a prisoner in Austria; but the simultaneous revolt in the Morea had been so successful that by August all Greece south of Thermopylae except for a few fortresses was in Greek hands. In mid-September Shelley, in a letter to Horace Smith, revealed the reason for his earlier unwonted lack of excitement. 'All public attention is now centred on the wonderful revolution in Greece. I dare not, after the events of last winter, hope that slaves can become freemen so cheaply.' He even praised Mavrocordato, and said that, if he was typical of the Greek rebels, all would go well. In this enthusiastic mood Shelley could once more celebrate the cause of liberty, and immediately he began writing his second lyrical drama, *Hellas*.

Again, as in *Prometheus Unbound*, Shelley followed Aeschylus, but now took the *Persae* for his model. This was most appropriate for several reasons. The more primitive dramatic form allowed the lyrical treatment which, with the war undecided, Shelley saw was alone acceptable. The wide, compassionate sympathy of Aeschylus, who had fought at Marathon, for the defeated Persians suited Shelley's humanity. Shelley's Prometheus summed up his recantation with a line quoted from Aeschylus:

> I wish no living thing to suffer pain.

Now Shelley, in spite of his eager wish for a Greek victory, could not suppress his pity for the human suffering that must precede it. To him, as to Wilfred Owen a century later, the poetry of war was in the pity.

Like Byron, he hoped against hope for the liberty of Greece, which he could but prophesy in the autumn of 1821. His only sources of information were what everyone heard, and in his preface he apologised 'for the display of newspaper erudition' to which he had been reduced. From such Byron had long been accustomed to make poetry, as Shelley observed during their tour of Lac Léman in the summer of 1816, but this was seldom Shelley's way. He wrote to John Gisborne this October, when he was just finishing *Hellas*: 'You might as well go to a ginshop for a leg of mutton, as expect any thing human or earthly from me.' His immediate reference was to *Epipsychidion*, but in the same paragraph he also wrote of *Hellas*. In *The Masque of Anarchy* and in *Swellfoot the Tyrant* he responded to contemporary events with satire, which was closer to Byron's method. But his response to the news of revolution in Spain and at Naples was idealistic. He saw these revolutions in the Mediterranean countries as reassertions of those human rights which were first conceived there, and his optimism led him to regard the progress of liberty as part of the inevitable continuing history of the human race. So in the *Ode to Liberty* which the revolution in Spain inspired, he saw man's original condition in Hobbesian terms; then Athens arose to establish the ideal of human liberty, which Rome for a time inherited. There followed a thousand years of oppression, induced by the priest-ridden rule of Christendom, until liberty returned once more in England and in Italy and at last in France. This same pattern of the progress of liberty informs the first great Chorus in *Hellas*, but with the further episode of its return to Greece. Shelley imagines the fear that the tyrannical governments of Europe feel now when they see

The panther, Freedom, fled to her old cover.

The apathy of their subjects was incomprehensible. 'We are all Greeks. Our laws, our literature, our religion, our arts have their root in Greece. But for Greece – Rome, the instructor, the conqueror, or the metropolis of our ancestors, would have spread no illumination with her arms, and we might still have been savages and idolaters.' Shelley may have forgotten that Dr Johnson had said much the same.

Interrupting the Chorus in this paean to liberty, Shelley contrives that a series of messengers bring to the Sultan, Mahmud, whose despondency is intensified by his religious fatalism, reports of the crumbling of Turkish power before new Greek victories. (It is here that he makes use of 'newspaper erudition'.) Then, to overcome the difficulty of writing when the war was still being waged, he introduces the Wandering Jew, Ahasuerus; and Mahmud is shown the future in 'such figures of indistinct and visionary delineation as suggest the final triumph of the Greek cause as a portion of the cause of civilisation and social improvement'. The whole drama was written very rapidly, as Shelley usually worked, and with the further incentive of getting it published while the Greek cause was undefeated. He wrote it, he told John Gisborne, 'without much care, in one of those few moments of enthusiasm which now seldom visit me'. Yet if his blank verse is at times somewhat turgid, the lyrical parts have a quality which none but he ever surpassed.

The choruses of *Hellas*, concerned as they are with the intellectual ideas which, for Shelley, determine historical events, preserve an optimism in spite of the uncertainty as to what the outcome would be, for

> . . . Greece and her foundations are
> Built below the tide of war,
> Based on the crystalline sea
> Of thought and its eternity . . .

Even if Greece were to fail in her present attempt, the cause of liberty must ultimately succeed. In the last chorus, one of the finest of all his lyrics, Shelley looks forward to a new Golden Age to follow a Greek victory; but even so he admits the possibility of the return of hate and death. As Medwin pointed out, this lyric,

> The world's great age begins anew,
> The golden years return,

owes much to Byron's 'The Isles of Greece' in *Don Juan* III. This is not coincidental, for Shelley had just been reading this for the first time, in the copy which Byron sent him in October. Shelley was yet again finding lyrical suggestion in a poem by Byron, and was again responding to Byron's pessimism with his own guarded optimism. And Byron in his poem recalled a passage from Aeschylus' *Persae*, which had given Shelley the suggestion for his drama.

Shelley thought of the modern Greeks as the descendants of Aeschylus' and Plato's contemporaries, and his small experience of them had not led to Byron's more realistic appraisal. Shelley had not much liked Prince Mavrocordato when he knew him in Pisa, but once he had taken the heroic course of joining the insurgents, where even now he was organising a provincial constitution for Western Greece at Missolonghi in the hope of overcoming the political chaos which he found on arrival, Shelley forgot his personal aversion. Mavrocordato was the only Greek whom Shelley knew who was participating actively in the war, and as such was a worthy representative of the ancient virtues of his nation. To him therefore Shelley dedicated *Hellas* 'as an imperfect token of the admiration, sympathy, and friendship of the author'. He dated this inscription 'Pisa, November 1, 1821.' That same day Byron arrived in Pisa.

CHAPTER EIGHT

The Pisa Circle is Formed

NOVEMBER 1821–JANUARY 1822: ITALY

FOR the first time in these five years of their friendship Byron, in coming to Pisa, was moving into a society of which Shelley was the centre. It is true that Teresa was there and the Gambas, but they had come to Pisa, out of all possible places in Tuscany, because Byron had decided to come there in order to be with Shelley; and they were remaining there near the Palazzo Lanfranchi which Shelley had recommended and rented for Byron. Shelley had recently furnished a flat in the Tre Palazzi di Chiesa, the first time since his arrival in Italy three and a half years before than he had felt settled enough to do so. The house was less that five minutes from the Palazzo Lanfranchi, on the opposite side of the river; it was much quieter, for their rooms faced south across the country away from the bustle of the town. They were at last beginning to put down roots, and there Shelley had the makings of that society of like-minded friends which he admitted was the practicable alternative to the romantic ideal of escape with Mary and their child to some remote and solitary island.

Besides, Shelley had long since declared that social enjoyment was the alpha and omega of his existence, and whatever longing for withdrawal from society the hostility of reviewers, the indifference of the public, and the slanders of such as Southey and Hoppner might from time to time induce, Shelley needed the stimulus of talk with his friends, and the encouragement of their pleasure in his poems. At Pisa, even before Byron came, Shelley had a number of friends about him:

John Taaffe, whom he had first met in November 1820; his cousin, Tom Medwin, who had arrived about the same time; Edward and Jane Williams, who, excited by Medwin's enthusiastic account of Shelley, came from the south of France early in 1821. The Masons, who had first attracted the Shelleys to stay in Pisa, were still living there, though Mrs Mason had somehow acquired, in Shelley's eyes, an annoying perverseness; but the Gisbornes, whose accessibility at Leghorn had once been a recommendation, had returned to England to live there permanently. Of the Italians whom the Shelleys got to know when they first came to Pisa, Francesco Pacchiani had soon shown himself to deserve his nickname of Il Diavolo; Emilia Viviani, recently married, was in the process of metamorphosis (in Shelley's classical imagination) from Juno into a cloud; and the *improvvisatore*, Tommaso Sgricci, whose company and whose talents they had enjoyed the previous winter, left Pisa at the end of January, and soon subsided into retirement on a pension from the Grand Duke. Prince Alexander Mavrocordato was by now acquiring heroic stature in Greece. Thus the cosmopolitan quality of Shelley's original circle at Pisa had been reduced by disillusion or removal, and only Dr Vaccà and Prince and Princess Argyropouli remained. But Byron's coming also brought Teresa Guiccioli and her father and brother.

His coming necessitated the departure of Claire, who had been staying at Pugnano with the Williamses in October. On 1 November she left for Florence. Near Empoli the carriage in which she was travelling met a grand unwieldy coach with its retinue of servants, and had to draw off the road to let it pass on its way. Claire recognised the coach: it was Lord Byron's. He is hardly likely to have noticed who was in the hired carriage.

Teresa was already on the most friendly terms with the Shelleys, and she was especially fond of Shelley, of whom Byron had often spoken to her. He was in every way unlike anyone else she had ever met, a Spirit rather than a man. Even in his dress he was extraordinary, for he generally wore a schoolboy's jacket, never any gloves, and unpolished shoes – 'yet among a thousand gentlemen, he would always have seemed the most accomplished.' Teresa met Mary in August, soon after Shelley called on her in Florence on his way back from Ravenna. From then on Mary and Teresa often saw one another, Mary coming in from the Baths of Pisa to visit Teresa in Casa Parra on the Lung' Arno, and Teresa returning her visits at Casa Prini. Occasionally they went out riding together, as they had been doing earlier in the day on which Byron had arrived. Mary told Maria Gisborne that Teresa was 'a nice pretty girl without pretensions, good-hearted and amiable' and, though there is something here of the patronising tone of twenty-four years considering twenty-one, it is apt enough. Jane Williams, who was twenty-three, sometimes accompanied them on their rides and visits, and the three young women enjoyed each other's company while the men were disposed to prefer their own. 'Our good cavaliers flock together,' Mary told Marianne Hunt after a few months, 'and. . . do not like "fetching a walk with the absurd womankind".' Monkbarns' phrase was a favourite with Byron, who greatly admired Scott's novels – when he moved to Pisa he kept them by him, after packing up the rest of his library – and often used expressions from them in his letters and conversation. Mary had recently been reading *The Antiquary* again, but she caught this trick of quoting Scott from Byron.

The womankind had reason to find sympathy together because of the somewhat unusual nature of their experience. Mary eloped at sixteen with Shelley, and bore him two children before Harriet's suicide set him free to marry her. Teresa was married at eighteen to a man nearly forty years older than herself, and had now left him to become the mistress of a man whose wife was living in England. Jane had married in India, also while still in her teens, an officer named Johnson;* they soon parted but without divorce; and she then became the mistress of Edward Williams, a Lieutenant in the Eighth Dragoons on service in India, who soon afterwards sold his

* See note 8, pp. 270–1.

commission. She had a son, now nearly two years old (a few months younger than Mary's Percy) and a daughter born the previous March, a couple of months after her arrival in Pisa. Mary was the most intellectual of the three – she had just completed her second novel *Valperga* – and the most serious; she was after all the daughter of two liberal intellectuals. Teresa found Mary a little alarming, and was more at ease with Jane; yet Mary was capable of gaiety, if not of frivolity. They were all three young and beautiful and could look forward now to many years of peace and happiness with the men they loved. And they must have been wonderful to see together: Teresa, with her high, pale forehead and auburn ringlets and her large, dark eyes; Jane, more serene in her beauty, with dark brown hair framing the perfect oval of her face, with her wide-spaced eyes and delicate mouth; and Mary, whose fair hair had a 'sunny and burnished brightness' in contrast with her calm, grey eyes, and whose features (as she once innocently remarked) 'somehow, people always remember'.

On the day after Byron arrived in Pisa Shelley called to see him in the Palazzo Lanfranchi, 'a very good spacious house', Byron called it, even if it was less quiet than the Palazzo Guiccioli in Ravenna. It is indeed a handsome sixteenth-century house, with a façade of white marble, and a finely carved cornice. There are five bays with plain classical pediments on the two lower storeys and scallop-shaped recesses above the windows of the top floor. Above the door is the bold coat-of-arms of the Toscanelli. Byron recognised the aristocratic distinction of the house, which had been built for one of the most famous of Pisan families, the Lanfranchi, and recently restored by the Toscanelli. He was grateful to Shelley for arranging everything so capably for him. Shelley had, it seemed, even taken care to provide a house full of ghosts, which terrified the servants, especially Byron's valet, Fletcher.

Byron gave Shelley the manuscript of *Cain* to take home, and Mary read it that evening. It made a great impression on her: 'Of some works one says, one has thought of such things though one could not have expressed it so well. It is not thus with *Cain*; one has perhaps stood on the extreme verge of such ideas, and from the midst of the darkness which has surrounded us the voice of the Poet now is heard telling a wondrous tale.' Byron had been writing it during the summer, and sent off the fair copy to Murray in September; he thought well of it – 'it is in my gay metaphysical style, and in the *Manfred* line' – and he must have thought that it would appeal to Shelley much more than *Marino Faliero*. He was right. Shelley read it at once, and was deeply moved: '*Cain* is apocalyptic – it is a revelation not before communicated to man'; it had in it the finest English poetry 'since *Paradise Regained*'. After its publication in December Byron showed Shelley some letters which he had received from Tom Moore, in which Moore said that he saw in *Cain* something of Shelley's influence on Byron's mind. This was perceptive of him, for 'the *Manfred* line' certainly owed much to Shelley in the beginning, however sincerely Shelley might now deny any part in the excellence of *Cain*. '*Cain* was *conceived* many years ago,' he told Horace Smith (who knew Moore), 'and begun before I saw him . . . at Ravenna; how happy should I not be to attribute to myself, however indirectly, any participation in that immortal work.' Moore, in commenting on Shelley's disclaimer in his *Life* of Byron, noted 'the good breeding, gentle temper, and modesty for which Shelley was so remarkable'. Though he had never met Shelley, he was quite won over by Shelley's friendly message to him through Horace Smith. His earlier warning to Byron of the harm to his reputation that association with Shelley would bring went unregarded.

This was a promising start. Byron was clearly prepared to renew the old intimacy with Shelley of that summer of 1816 at Geneva, and there seemed no reason why they should not remain together in Pisa indefinitely. Those two months in the autumn of 1818 could not have been much further prolonged even if Claire had then left them; for, in spite of the creative excitement brought by the renewal of friendship, Byron was still defiantly given over to dissipations of a kind that nauseated Shelley, and had they remained long in each other's company they must have quarrelled. But now Claire had gone away; Mary was happy; and Teresa had rescued and domesticated Byron without in any way lessening the fascination of his company. Shelley at once recognised the change that had come upon Byron when, after nearly three years absence, he saw him again in Ravenna in August, and he knew that he must thank Teresa for it. Byron with Teresa at hand to protect him from the insolence and pride of his own temperament was a very different man from Byron subjected to the violent passions of La Fornarina. Confronted by that Byron, Shelley's sensitive and unworldly spirit withdrew in alarmed disgust; but Teresa's Byron was much more like the Byron whom he had first known. This was a friend with whom he could never tire of talking, because they could talk of anything under the sun with the certainty that, whatever it was, they would always approach it from opposite sides. Talking to Byron, Shelley forgot his deference to the most famous poet of the age, and was incited to employ the full power of his extraordinary intellect. Byron knew that he was no match for Shelley in dialectical skill or in learning, but that mobility of mind which could draw so deftly on so rich stores of experience enabled him to divert rather than to meet Shelley's arguments. Perhaps there is some analogy here with those conversations to which men had delightedly listened two centuries before in the Mermaid Tavern; but no more than that to those who were privileged to hear Byron and Shelley, as to those who heard Shakespeare and Jonson, such talk seemed the perfect interchange between two men who had been born thus to stimulate and to respond to each other.

The first of Shelley's Pisan friends to meet Byron was Williams. He arrived from Pugnano with Jane on 4 November, and next day Shelley introduced him to Byron. Williams, who had perhaps discounted Shelley's partiality in favour of the common opinion about Byron, was surprised and pleased at his reception: 'So far from his having a haughtiness of manners, they are those of the most unaffected and gentlemanly ease – and so far from his being (as is generally imagined) wrapt in a melancholy gloom he is all sunshine and good humour, with which the elegance of his language and the brilliancy of his wit cannot fail to inspire those who are near him.' When they left Byron lent them a copy of the *Annuaire historique universel*, in which, he said, they would find something to amuse them, 'for at the end it takes infinite pains to prove that I am the Devil'. The Williamses took a flat in the same house in which the Shelleys were living, and next day Byron called with Teresa and her brother Pietro. He had a fresh libel against himself to regale them with: he had been accused, he told them, of earning £500 by writing puffs for Day and Martin's blacking. (The allegation was self-evidently ludicrous then, before a century of progress persuaded men of letters to be photographed for advertisements of 'My *Daily Mail*'.) Byron must have taken to Edward Williams, the son of an officer in the East India Company's army who, after a short period at Eton, had gone into the Navy, and thence into the Eighth Dragoons. He was handsome and masculine, and delighted Teresa with his accounts of big-game hunting in India; Byron also would have enjoyed these, for he always liked the adventurous. He asked Williams round on the 7th to practise pistol-shooting in his garden, a favourite sport of his and Shelley's; but the Governor of Pisa, Emilia Viviani's father, forbade shooting within the city walls.

Williams had other talents than those of a sporting officer. He was a more than competent water-colourist, and in the summer painted a miniature of Mary; she sent it to Shelley as a birthday present while he was staying with Byron in August. Like many others of Shelley's acquaintance, he aspired to be a writer, and while he was at Pugnano he wrote a play called *The Promise, or a Year, a Month, and a Day*. Now, on his arrival in Pisa, Shelley got his assistance in a translation of Spinoza's *Tractatus Theologico-Politicus* which he had begun long before. As was his custom with the Greek dramatists or Calderón, Shelley translated directly aloud; Williams then wrote to his dictation, as Mary had done in the earlier stages. Byron was interested in this too, and offered to write a life of

Spinoza to introduce the translation. Byron's name would thus help to gain attention for the work. Shelley completed the translation that winter, but it remained unpublished.

Shelley must have introduced another of his friends, John Taaffe, to Byron soon after his arrival. He was a Catholic Irishman of distinguished lineage, and he had been living in Pisa for five or six years; he had two small children, but his wife had died in 1819 in giving birth to the second. Like Byron he had travelled over much of the Mediterranean and had written about his travels; and he was acquainted with Madame de Staël. It is scarcely necessary to add that he had literary ambitions. At the moment these concerned the publication of a translation from Dante with an elaborate commentary on the *Commedia*. Shelley thought little of the translation but praised the commentary, and had already tried to interest his own publisher, Ollier, in it. This came to nothing, but Taaffe was not the sort of man to take No for an answer, and very soon Byron was writing to another Irishman, Tom Moore, to invite his interest. 'There is here Mr. Taaffe, an Irish genius, with whom we are acquainted. He hath written a really *excellent* Commentary on Dante, full of new and true information, and much ingenuity. But his verse is such as it hath pleased God to endue him withal.' Taaffe misguidedly tried to insist on having his translation published with the Commentary, in spite of Byron's efforts to dissuade him. Eventually, thanks to Byron's recommendation, Murray published the first volume of the Commentary, which covered the first eight cantos of the *Inferno*, but without the translation.

Taaffe, though a sincere and well-read and well-travelled man, Byron could never take quite seriously, as this first reference to him in a letter to Moore shows. He was indeed somewhat ridiculous. Like a true Irishman he prided himself on his horsemanship, 'that most delicate and momentous of subjects', though without much justification, as Byron was unkind enough to notice; his confidence in the merits of his verses was of the same order, and was mocked by Mary, who called him the poet laureate of Pisa, as well as by Byron.

Taaffe seems not to have understood that Mary laughed at him, for in the summer when he sent her some guinea-pigs, presumably as pets for her little boy, he sent her a note which concluded: 'O that I were one of those guinea-pigs, that I might see you this morning!' Shelley could laugh at those absurdities too, but he saw that there was some more serious quality in him, and he responded to Taaffe's loving admiration. 'If he disdained to be understood,' Taaffe said of Shelley, 'it was more in his printed books than in his conversation, which was almost always eloquent, singularly mellifluous and full of heat and in a most wonderful and attractive degree uniting gentleness and vigour – his unquenchable courage contrasting strangely with his feeble frame and girlish voice.' He rejected Shelley's youthful assertion of atheism, and considered that he had been most unjustly persecuted. Like Williams, he was fascinated by Shelley's gift for language – 'he knew English better than any person I ever met with,' he said; and he genuinely admired his poems.

Before November was out Shelley introduced to Byron another of his friends, Tom Medwin, who returned to Pisa from Geneva on the 14th. He had spent about four months there the previous winter, and though welcome at first, he had in time proved something of a bore: 'common place personified', in Mary's eyes. He had the maddening habit of interrupting them when they were reading or writing in order to read out to them some fine thing he had just come across. He was Shelley's second cousin, and had served for some years in India in the 24th Light Dragoons. While in India, when he had not seen Shelley for several years, he came across a copy of *The Revolt of Islam* in a lot of remainders on a Parsee bookstall, and thenceforward was an ardent admirer of his poetry. This was an improbable taste in a young cavalry officer, but Medwin had a receptive and inquiring mind, and like Williams (whom he introduced to Shelley) had many interests other than those of a soldier and sportsman. He had some literary talent to support the literary ambition which seemed inescapable among Shelley's friends, and as soon as he met Lord Byron he decided to make a record of his conversations. He was not a Boswell, but even Boswell might have been at a loss to record such swift and volatile talk as Byron's, which was totally different from the pontifical laying down the law which usually constituted Dr Johnson's more memorable remarks. Byron's wit was gayer, more good-humoured, more provocative to response and repartee. He hoped for a reply, where Johnson preferred conclusion. Medwin's too notorious unreliability derives in part from this difference between his subject and Boswell's, since it is much easier to recall some observation that brings an argument to a close, than to recollect some quick and witty intervention in a many-sided conversation. Of those best qualified to judge, from their own knowledge of Byron, most agreed that Medwin succeeded in conveying the characteristic qualities of Byron's talk.

Shelley took Medwin to the Palazzo Lanfranchi on 20 November. Tiger, the bulldog which guarded the head of the staircase, knew Shelley and let them pass with no more than an admonitory growl at Medwin. Byron was writing to Douglas Kinnaird in Rome when Shelley and Medwin were announced. 'His reception was frank and kind; he took me cordially by the hand, and said: "You are a relation and schoolfellow of Shelley's – we do not meet as strangers – you must allow me to continue my letter on account of the post. Here's something for you to read, Shelley, (giving him part of the MS of *Heaven and Earth*); tell me what you think of it." ' *Heaven and Earth* Byron began at Ravenna on 9 October and completed before leaving for Pisa. A few days before Medwin saw him he sent the fair copy to Murray, who declined to publish it, in spite of Byron's assurance that it was pious enough, 'at least some of the Chorus might have been written by Sternhold and Hopkins themselves for that, and perhaps for melody.' Shelley, however, much admired the lyrical parts.

Next day Medwin called without Shelley. Byron knew Medwin had just been at Geneva, and he gave him some account of the summer that he had spent there with Shelley; he also told him that he had recently thought of going back there, 'but Shelley, when he came to visit me at Ravenna, gave me such a flattering account of Pisa that I changed my mind.' Byron showed Medwin his pet monkey – later he acquired a second, after seeing it cruelly treated in the street – and they played billiards. They rode out to practise pistol-shooting at the farmhouse at Cisanello to which they resorted after the Governor's ban on shooting within the city. The farm, which lay in the rich alluvial land between the Arno and Colle Pisano, belonged to a family who were friends of Dr Vaccà, and he had recommended it to them. Williams joined them, but not Shelley on this occasion, though he too enjoyed the sport. These pistol-shooting excursions took place frequently; they used coins inserted in the tops of canes for targets, giving the farmer on whose land they met the counterpart of every coin struck. As Medwin said, he was making a small fortune this way. Once Williams noted, Byron's 'last shot struck the piece of money so exactly in the centre that it was afterwards found with the ball enclosed within it – the sides being drawn to the centre like a three-cornered cocked hat'. Such coins Byron kept for his 'Museum'. He was a great hoarder of these things, and his pockets were generally full of bent nails, bits of cast horseshoes and so forth. Shelley, as Byron told Medwin, was a much better shot than he, even though 'he is thinking of metaphysics rather than of firing.' From Williams' diary it seems that, in spite of this absent-mindedness, he was the best shot of the four of them. He was never quite what anyone expected.

The daily routine did not vary much. Byron, as was always his habit, got up late, spent the afternoon in talking with his friends, reading, playing billiards. Then, to avoid the stares of English visitors,* he drove out of Pisa in his carriage to where his horse and groom were waiting. He rode the last part of the way to the farm to practise pistol-shooting, returning to dine half an hour after sunset. He spent the evening with

* And not only these. Mary Shelley told Tom Moore of seeing the Grand Duke of Tuscany and his family walking past the Palazzo Lanfranchi to get a glimpse of him.

Teresa at Casa Parra, and after getting home again read or wrote till the early hours of the morning. Shelley got up early, read or wrote till two, then went to Byron's to ride and shoot with him if the weather was fine, or to play billiards if it was not. In the evening he read or talked with his friends – 'whoever happens to drop in', he told Peacock. There was a dinner-party every Wednesday at the Palazzo Lanfranchi, which Shelley enjoyed rather more than his account of these occasions to Horace Smith at first suggests: 'my nerves are generally shaken to pieces by sitting up, contemplating the rest making themselves vats of claret, etc. till 3 o'clock in the morning.' Smith would have recognised with amusement the analogy with Socrates' sobriety at the Symposium which Plato described. Shelley, who had translated the dialogue, no doubt meant that Smith should take the point, for elsewhere he paid tribute to Byron's excellence as a host. 'Never did Byron display himself to more advantage than on these occasions; being at once polite and cordial, full of social hilarity and the most perfect good humour; never diverging into ungraceful merriment, and yet keeping up the spirit of liveliness throughout the evening.'

This was what he had been hoping for when he persuaded Byron to come to Pisa. 'We are constant companions,' he told Peacock, 'no small relief this after the dreary solitude of the understanding and the imagination in which we passed the first years of our expatriation, yoked to all sorts of miseries and discomforts.' He realised how much he had missed Byron's company during the years apart, at least the company of this delightful Byron of Teresa's reformation. And, in addition to his companionship and his conversation, the pleasure of being with him, there were his new poems to read: *Cain*, which seemed to him the finest poem in English for a century and a half; *Heaven and Earth*; and *The Vision of Judgment*.

Byron took this up again as soon as Shelley left Ravenna and he gave it to Shelley to read immediately he reached Pisa. On 9 November Shelley read it aloud to Mary and the Williamses. Williams, recording the occasion in his diary, somewhat solemnly called the poem 'a sublime composition which displays the greatness of his genius above any other of his works'. Shelley with his personal interest in the discomfiture of Southey, yet with his lack of rancour, must have been no less delighted with its good-humoured demolition of the sour and vindictive poet laureate. With what pleasure he would have come to the final scene in Byron's poem where Southey, after offering his services as biographer to Satan – for had he not just written a life of John Wesley? – draws forth the manuscript of his *Vision of Judgment* and begins to read it to the celestial host:

> Those grand heroics acted as a spell;
> The Angels stopped their ears and plied their pinions;
> The Devils ran howling, deafened, down to Hell;
> The ghosts fled, gibbering, for their own dominions –
> (For 'tis not yet decided where they dwell,
> And I leave every man to his opinions);
> Michael took refuge in his trump – but, lo!
> His teeth were set on edge, he could not blow!

Byron had not yet begun any new poem since reaching Pisa, for *Don Juan* was still forbidden. Now that he was coming back to Teresa he remembered her words when she laid the ban, that she would rather have the fame of *Childe Harold* for three years than an immortality of *Don Juan*. After all, what did fame matter?

> Oh Fame! if I e'er took delight in thy praises,
> 'Twas less for the sake of thy high-sounding phrases,
> Than to see the bright eyes of the dear One discover
> She thought that I was not unworthy to love her.

A few days later, when he had seen her again, he added a final stanza.

> *There* chiefly I sought thee, *there* only I found thee;
> Her glance was the best of the rays that surround thee,
> When it sparkled o'er aught that was bright in my story,
> I knew it was Love, and I felt it was Glory.

Such placidity was not very likely to last, but while it did it was good.

During November and December Shelley wrote little. He sent off *Hellas* to Ollier on 11 November with a request that it should be published immediately, because such interest as it had was topical, or so he thought. In spite of the slowness of the post, Shelley could reasonably hope for publication within a few weeks. But he became increasingly irritated, as many another author has been, by his publisher's dilatoriness. (*Hellas* was eventually published in February, three months after he sent it. The technological progress of the last one hundred and fifty years would make such an achievement now out of the question.) And he could get no news of the success or failure of *Adonais*. He was very anxious to hear how it was received in the reviews (which it had attacked), and he was bold enough to confess that he would be surprised if that too, like his other poems, 'were born to an immortality of oblivion'. But only three reviews noticed it at all; of these *The Literary Chronicle* was favourable, but *The Literary Gazette* continued its attack on Shelley's impious nonsense, and Blackwood's *Edinburgh Magazine* was viciously contemptuous. Before Shelley had seen these reviews, he admitted to Leigh Hunt how much he had hoped for some more favourable interest for *Adonais*. If that too 'had no success and excited no interest what incentive can I have to write?' Mary's diagnosis the previous year had been correct: he needed some public interest in his poetry if he was to continue. But self-exiled in Italy he was unaware that such an interest was indeed growing, for he seems never to have seen the reviews of *The Cenci*, which went into a second edition this year, nor of *Prometheus Unbound*. Some of these continued the old uncomprehending hostility, but others were complimentary, and even enthusiastic about 'one of the most stupendous of those works which the daring and vigorous spirit of modern poetry has created'. Shelley did not expect popularity – he had too clear a knowledge of his own genius for that – and the encouragement which some of the current notices of his poetry provided would have more than satisfied his need. But his publisher and his friends in England, even Leigh Hunt and Peacock, failed to send him the reviews, and more and more he felt isolated in a wilderness of contempt and misunderstanding. Peacock gave him admirable advice. 'When you write,' he told Shelley, 'you never think of your audience. The number who understand you, and sympathise with you, is very small. If you would consider who and what the readers of poetry are, and adapt your compositions to the depth of their understanding and the current of their sympathies, you would attain the highest degree of poetical fame.' Shelley knew this well enough: he always wrote, as he himself said, 'with a total ignorance of the effect that I should produce'. If he had only realised it, the admired poets of Greece and Elizabethan England had always considered their audience, and it need not have derogated from his integrity if he had followed their example.

His friends in Pisa certainly admired his poetry and encouraged him, but Byron later remarked to Trelawny that 'if Shelley cast off the slough of his mystifying metaphysics he would want no puffing' – on this being of one mind with Peacock. But it was the characteristic Romantic failing to be inconsiderate of the readers of poetry; to expect the unawakened earth to respond gratefully to the trumpet of a prophecy, instead of realising that it would be far more likely to grumble, or to pull the blankets up over its ears. Byron, as Shelley saw, had not disdained his public, but now even Byron's presence failed to stimulate him to the writing of poetry. Byron provided a most welcome relief from what, by contrast, seemed the three years' traverse of a desert of the intellect and imagination. But there was, inevitably, the other contrast between Byron's unequalled fame and his own neglect. Shelley had a just enough estimate of his own powers to realise that Byron alone among living poets was worth attempting to rival. But surely it was ludicrous, in view of the reception of his poems, even to think of this? Shelley had had so many disappointments that his confidence seemed to have altogether vanished; probably it was best to accept the inevitable, and return to the translation of Spinoza. Byron's name on the title-page would be enough to associate him in some sort of success, even if only as the translator of a work of prose. As Williams shrewdly remarked Shelley's 'greatest fault is ignorance of his own worth'; or perhaps it would be nearer the truth to say that it was the modesty which made him accept others' disparagement. That, and the uncompromising integrity which prevented him approaching a wider audience.

Byron himself wrote nothing during these first weeks in Pisa, but he did not share Shelley's impatience. In spite of his reluctance to leave Ravenna he very quickly settled down to this quite different life of Pisa. He was happy to be reunited with Teresa, and he always enjoyed Shelley's company. The two young soldiers from India were much to his liking too, and even John Taaffe was acceptable. With these he was content, and he did not care to meet other visitors to Pisa, as Shelley sometimes did. Life was, in the main, quiet and uneventful, for Byron was no longer involved, as he had been in Ravenna, in Italian politics, and in spite of the continuing good news from Greece he remained sceptical of final success. On 11 November Prince Argyropouli brought Shelley news of the capture of Tripolitza, which had been mercilessly sacked after its surrender, and of a Greek naval victory. (In fact the Greeks had suffered a severe defeat of their naval forces at Galaxidion, though they destroyed an Algerian brig a few days later.) Three days afterwards Shelley introduced him to Byron. A month later again the news was still better: the whole of the Morea was liberated from the Turks. Prince Mavrocordato was taking an active part and presided over the National Assembly which met at Piada in December.

In the middle of the month an opportunity for supporting the cause of liberty near at hand presented itself. On 12 December Medwin, while in Moloni's bookshop, heard a rumour that a man who had taken the consecrated wafers off the altar in a church in Lucca, and scattered them on the floor, was to be burnt at the stake. He immediately went to tell Byron. 'Is it possible?' said he. 'Can we believe that we live in the nineteenth century?' How were they to prevent the auto-da-fé? Byron remembered that Lord Guilford had just arrived in Pisa and that he was a personal friend of the Grand Duke; they must get his help. And then surely the Grand Duke, who had never yet signed a death-warrant, would intervene?

While they were discussing what to do, Shelley came in. He had heard the story too, and with his usual quixotic impulsiveness, 'proposed that we should mount and arm ourselves as well as we could, set off immediately for Lucca, and endeavour to rescue the prisoner when brought out for execution'. This, he had heard, was to be on the very next day. Byron, calmer and more practical than Shelley, saw that his plan was not very likely to succeed, though, if all else failed, he said he would join them. In the meantime, let them try to get all the English residents in Pisa to sign a petition to the Grand Duke, and then meet again in the evening.

Shelley and Medwin returned after dinner to the Palazzo Lanfranchi, and Byron sent off a note to Taaffe, the only Roman Catholic in the group of friends, to solicit his help. Shelley got back home at two in the morning, and Byron sent a servant round with Taaffe's reply as soon as he received it. Taaffe, from his knowledge of the Lucchesi, was not disposed to believe the story. Byron himself replied to Taaffe: 'Your reasons may be good and true, but ought not to weigh against the possibility even of saving a human creature.' And he urged him to go over to Lucca, which he knew well. In his note to Shelley Byron asked him to write at once to Lord Guilford, whom he had met in Rome in 1819. But he must be quick, as Lord Guilford was leaving next morning. Shelley wrote as soon as he had Byron's note and gave it to Byron's servant to deliver. Taaffe replied to Byron's second note at two in the morning, and promised to go over to Lucca to find out the truth of the matter, and to take whatever action might be necessary. Arrived there, he discovered that the prisoner, who was a Florentine, had surrendered to the Tuscan police.

Even before Taaffe got back to Pisa Shelley learnt that the danger of an auto-da-fé was over. He wrote a note to Byron: 'I hear this morning that the design which certainly had been in contemplation of burning my fellow serpent has been abandoned and that he has been condemned to the galleys.' Lord Guilford had apparently already left for Leghorn, but there was no longer any need to appeal to him. Byron wrote to Tom Moore on the back of Shelley's note, and also sent him Taaffe's second note, in which he promised to go to Lucca, as the easiest way of telling him a story he would enjoy. He explained Shelley's allusion to his fellow serpent. 'Goethe's Mephistopheles calls the serpent who tempted Eve, "my Aunt the renowned Snake," and I always insist that Shelley is nothing but one of her nephews walking about on the tip of his tail.'

On 2 January news reached Byron of the suicide of Polidori, which had taken place the previous August. Byron attributed it to disappointment of his hopes for literary success, following on the publication of *The Vampyre*. (In fact it was due to gambling losses.) The day was also Byron's wedding-day, 'the most wretched day of my existence', he called it, on which the receipt of bad news was appropriate. Besides, Taaffe had been in 'with a most portentous and obstetrical countenance, and it seems he has been bringing forth an ode. . . . He threatened to inflict, as Shelley calls it; but I fought off.' Even though the melancholy anniversary of his wedding fell on a Wednesday this year, Byron would not put off the weekly dinner-party. In addition to the usual company – Shelley, Medwin, Williams and Taaffe – Counts Ruggero and Pietro Gamba were present, and also a newly arrived visitor to Pisa, Captain John Hay. This was exceptional, for Byron preferred to avoid the visiting English, but he was delighted to see Hay, who was an old friend from the years of fame in London. Besides, there was an ironic propriety in his presence at the dinner-party this evening, for Byron once betted him fifty guineas that he would never marry; perhaps it was Hay who now rose to propose the hearty toast to Lady Byron's health. 'We all drank it in bumpers,' says Medwin. But Byron was not at his best on this occasion; his gaiety was forced and unnatural, and he could not help coming back to the topic of his marriage and separation.

Normally on these occasions he was in the liveliest spirits, and the conversation would be of less melancholy matters:

their different attitudes to religion, for example. 'You are a Protestant,' he said to Shelley, 'you protest against all religions.' For himself, he wished he had been born a Catholic, like Taaffe, instead of a Calvinist. 'That purgatory of theirs is a comfortable doctrine; I wonder the reformers gave it up, or did not substitute something as consolatory in its room. It is an improvement on the transmigration, Shelley, which all your wiseacre philosophers taught.' Shelley would have recognised this as a prelude to another attack on Plato, and on his addiction to Platonism. 'You believe in Plato's three principles,' Byron went on. 'Why not in the Trinity? One is not more mystical than the other.' Or Byron might talk about the Italian custom of *serventismo* in which to his own ironic amusement he had become involved: 'Cavalier Servitude,' he called it, 'a man actually becomes a piece of female property,' and he could not help laughing at his own subjection to Teresa, learning to 'double a shawl with considerable alacrity', and so forth.

Then there were literary plans to talk of, with Shelley alone for the most part, since his judgment was the only one that mattered. Above all there was Byron's proposal, with which Shelley most gladly concurred, that Leigh Hunt should come out to Italy to edit a journal. He had made a similar suggestion some months before to Tom Moore, when he was thinking of returning to England – Moore had proposed such a venture to Byron in 1812 – but Byron did not return to England, and nothing came of it. But when Shelley visited Byron at Ravenna in August, they talked of the idea again, and Hunt was suggested as editor in place of Moore. It seemed to be an excellent suggestion, for Hunt was an experienced and capable editor, and though Byron did not admire his writings he respected his character and his liberal opinions. Indeed he and Shelley had discussed inviting Hunt to come out to Italy when they had been together in Venice three years before. As soon as Shelley got back to Pisa he wrote to Hunt to tell him of Byron's proposal, and to urge him to accept:

He proposes that you should come and go shares with him and

me, in a periodical work, to be conducted here; in which each of the contracting parties should publish all their original compositions, and share the profits. He proposed it to Moore, but for some reason it was never brought to bear. There can be no doubt that the profits of any scheme in which you and Lord Byron engage, must, from various yet cooperating reasons, be very great. As to myself, I am, for the present, only a sort of link between you and him, until you can know each other and effectuate the arrangement; since (to entrust you with a secret which, for your sake, I withhold from Lord Byron), nothing would induce me to share in the profits, and still less in the borrowed splendour, of such a partnership.

Shelley's modesty was not the only motive here; he always refused to incur any obligation to Byron, and, as he told Hunt in this letter, he had not cared to ask Byron to lend Hunt the money for the passage to Italy. If he needed help, Horace Smith would oblige.

Hunt replied on 7 September, disinclined to accept the proposal; but a fortnight later he changed his mind. 'We are coming,' he wrote to Shelley and Mary, 'we hope to set off in a month from the date of this letter.' Shelley wrote as soon as he had Hunt's letter, advising him in response to Hunt's inquiry, to come by sea direct to Leghorn: 'Lord Byron is expected every day, and I know will be delighted to hear of your coming.' Shelley would find lodgings for the Hunts as soon as he knew when to expect them. They sailed from London on the *Jane* on 16 November, but bad weather made them put in first to Ramsgate and then to Dartmouth. Postal delay prevented news of this reaching Shelley, and on 11 December he was expecting them daily. By this date Byron had agreed to let them have apartments in the Palazzo Lanfranchi. (Shelley, who was well aware of the size and unruliness of Hunt's family might have warned him against this.) By 31 December there was still no news of them, and Shelley was anxious for their safety, for the weather had been violently stormy. 'The wind was beyond anything I ever remember, and all the shores of the Mediterranean are strewn with wrecks.' Was Hunt's ship among these? Ten days later there was still no news. 'We expect Hunt here every day and remain in great anxiety on account of the heavy gales which he must have encountered at Christmas.' (The Hunts were spending Christmas comfortably ashore in England.) 'Lord Byron,' Shelley told Peacock, 'has fitted up the lower apartments of his palace for him, and Hunt will be agreeably surprised to find a commodious lodging prepared for him after the fatigues and dangers of his passage.' But Hunt did not finally set sail for another four months.

In December Byron and Shelley both began writing again, and both took up tragedies on subjects long considered. Twenty years before, Byron, then a thirteen-year-old schoolboy, read the story of Kruitzner in Harriet Lee's *Canterbury Tales* and attempted to make it into a drama, which he called *Ulric and Ilvina*. This he destroyed, but in 1815 he tried again, but again abandoned it and left the manuscript behind in England when he went to Switzerland. Now he thought of it once more, and in October asked Hobhouse to see if he could find the old manuscript of the first act. Hobhouse could not, so Byron rewrote it and completed the play of *Werner* in six weeks. He gave Shelley the manuscript to read as he completed each act, and during January Mary read it to Shelley and the Williamses. Shelley's interest in the subject of Charles I for a tragedy dated at least from 1818 when he was urging Mary to attempt it. When she would not, as with *The Cenci*, which at first he wished her to write, Shelley himself decided to make the attempt, and, though in February 1821 he had not yet begun writing, he told Ollier that 'when once I see and feel I can write it, it is already written'; and he sent to England for some histories of the time. He was still considering the subject, but had not begun writing, in September; but a few weeks later, encouraged by his rapid progress with *Hellas*, he told Ollier it would be ready in the spring. In January he repeated this promise. By then he had begun writing, but was not finding it easy: 'I am now engaged in Charles the 1st,' he told Peacock, 'and a devil of a nut it is to crack.' On 7 January he read what he had written to Williams, who decided that, if he continued as he had begun, it would be the best historical play since Shakespeare.

A week later, on 14 January, another Englishman, whom Medwin and Williams had met at Geneva in the summer of 1820, arrived in Pisa, Edward John Trelawny. He had been back in England since the late autumn of 1820, but Williams kept up a correspondence with him, and Medwin's account of Shelley, when they were together in Geneva, made him eager to meet so unusual and so gifted a being. Trelawny, a Cornishman of good family, had cast himself for the role of a romantic Byronic adventurer, and he looked the part. He was the same age as Shelley. Mary soon saw through his histrionics and summed him up in her journal five days after he arrived.

Trelawny is extravagant – un giovane stravagante (though not as the Venetian gondoliere meant) partly natural and partly perhaps put on, but it suits him well, and if his abrupt but not unpolished manners be assumed, they are nevertheless in unison with his Moorish face (for he looks Oriental yet not Asiatic) his dark hair, his Herculean form, and then there is an air of extreme good nature which pervades his whole counenance, especially when he smiles, which assures me that his heart is good. He tells strange stories of himself, horrific ones, so that they harrow one up, while with his emphatic but unmodulated voice, his simple yet strong language, he portrays the most frightful situations. [In fact he had served in the East with the Royal Navy.] Then all these adventures took place between the ages of thirteen and twenty. I believe them now I see the man, and, tired, with the everyday sleepiness of human intercourse, I am glad to meet with one, who, among other valuable qualities, has the rare merit of interesting my imagination.

There spoke the novelist, as well as the woman excited by Trelawny's masculinity. It was intriguing to have a creature of Albe's imagination put on flesh and blood.

Trelawny for his part expected to be excited by the company in which he now found himself. His description of first meeting

Shelley is well known, but must be quoted again. Trelawny arrived late and, after dining, went round to the Tre Palazzi to see the Williamses:

... We had a great deal to communicate to each other, and were in loud and animated conversation, when I was rather put out by observing in the passage near the open door, opposite to where I sat, a pair of glittering eyes steadily fixed on mine; it was too dark to make out whom they belonged to. With the acuteness of a woman, Mrs. Williams's eyes followed the direction of mine, and going to the doorway, she laughingly said,

'Come in, Shelley, it's only our friend Tre just arrived.'

Swiftly gliding in, blushing like a girl, a tall thin stripling held out both his hands; and although I could hardly believe as I looked at his flushed, feminine, and artless face that it could be the Poet, I returned his warm pressure. After the ordinary greetings and courtesies he sat down and listened. I was silent from astonishment: was it possible this mild-looking, beardless boy, could be that veritable monster at war with all the world? – excommunicated by the Fathers of the Church, deprived of his civil rights by the fiat of a grim Lord Chancellor, discarded by every member of his family, and denounced by the rival sages of our literature as the founder of a Satanic school? I could not believe it; it must be a hoax. He was habited like a boy, in a black jacket and trowsers, which he seemed to have outgrown, or his tailor, as is the custom, had most shamefully stinted him in his 'sizings'. Mrs. Williams saw my embarrassment, and to relieve me asked Shelley what book he had in his hand? His face brightened, and he answered briskly:

'Calderon's Magico Prodigioso, I am translating some passages in it.'

'Oh, read it to us!'

Shoved off from the shore of common-place incidents that could not interest him, and fairly launched on a theme that did, he instantly became oblivious of everything but the book in his hand. The masterly manner in which he analysed the genius of the author, his lucid interpretation of the story, and the ease with which he translated into our language the most subtle and imaginative passages of the Spanish poet, were marvellous, as was his command of the two languages. After this touch of his quality I no longer doubted his identity; a dead silence ensued; looking up, I asked,

'Where is he?'

Mrs. Williams said, 'Who? Shelley? Oh, he comes and goes like a spirit, no one knows when or where.'

So began a devotion which would last unimpaired until, after a life of nearly ninety years, Trelawny's ashes were interred in the grave which he had chosen, next to Shelley's.

CHAPTER NINE

The Pisa Circle

JANUARY–MAY 1922: ITALY

On the day after Trelawny's arrival in Pisa Shelley and Williams introduced him first to Taaffe, and then, when they judged Byron would be up and about, they took him over to the Palazzo Lanfranchi. Byron at once detected the source of Trelawny's romantic appeal. He told Teresa: 'I have met today the personification of my Corsair. He sleeps with the poem under his pillow, and all his past adventures and present manners aim at this personification.' Teresa said she was curious to see him. 'You will not like him,' said Byron. And indeed when she did see him she was so alarmed that she asked Byron not to go on meeting him. Byron laughed at her, and took no notice. For Trelawny this scepticism was embarrassing: Byron, he considered, should show more respect to his own creation, and not regard him as so palpably fictitious. Fortunately, characters imagined by poets seldom assume human shape to confront their creators. 'I had come,' Trelawny admitted, 'prepared to see a solemn mystery, and so far as I could judge from the first act it seemed to me very like a solemn farce.' The poet who had invented Trelawny ought, in Trelawny's opinion, to take him seriously as a real, living human creature, and to remember that *The Corsair* was not a comedy. What if Trelawny's interpretation of the role were false? Or if Byron should perceive that Trelawny, with his fierce aspect and booming voice, had rendered it comic? Perish the thought! But under the sharp and humorous observation of Byron such thoughts refused to perish.

Whatever doubts Byron, and Mary too, had about the genuineness of Trelawny's character, or the truth of his stories of his experiences, they all realised that he knew more about boats and sailing than anyone else in their circle. Williams, from the spring of the previous year, soon after he came to Pisa, had shared and encouraged Shelley's enthusiasm for boats, and now Trelawny could bring some professional expertise to guide their amateurish efforts. In April 1821 Shelley acquired at Leghorn through Henry Reveley a flat-bottomed boat about ten feet long, into which he promptly had a keel put and a mast and sail. The same evening Shelley and Williams left for Pisa by the canal, accompanied by Henry. Williams soon showed his ineptitude in a boat by standing up and clutching at the mast to steady himself, with the result that the boat capsized. 'I nearly put an end to the Poet and myself', Williams wrote to Trelawny. It was fortunate that Reveley had gone with them, for though Williams could swim, Shelley could not. 'I caught hold of Shelley,' Reveley said, 'and told him to be calm and quiet and I would take him on shore. His answer was: "All right, never more comfortable in my life; do what you will with me." But as soon as I set him down on shore, he fell flat down on his face in a faint.' A peasant family took them in and dried their clothes, and no harm was done. Shelley wrote to his rescuer next day, on getting back to Pisa. 'Our ducking last night has added fire instead of quenching the nautical ardour which produced it: and I consider it as a good omen in any enterprise that it begins in evil: as being more probable that it will end in good. I hope you have not suffered from it.' And he sent further instructions for the boat, to which he added a day or two later. Henry Reveley brought it to them, after repairs and alterations, on 30 April.

During the following months Shelley and Williams spent many happy hours with their boat, generally on the river Arno at Pisa, or on the canal that runs between Pisa and the Baths of Pisa, or on the Serchio. The Italians were astonished at these mad Englishmen, and could not understand how anyone could take pleasure in an exercise that risked life. 'Ma va per la vita!'

they exclaimed. Occasionally Shelley and Williams adventured* on the sea. Generally they were alone, but sometimes Mary or Jane would go with them. Shelley's fragmentary poem, *The Boat on the Serchio*, gives an idealised account of an excursion with Williams (Melchior to Shelley's Lionel), and captures the carefree holiday spirit of these adventures of two friends who

> from the throng of men had stepped aside.

Into his vivid painting of the scene Shelley inserts a quotation from Dante about the hill, the Colle Pisano,

> whose intervening brow,
> Screens Lucca from the Pisans' envious eye,

a passage immediately followed by a reference to the Lanfranchi.† He contrasts his own imaginative relishing of the idle movements of the sleeping boat with Williams' active concern to get her under way. For to Shelley a boat had always been a means of directly experiencing the forces of nature through the wind in the sails or the movement of the tiller, the pull of a stream or the slapping of waves. He conveyed something of this feeling to Williams, so that they both seem to have been exhilarated rather than alarmed by rough weather; but no further mishap yet marred their pleasure, and it was to be expected that they would wish in time to have a better boat.

Trelawny knew from Williams' letters of this interest before he came to Pisa, and he brought with him a model of an American schooner which he had obtained from Captain Daniel Roberts R.N., whom he and Williams and Medwin had known at Geneva. Roberts was now at Genoa and had access to a boat-builder's yard where, Trelawny assured Williams and Shelley, he could build a similar boat for them. The two friends were so taken with the design that they asked Trelawny to write at once, the day after he had arrived in Pisa, to request Roberts to put the work in hand for them. Mary and Jane were told of the discussion, in which they took no part. 'Our

* This was Shelley's word.
† See note 9, p. 271.

husbands decide without asking our consent, or having our concurrence,' Mary said to Jane; 'for, to tell you the truth, I hate this boat, though I say nothing.' 'So do I,' said Jane,'but speaking would be useless, and only spoil their pleasure.'

Next day, when Trelawny saw Byron, he told him that Shelley and Williams were thinking of spending the summer on the Gulf of Spezia, and that they were having a boat built for them in Genoa. Byron, who already knew of their plans, at once told Trelawny that he intended to join them, and asked him to arrange for Roberts to build a second boat for him. Trelawny, warned by Shelley that Byron was very likely to change his mind, waited some days before writing to Roberts on his behalf. But Byron liked the prospect of Shelley's company too much to wish to defect, and he entered into the spirit of competition over the boats. Trelawny, the expert, conducted all the correspondence. For Shelley and Williams, Roberts was instructed to lay down 'a small, beautiful boat about 17 or 18 feet – to be a thorough *Varment* at *pulling* and *sailing*! Single banked oars, say four or six; and we think, if you differ not, three luggs and a jib – *backing ones*! She will be used for fishing, shooting, and as a tender for the other.' The other, Byron's boat, was to be a much grander affair: 'She is to have *Iron Keel*, copper *fastenings* and *bottom* – the Cabin to be as *high* and *roomy* as possible, no *expence* to be *spared* to make her a complete BEAUTY! We should like to have four guns, one on each bow and one on each quarter, as *large* as you think *safe* – to make a devil of a noise! – fitted with locks – the swivels of brass! – I suppose from one to three pounders.' Throughout the early months of the year the boats were constantly in the hopes and plans for the summer which the four men looked forward to spending together.

In the meantime Shelley and Williams continued to sail, regardless of the weather and various mishaps. Once, Williams noted in his journal, they reached the banks of the Arno only just in time – the weather was windy and wet; another time, 'In the afternoon I made an effort with Jane in the boat to put to sea, which appeared quite calm in the offing, but a sea struck her on the bow while launching and a second on the broadside almost swamped her. I got her out however and landed Jane half drowned on the rocks.' Whatever Jane may have thought, Williams and Shelley seem to have regarded such incidents as part of the fun of sailing. Trelawny, 'the crew' as Mary sometimes called him in her journal, seldom accompanied them and so had no chance of teaching them to read the weather and to fear the sea.

There were other pleasures during these early months of 1822. Trelawny's vivid anecdotes of his early life, authentic or not, amused them, Mary most of all; she found him a relief after Medwin and Taaffe, who bored her. Shelley began a poetical drama based on Trelawny's adventures:

An Enchantress, living in one of the islands of the Indian Archipelago, saves the life of a Pirate, a man of savage but noble nature. She becomes enamoured of him; and he, inconstant to his mortal love, for a while returns her passion; but at length, recalling the memory of her whom he left and who laments his loss, he escapes from the Enchanted Island, and returns to his lady. His mode of life makes him again go to sea, and the Enchantress seizes the opportunity to bring him, by a spirit-brewed tempest, back to her island.

Unfortunately Shelley wrote only about 250 lines of the play so that we cannot tell how he intended to transform the Byronic Corsair into a noble savage derived from Rousseau's imagined ideal. And the company of friends in Pisa never had the opportunity of presenting a play by one of their number, though Williams was writing plays there, as well as Shelley and Byron.

Byron said that his own plays were not intended for the stage. Shelley thought this an affectation, for there was nothing he himself wished more than to have a play produced, and he had been disappointed at the rejection of *The Cenci*. Byron knew this, and probably suggested to Shelley that he might write a play for his friends to act, and certainly it was Byron who proposed in February that they should produce *Othello* in the hall at the Palazzo Lanfranchi. He himself would play the part of Iago. Trelawny was to act Othello, Williams Cassio, Medwin Roderigo; Mary should play Desdemona, and Jane Emilia. Williams would be responsible for the décor. No part was assigned to Shelley, who is not likely to have had much talent as an actor, nor to Teresa, who could not have memorised the English lines. Byron, who had once been on the sub-committee of management for Drury Lane Theatre, might 'have made the finest actor in the world', Medwin thought. 'His voice had a flexibility, a variety in its tones, a power and pathos beyond any I ever heard; and his countenance was capable of expressing the tenderest, as well as the strongest emotions.' Mary agreed.* Besides, Byron had seen Kean act Iago in 1814 and greatly admired the performance. He was a talented mimic, and remembered enough of Kean's interpretation to follow him. Both Medwin and Trelawny were much impressed by his acting in the few scenes they rehearsed. But Teresa, for some private reason, disapproved, and after ten days or so the production of *Othello* was called off. Shelley repeated to Medwin a remark which Byron's valet, Fletcher, once made: 'That it was strange every woman should be able to manage his Lordship, but her Ladyship.'

Amateur theatricals might come under the ban of La Guiccioli, and boat-building might incur the displeasure of Mary and Jane, but Byron and Shelley, Williams and Trelawny, Medwin, Taaffe, Hay and the Gambas continued to find plenty of diversion to suit their varied masculine tastes. Captain Hay and the Gambas enjoyed shooting, and went off to the Maremma. Neither Byron nor Shelley approved of blood-sports, but they had better manners than to interfere with their friends' pleasures. Shelley's objection to shooting was not only humanitarian: 'this amusement of shooting,' he

* On 26 February 1825 Mary and Jane went with Godwin to see Kean in *Othello*. Mary wrote to Trelawny about it: 'Do you remember when delivering the killing scene you awoke Jane as Othello awakens Desdemona, from her sleep on the sofa? . . . I wish we had seen it represented, as was talked of at Pisa – Iago would never have found a better representative than that strange and wondrous creature, whom one regrets daily more – for who here can equal him?'

once wrote to Hogg, 'familiarises people with the society of inferiors and the gross and harsh habits belonging to those sort of pursuits.' Hay was the more successful shot, and sent Byron presents of game to distribute among the company. On 20 January Mary invited Edward and Jane Williams, Medwin and Trelawny to dine off a wild boar which Hay had sent. A fortnight later Byron was thanking him for a further gift. Trelawny, who had at first assumed that Shelley and Williams would use their boat, among other things, for shooting parties, would no doubt have welcomed an invitation to join Hay; but Williams had already been converted, through his friendship with Shelley, from the taste for big-game hunting which he had acquired in India, to the writing of plays. Shelley did not encourage Williams to believe that he had much dramatic talent; but Byron offered to write a prologue and epilogue to his second play, to help him to get it accepted for production in London.

There were frequent visits to the opera, which Shelley and Mary always enjoyed, in January and February, and to the theatre in March. Byron seems never to have gone because of his dislike of being stared at, but the Shelleys and Williamses often went to the opera together, and sometimes took Trelawny with them. On 19 January they saw Pacini's new opera, *Il Gioventù di Enrico V*, which Williams judged 'a dull insipid concern'. Rossini was all the rage now, 'talked of, written of, copied, sung, hummed, whistled, and demi-semi-quavered from morning to night', as Leigh Hunt put it. On 18 January Mary confessed that she could not get out of her head the duet, 'Nati in ver noi siamo', from his *Ricciardo e Zoraïde*, which she had seen when it was first produced at Naples in December 1818, and which she had probably just seen again (for she had been to the opera three times in the previous week). A young Scottish tenor named John Sinclair, who was singing in the opera, was much admired. Mary wished to arrange a musical evening, at which he should sing; the prospect terrified Shelley so much that he asked Williams to intercede for him with Mary. 'I will submit to any other species of torture than that of being bored to death by idle ladies and gentlemen.' However, both Shelley and Byron agreed to write words to an air which Jane used to play to them, for Sinclair to sing. Byron's poem defeated even Teresa's loyal attempts to sing it and may be charitably left unquoted. Shelley's is not, as Trelawny thought, the *Lines to an Indian Air*, for he wrote that in 1818 for Sophia Stacey. It may be 'When the lamp is shattered'.

Jane's musical talents more than anything else 'reconciled' Shelley to her after some initial doubts. By January 1822, when he had known her for a year, she was 'a sort of spirit of embodied peace in our circle of tempests', and he wrote to Horace Smith, at Versailles, to ask him to buy a good pedal harp (her favourite instrument) for him to give her. Horace Smith tactfully declined to make a loan for this purpose, and instead Shelley bought in Italy the guitar which he gave to Jane early in April (when the circle of tempests had recently been especially violent), with the exquisite accompanying poem, 'Ariel to Miranda'.

This was not the first of his poems to Jane. On 2 February Shelley with Mary and Jane took a walk through the pine forest of the Cascine to the sea, which Shelley commemorated in a poem subsequently revised into two poems, *To Jane – The Invitation* and *To Jane – The Recollection*. Another poem, *The Magnetic Lady to her Patient*, is about Jane, who learnt from Medwin the skill of hypnotism, then called 'animal magnetism', and who, when Medwin left, used this, as he had done, to relieve Shelley's attacks of pain. (These were probably due to a stone in the kidneys.) On 26 January Shelley sent Edward Williams the poem which begins

The serpent is shut out from Paradise,

together with a note in which he says, 'If any of the stanzas please you, you may read them to Jane, but to no one else, – and yet on second thought I had rather you would not.' The poem, in spite of the humorous reference to Byron's nickname for him in the opening line, is a sad poem; but it is absurd to suppose that this sadness derived from some objection by

Mary to his intimacy with the Williamses. There was no such objection. They lived in the same house and saw each other daily. On this very day Mary went for a walk with Jane, and in the evening Edward and Jane Williams, together with Trelawny, dined with the Shelleys. Mary dated the poem 1821, and Shelley's note to Williams implies, at least, that it had not just been written. It is chiefly concerned with Shelley's despondency over the reception of his poems in England, and the lack of confidence in his own powers that had resulted from it. The last stanza perhaps represents talk with Mary on this recurring topic.

> I asked her yesterday, if she believed
> That I had resolution. One who *had*
> Would ne'er have thus relieved
> His heart with words, – but what his judgement bade
> Would do, and leave the scorner unrelieved.

This was advice which Shelley knew to be in accordance with his own integrity. It was the sort of advice he himself gave Byron at this very time, 'Write nothing but what your conviction of its truth inspires you to write; you should give counsel to the wise, and not take it from the foolish. Time will reverse the judgment of the vulgar. Contemporary criticism only represents the amount of ignorance genius has to contend with.' Mary may have chosen an inopportune moment to offer this advice, when Shelley was feeling more in need of comfort than of such stern stuff, but we need not deduce from this some new estrangement between him and Mary.

Byron frequently consulted Shelley about his own poetry, giving him poems to criticise even before he had finished them. He began *Werner* on 21 December and finished it on 20 January, but Mary read it to Shelley and the Williamses on 8 January. She was reading it again to Jane on the 16th while the men were at their Wednesday dinner-party in the Palazzo Lanfranchi. Williams notes a further reading, this time presumably of the completed play, a week later. Medwin's story of Byron handing to Shelley the manuscript of his next play, *The De-*

formed Transformed, on which Shelley is supposed to have commented that he liked it least of anything he had seen of Byron's, 'and besides, there are two entire lines of Southey's in it' (upon which Byron threw the manuscript into the fire), cannot be accepted. Byron did not begin *The Deformed Transformed* until some weeks after Medwin left Pisa; there are no echoes from Southey in it; and he did not destroy the manuscript. But Medwin's impression of Shelley's candour in discussing Byron's poetry with him is true. He was always candid, and Byron respected his criticism.

Most of all Shelley wished to bring Byron back to *Don Juan*. But first he must get Teresa to withdraw her ban. Eventually he succeeded, and Byron began the sixth canto on 14 April. 'I obtained a permission from my Dictatress to continue it,' he told Murray, '*provided always* it was to be more guarded and decorous and sentimental in the continuation than in the commencement.... The embargo was only taken off upon these stipulations.' But it needed Shelley's diplomacy to negotiate even those terms.

Byron's respect for Shelley and Shelley's tact in handling Byron received further confirmation at this time. In January Prince John of Saxony was on a visit to the Grand Duke of Tuscany, and one of his A.D.C.s, Freiherr von Lützerode, an enthusiastic admirer of Byron's poetry, wished to translate *Cain* into German. Byron had declined going to the Grand Duke's Court and therefore thought it etiquette to decline a visit from the Grand Duke's guests. But von Lützerode called on Shelley on several occasions, and through him obtained Byron's consent to the translation. Some time later, when he had returned to Dresden, Shelley received from him a version of the first act of *Cain*, submitted for his approval, since Byron could not himself read German, in the hope that permission would be given not only to complete *Cain* but also to translate the other dramas which Byron had recently written. Byron especially envied Shelley his ability to read *Faust* in the original; he was at this time making his translation of the Hartz Mountain scene. He also translated to Byron Goethe's

Dichtung und Wahrheit. Freiherr von Lützerode also wrote poetry of a kind, and he wished Shelley to translate his *Swan-Song of the Priest-Murderer*, a task in which Shelley, perhaps because of merriment at the absurd title, failed. A little belatedly, when sending his attempt at *Cain*, he asked Shelley to tell him the titles of his own published works. He assured him that he would never forget 'the methophisical english hospitality of Pisa'.

At the Wednesday evening dinner-parties in the Palazzo Lanfranchi the talk was often of poetry, Greek and Latin, Italian, Spanish, German, English. On one such occasion someone asked what was the best ode written in their own day. Shelley proposed Coleridge's,

> Ye Clouds! that far above me float and pause.

Byron fetched a magazine, and read from it *The Burial of Sir John Moore*, which he greatly admired, especially the third stanza. This he repeated:

> No useless coffin confined his breast,
>   Nor in sheet nor in shroud we wound him;
> But he lay like a warrior taking his rest,
>   With his martial cloak around him.

None of them knew who was the author. Shelley suggested Campbell. 'No,' said Byron, 'Campbell would have claimed it, if it had been his.' (It was by Charles Wolfe.) The choice which the two poets made was entirely characteristic, and worthy of both.

There were social occasions which prompted poems too: a walk in the pine forest of the Cascine with Jane and Mary; the gift of the guitar to Jane; the words to music for Sinclair to sing; and another which provided better scope than this for Byron's genius. Mary and Jane had taken to attending religious services which Dr G. P. Nott conducted on the ground floor of the house in which they were both living – 'for good neighbourhood's sake,' said Mary, apologetically. Jane asked him to baptise her daughter, and Mary stood godmother. Nott was a prebend of Winchester Cathedral, and his chief claim on our remembrance is as the editor of the poems of Sir Thomas Wyatt and the Earl of Surrey. He took his pastoral duties seriously enough to invite Mary to a course of three sermons against atheism, though, when asked, he denied that he was intending to attack Shelley. For good measure, he also attacked heresies in Byron's *Cain.* Byron observed that he seemed to have revised the ninth commandment to read, 'Thou shalt, Nott, bear false witness against thy neighbour.' Nott also shared the contemporary taste for puns, and was heard to refer to 'Shelley lo scelerato'. Shelley laughed, but Byron was prompted to compose, to the tune of *The Vicar of Bray*, a satirical song beginning,

> Do you know Dr. Nott?
> With 'a crook in his lot' . . .

One evening when Shelley and Mary were sitting together, before the servant had brought in the candles, she heard an owl cry, and drew Shelley's attention to it, using the Italian name, *aziola.** Shelley did not know the name and thought it must be an Italian friend of Mary's, 'some tedious woman'. He asked her who Aziola was.

> And Mary saw my soul,
> And laughed, and said, 'Disquiet yourself not;
> 'Tis nothing but a little downy owl.'

Another evening he walked along the river to the Ponte al Mare and jotted down some lines there as he watched the reflections of the houses in the river, or saw the dust and straws whirled about the pavements in the breeze. And he noted the bats, which by now had taken the place of the swallows over the river, bats which still flit silently and swiftly over the Arno, bats which alarmed D. H. Lawrence when he saw them, but which to Shelley were welcome denizens of the quiet summer evening.

Some time in 1821 the Italian sculptor Lorenzo Bartolini wrote to ask Byron to sit to him for a bust. Byron agreed, if Bartolini would at the same time take a bust of Teresa. Early in

**Assiolo*: Scops Owl. *Aziola* is Shelley's or Mary's mishearing of this.

January Bartolini arrived and began work on the clay model. During the sittings some of Byron's friends would go in to talk to him. Bartolini came to Byron's Wednesday dinner-parties while he was in Pisa, and once accompanied the Shelleys to the opera. Medwin thought the clay model an admirable likeness, but he did not see the marble bust, which was not finished until September. 'It may be like for aught I know,' was Byron's comment, 'as it exactly resembles a superannuated Jesuit.'

Apart from welcoming occasional visitors such as Captain Hay and Bartolini, Byron and Shelley were very much inclined to keep to their own small circle of friends, and especially to avoid English visitors. Sometimes one might briefly intrude, only to be dismissed as a bore. Such was the fate of Maria Edgeworth's brother, who was in Pisa during the winter; and when Samuel Rogers visited Byron in the spring he fared little better. On his way to Pisa in the autumn Byron met Rogers at Bologna and crossed the Apennines in his company before parting at Florence. Byron had known Rogers in London, and though he had written some cruel verses on him in 1820, he had some sympathy for his Augustan preferences in style and manner. Shelley also had gone to see him once in London, when trying to raise a loan from him in his capacity as banker, to assist Leigh Hunt; he could not share Byron's estimation of his poetry. But Rogers, like everyone else who met Shelley, was delighted with his courtesy: 'both in appearance and in manners', he remarked, 'Shelley was the perfect gentleman.' At dinner in the Palazzo Lanfranchi, when Shelley and Trelawny were present, Byron, to bait Rogers, began running down Shakespeare. Rogers was not to be drawn. 'But Shelley,' he afterwards recalled, 'immediately took up the defence of the great poet, and conducted it in his usual meek yet resolute manner, unmoved by the rude things with which Byron interrupted him, – "Oh that's very well *for an atheist*," and so on.' Shelley, when he chose, could give as good as he got: once, when Byron was discussing *Cain*, Shelley exclaimed, 'I do believe, Mary, that he is little better than a Christian!'

In Pisa this winter was living a half-sister of the Irish patriot Lord Edward Fitzgerald, Mrs Beauclerc, an old friend of Medwin, who eventually prevailed upon Shelley to visit her. She 'did me the favour to caress me exceedingly,' he told Claire; 'unless she calls on Mary, I shall not repeat my visit.' But if Shelley remained cold to her fashionable gaiety, Mary was not so aloof, and accepted invitations to dine at her house, and once, while Shelley was away at La Spezia looking for a house for the summer, she even went to a ball there. Trelawny was her escort, and Mary was so excited by the unusual experience that she made long entries in her journal for that day and the next.

The enthusiast suppresses her tears, crushes her opening thoughts, and – But all is changed; some word, some look excites the lagging blood, laughter dances in the eyes and the spirits rise proportionably high.

> The Queen is all for revels, her light heart,
> Unladen from the heaviness of state,
> Bestows itself upon delightfulness.*

A day or two later Mary wrote of Trelawny to Maria Gisborne:

He is a strange web which I am endeavouring to unravel. I would fain learn if generosity is united to impetuousness, nobility of spirit to his assumption of singularity and independence. He is six feet high, raven black hair, which curls thickly and shortly like a Moor's; dark grey, expressive eyes, over hanging brows, upturned lips, and a smile which expresses good nature and kindheartedness. . . . His company is delightful for he excites me to think, and if any evil shade the intercourse, that time will unveil. The sun will rise or night darken all.

Poor Mary! After Shelley's failure to arrange for her presentation to the Grand Duchess, his ban on her musical evening for John Sinclair, and his steady refusal of any other social intercourse than the weekly dinner-parties at the Palazzo Lanfranchi, to which ladies were not invited, it must indeed

* Gervase Markham and Lewes Machin; *The Dumb Knight* IV 1.

have seemed an enchanting glimpse of another world to go to Mrs Beauclerc's in the company of so handsome, so virile, so uncomplicated a man as Trelawny. Besides, it was some compensation for being denied the opportunity to play Desdemona to Trelawny's Moor of Venice.

About this time, towards the end of February, Shelley again became temporarily disillusioned with Byron, and the fierce denunciation to which from time to time he subjected so many of his friends – Elizabeth Hitchener, Emilia Viviani, the Gisbornes, Mrs Mason – now came again into his letters when he referred to Byron. He did not, on this occasion, go so far as to hope for his assassination, as in the autumn of 1818, yet he could tell Leigh Hunt in a letter of 17 February that 'many circumstances have occurred between myself and Lord B. which make the intercourse painful to me.'

In writing thus to Hunt he was, for once, not being very candid. Only two days before, in forwarding to Byron a letter from Hunt requesting further supplies of money, he said that he thought Byron had done enough already in fitting out apartments for Hunt and his family in the Palazzo Lanfranchi. To his embarrassment Shelley himself could not help Hunt at this time. He ended his letter with a paragraph which suggests nothing of the disillusion of which he told Hunt: 'I do not think poor Hunt's promise to pay in a given time is worth very much; but mine is less subject to uncertainty, and I should be happy to be responsible for any engagement he may have proposed to you. I am so much annoyed by this subject that I hardly know what to write, and much less what to say; and I have need of all your indulgence in judging both my feelings and expressions.' To Byron Shelley was complaining of Hunt's behaviour, and to Hunt of Byron's. He soon realised the duplicity of this, and a fortnight later he was asking Hunt to 'let my last letters, as far as they regard Lord Byron, be as if they had not been written'. In a letter in which he described Byron as Proteus, Shelley could hardly admit the resumption of an intimate friendship so lately anathematised, but there is no evidence of any serious estrangement between them. Byron provided the sum for which Hunt had asked, and promised not to require repayment until after the death of Sir Timothy Shelley. And, in spite of the warnings he received from his friends in England against associating with Shelley and Hunt – 'You could not give your enemies . . . a greater triumph than by forming such an unequal and unholy alliance,' Moore wrote at this time – he was firm in his purpose to go on with the plans for their journal, *The Liberal.*

Byron's letters of this time have no suggestion of any coolness in their friendship. On the contrary, he went out of his way to defend Shelley in a letter to Tom Moore. 'As to poor Shelley, who is another bugbear to you and the world, he is, to my knowledge, the *least* selfish and the mildest of men – a man who has made more sacrifices of his fortune and feelings for others than any I ever heard of.' Byron was quite unconscious of having upset Shelley, and Williams, in his diary, is ignorant of any offence given or taken. The estrangement was invented by Shelley's imagination, and existed only while he was writing to Hunt.

The cancellation of the production of *Othello* cannot in itself have upset Shelley, who was not to have taken part, though Teresa's ban is said to have been prompted by some trouble over Desdemona. Had she observed Mary's excited response to Trelawny, and feared that Desdemona's passion for Othello might lead to jealousies? If so, it would have been too much to expect Byron to refrain from comment; he might even find here a frivolous justification for his too ready acceptance of Hoppner's slander.

Sudden revulsions of feeling were part of Shelley's nature. Often they arose from his realisation that someone whom he had idealised in his imagination was no more than another imperfect human being. Shelley was well aware of this trait:

> In many mortal forms I rashly sought
> The shadow of that idol of my thought.

So he had written in *Epipsychidion*, and when in June he was writing to John Gisborne about this poem, which he could no longer bear to look at, he came back to this. 'I think one is always in love with something or other; the error, and I confess it is not easy for spirits cased in flesh and blood to avoid it, consists in seeking in a mortal image the likeness of what is perhaps eternal.' Disenchantment, when it came, as it had by then come with Emilia, was total. But he had always had a realistic appraisal of Byron's character, and his chief criticism of him in the past had nearly always arisen from his fear that Byron might not fulfil the magnificent promise of his genius. In this spring of 1822 he was very far from doubting this. 'What think you of Lord Byron now?' he asked Gisborne. 'Space wondered less at the swift and fair creations of God, when he grew weary of vacancy, than I at the late works of this spirit of an angel in the mortal paradise of a decaying body.' And there was more to this effect, which his *Sonnet to Byron* sums up with the same comparison.

> If I esteemed you less, Envy would kill
> Pleasure, and leave to Wonder and Despair
> The ministration of the thoughts that fill
> The mind which, like a worm whose life may share
> A portion of the unapproachable,
> Marks your creations rise as fast and fair
> As perfect worlds at the Creator's will.

Shelley could scarcely avoid comparing Byron's popular success (in spite of the hostile reception of *Don Juan* and *Cain*) with the neglect of his own poetry in England. Jealousy or envy were not a normal part of Shelley's mild and generous nature, but in April, when the brief revulsion against Byron was already past, Shelley could admit, with regret, to a recent jealousy of Byron which, he said, he had allowed to affect the financial arrangements they were making for Leigh Hunt. 'Lord Byron,' he told Hunt, 'has made me bitterly feel the inferiority which the world has presumed to place between us.' But this was not due to some deliberately insulting comparison which Byron had made, for he not only admired much of Shelley's poetry, but was himself more and more coming to accept Shelley's attitude to the writing of it. As he told Moore early in March:

'I think society, as now constituted, *fatal* to all great original undertakings of every kind. I never courted it *then*, when I was young and high in blood, and one of its "curled darlings"; and do you think I would do so now, when I am living in a clearer atmosphere?' Shelley's clarifying intellect had thus influenced Byron, but the bitter feeling of inferiority to him was created by and existed only in Shelley's imagination. Byron's constant presence was enough to arouse it.

Besides, there was always Claire to drip poison into the relationship between Byron and Shelley. She was at Florence, but was being, even for Claire, exceptionally irresponsible. She was planning to kidnap Allegra from Bagnacavallo, and as a part of this plan proposed that Shelley should forge a letter from Byron to the Mother Superior. Shelley wrote to Claire with sharp common sense:

Your late plan about Allegra seems to me in its present form pregnant with irremediable infamy to all the actors in it except yourself; in any form wherein I must actively cooperate, with inevitable destruction. I *would not* in any case make myself the party to a forged letter. I *could not* refuse Lord Byron's challenge; though that, however to be deprecated, would be the least in the series of mischiefs consequent upon my fraudulent intervention in such a plan. I say this because I am shocked at the thoughtless violences of your designs, and I wish to put my sense of their madness in the strongest light.

Mary attempted to calm Claire, by telling her that Bagnacavallo was an exceptionally healthy place, and that Allegra was well looked after there. But a correspondence of this kind with Claire after a quiescent period must have distressed Shelley. Allegra, whose conception had led to the first meeting of Byron and Shelley, seemed destined always both to bring them into friendship and to disturb that friendship.

In one of his letters to Claire, Shelley regretted that owing to his current lack of means (which was largely due to his generosity to Hunt) he could not help her even with any practical plan to rescue Allegra. Byron's means were far beyond his own, and gave him increased power to frustrate any of Claire's projects. Besides, Byron's income had lately been much increased by the death of his mother-in-law, Lady Noel. On Christmas Day – the pun would have appealed to them both – as they went into dinner, Byron and Shelley each undertook to pay the other £1000, whoever first came into his estate. This was tantamount to a bet on the powers of survival of Lady Noel and Sir Timothy Shelley. News of Lady Noel's death, and therefore of his inheritance, reached Byron on 15 February; but he failed to pay Shelley his £1000. Although it seems out of character for Shelley to resent this, yet a quarrel with the Gisbornes two years before had arisen over their failure to reimburse him for his expenditure on Henry Reveley's steamboat, and his present shortage of cash, which even prevented Mary going over to Florence to see Claire, must have caused some irritation with Byron. There are few things which are more certain to cause ill-feeling in a needy creditor than the failure of a rich debtor to pay a debt. Williams, Shelley's most constant companion, thought Byron ought to have paid up promptly, and Mary also regarded it as a valid debt. Yet it would have been undeniably odd, if Byron had paid Shelley, for Shelley then to have used the money to help Claire to remove Allegra from Byron's control. His excuse to her, 'the attempt even is impossible; as I have no money,' was conveniently true, but, as he made clear, there were more serious objections. The regret which he expressed to Leigh Hunt in April was as much for allowing himself to be affected by financial concerns as for succumbing to a temporary jealousy of Byron's success and good fortune. He had fallen below his own best standards, and he admitted it. But, even for a Christian, repentance does not imply the abrupt dismissal from his mind of all recollection of the fault.

Perhaps it was fortunate therefore that these introspective distresses were suddenly flung aside through an incident of violent action in which Shelley and Byron were involved together on Sunday 24 March. They had been out to Cisanello with Trelawny and Hay and Pietro Gamba for their usual pistol-shooting. Williams had remained at home with Jane, and Medwin had left Pisa a few days before. Taaffe had been out riding with a Turkish friend, Mehemet Effendi, but on leaving him he rode out to meet Byron and his party. Mary and Teresa drove out in Teresa's carriage also to meet them. They all met not far outside Pisa, and began to return together towards the Porta alle Piagge. The carriage led the way, followed by Taaffe, Byron, Shelley and Trelawny riding abreast across the width of the road, and behind them came John Hay and Pietro Gamba. In the rear rode Byron's Swiss groom, Giuseppe Strauss. They were ambling quietly home on this fine spring evening, deep in conversation, when suddenly another rider galloped past Taaffe, who was on the left of the four in front, startling his horse, which he could not control. Taaffe's horse bumped into Byron's. 'Have you ever seen the like of that?' Taaffe exclaimed; he was taken by surprise for none of them had heard the approach of this other rider, and, knowing Byron's opinion of his horsemanship, he was prompt to excuse another show of incompetence. Byron at once set off in pursuit of the unknown rider, who was in military uniform; Shelley, Trelawny and the others followed. Taaffe's horse bolted, and he lost his hat. An old peasant woman by the roadside picked it up and handed it to him when he had brought his horse under control; the hat was covered with dust, and Taaffe, fearing that Byron would regard it as evidence that he had fallen yet again, stopped to brush it off. By now Byron and the others were out of sight. Taaffe made no haste to follow.

Just short of the city gate Shelley overtook the cavalryman – he was in the Tuscan Royal Light Horse, and his name was Stefano Masi – and reined in his horse across Masi's path. Masi asked Shelley what was the trouble. Trelawny now came up with Shelley. Shelley politely asked Masi to explain his conduct in dashing through their party. Masi, who had been out to dine with some friends and was in a hurry to return to duty, became truculent and abusive; Shelley thought he was probably drunk. Byron and the others (except Taaffe, who was brushing his hat) now came up. 'Why have you insulted us in this manner?' Byron asked. Masi replied with more abuse. Some Italians who were standing about by the gate, among them a soldier named Tommaso di Marco, observing that a row was in prospect, naturally came down the road to join in. Byron and Trelawny, who both supposed that Masi was an officer, gave di Marco their cards to hand on to him, and Shelley (who had none on him) told Masi his name. Hay alone recognised Masi's badges of rank, and told the others to let him go, as he was not an officer; he could not therefore be called to account for failing to behave like one. Pietro Gamba got excited and joined in the clamour of Italian abuse, and he struck Masi with his riding whip. Masi turned to ride into the town, followed by the English party. As they got to the gate Masi, prompted by di Marco, called out to the guards to arrest the Englishmen. Byron laughed at him and rode on with Pietro. The guards showed no enthusiasm for obeying Masi's orders, which no doubt infuriated him still further. He thereupon blocked Trelawny's way and shook his fist in his face. Trelawny ignored him and rode on, but Masi drew his sabre and cut at him, while di Marco caught Trelawny's bridle and struck at his legs with the flat of his sabre. Shelley seeing what was happening tried to get between Masi and Trelawny, but by now Masi had lost his head, and he slashed at Shelley. Hay deflected the blow with his cane, but it struck Shelley on the back of the head and knocked him off his horse. Masi struck at Hay, wildly enough, for his sabre hit part of the gate, but Hay received a cut on the face. Masi and di Marco then attacked Strauss and badly bruised his chest. Shelley remounted and joined Trelawny just inside the gate. Mary and Teresa in the carriage had seen the fight going on, but they passed through the gate unmolested just behind Shelley. Trelawny and Shelley then realised that Hay was missing. They turned round to find him, but Shelley rode a few paces by the carriage to reassure Mary and Teresa. 'Sta tranquilla,' he said to Teresa, who was in a state of great alarm, though Mary was self-controlled enough. While he turned to do this Trelawny went on ahead and met Masi, who again began to shout insults at him. Shelley then came up with Trelawny, and Masi rode off. They went on to the gate where they found Hay faint from shock and loss of blood; they helped him to remount and escorted him back to the Palazzo Lanfranchi, which was only a quarter of a mile away. When the affray was all over Taaffe arrived at the gate and lectured the Italians there on the cowardice of using weapons against unarmed men.

So far the affair was distressing enough. In Italian eyes the English had behaved with their customary insufferable arrogance. In English eyes the Italians had behaved with their customary hysterical violence. Byron had stood on his dignity as an English nobleman, resenting an affront to a companion. Shelley, 'whose blood always boils at any insolence offered by a soldier' as Mary said, had backed him up, and had revealed a dashing courage quite different from the calm courage which Byron had long known him to possess. The gallant Hay had been wounded, but not seriously, and the whole incident might have blown over in a few days with no worse result than a confirmation in the minds of participants and witnesses of traditional English and Italian beliefs about Italians and Englishmen.

Unfortunately more was to follow. As soon as Byron and Pietro Gamba had passed the gate, Byron asked Pietro to gallop on to the Palazzo Lanfranchi to tell his secretary Lega Zambelli to go immediately to report the affair to the police. Byron meanwhile rode slowly home along the Lung' Arno. Strauss, having escaped from the attack of Masi and di Marco, galloped past him to the Lanfranchi, calling out to Byron's servant Tita to hurry to his master's assistance. Strauss ran into the palazzo, and returned a moment later with a black sword-stick which he handed to Byron, who had now come up. Byron started back towards the scene of the affray followed by Strauss and by Tita, who had armed himself with a couple of sabres. As they left Mary and Teresa drew up in the carriage. Mary had the presence of mind to tell one of Byron's servants, Antonio Mallucelli, to inform Williams what had happened. Byron soon encountered Masi, riding towards him along the

Lung' Arno. Masi's hand went to his sabre. 'Don't draw!' Byron called out. 'I shall not draw,' Masi replied, 'but I want satisfaction.' Byron in reply demanded his name and rank, as he spoke half-drawing his sword-stick to warn Masi that he was now armed. He had turned his horse to ride alongside of Masi, who put out his hand to seize Byron's and to prevent him drawing his sword. 'My name is Masi,' he said, 'and I am a sergeant-major.' Byron is reported to have said, 'We shall see each other tomorrow,' which seems unlikely, after Masi's acknowledgment that he was not an officer. At this moment the huge, black-bearded Tita ran up, seized Masi's bridle with one hand and offered Byron a sabre with the other. Byron, still perfectly calm, refused the sabre and told Tita to release Masi's bridle.

As soon as he did so Masi galloped off, within a few seconds passing the Palazzo Lanfranchi, where various servants of Byron's were gathered by the entrance together with Pietro Gamba. Byron came up shortly afterwards, and saw Masi's casque and *berretta* lying in the road. He told Tita to pick them up. He did not like the look of the crowd which had gathered – one man tried to prevent Tita getting the *berretta*, and the barrow-boy who had his stand just outside the palace, Matteo Giuntini, was fighting to prevent his fruit being stolen – and he ordered everyone into the house. As soon as he got indoors he found Mary trying to calm Teresa. Almost at once Shelley and Trelawny came in with the wounded Hay, to whom everyone's attention now turned. Hay asked Byron if he thought the wound would disfigure him. While they were attending to Hay, Taaffe came in. Byron asked him to go off to report to Governor Viviani who lived a few doors away; on his way there Taaffe heard that Masi had been wounded by a lance-thrust in the side as he was passing the Palazzo Lanfranchi. This was still unknown to those in the Palazzo, for, though Byron was not far off when it happened, his view had been obscured by the milling crowd.

In spite of Mary's message Williams did not come; Antonio had failed to find him, for he and Jane had already gone upstairs to the Shelleys' flat, where they were to dine, and the nursemaid, with the children, was at the back of the house, where she could not hear Antonio's knock. The first news Williams had of the affray was from Trelawny, who came to find him. 'Trelawny had finished his story when Lord B. came in – the Countess fainting on his arm – Shelley sick from the blow – Lord B. and the young Count foaming with rage – Mrs. Shelley looking philosophically upon this interesting scene – and Jane and I wondering what the devil was to come next.' Teresa provided the answer by going into convulsions, and a surgeon, Foscarini, was sent for to attend her. An assistant who came with him gave Byron the first, garbled, account of Masi's wounding. Masi had been wounded in the shoulder by a pistol-shot, he said. Foscarini advised sending Teresa back to her own house, where Byron and Mary accompanied her. Mary, unruffled as ever, stayed with her, while Byron returned home.*

There Taaffe came to report back after his visit to the Governor. He was ill, but Taaffe reported to one of his officers, Captain Bini. Taaffe brought the alarming news that Masi was not expected to live through the night. Byron thereupon asked Pietro Gamba and Shelley, who must have returned to the Lanfranchi while Byron was taking Teresa home, to go to report further to Captain Bini. He asked Hay, in spite of his wound to go too. Lega Zambelli accompanied them. 'All soon again sallied forth to be the first to accuse, and according to Italian policy not wait to be accused,' as Williams noted. This shows Byron's common sense in understanding what was needed in Italy if they were not to have a charge of murder brought against them. It was a shrewd move to have their injured man exhibited first, especially as Hay's still unbandaged wound must have looked worse than it was. Facial wounds are indeed usually rather sensational. On their return Hay at last got proper attention, from an English physician, Dr John Todd, who was living in Pisa; Byron ordered Lega to request Foscarini to look after Masi, at his expense. By nine

* See note 10, p. 271.

o'clock, perhaps three hours after the affray, the rumour in Pisa was that the English had led an armed insurrection of peasants against the heroic guard at the gate, who had been defeated by overwhelming numbers. 'One Englishman whose name was Trelawny left dead at the gate, and Lord Byron mortally wounded, who is now', Williams records, 'telling me the tale, and Trelawny drinking brandy and water by his side.'

The English could laugh at Italian hysterics, but if Masi were to die they might find themselves in serious trouble. Byron had long been under suspicion for his known association with the Carbonari and he was, as he knew, under police surveillance. His friends must also incur suspicion by that fact, quite apart from their extraordinary habits: sailing a frail boat on the Arno, practising pistol-shooting almost daily in the seclusion of a farm, and so forth. The Gambas had already been in trouble at Ravenna, and were exiles from their own home. And Trelawny – well, anything might be expected of a ferocious giant like that. As for the gigantic and hirsute Tita, a Venetian gondolier of all things! One had only to look at him, or to hear that terrible accent. . . . 'Mamma mia! e veramente un mostro mirabile!'

Masi's condition remained serious for five or six days, during which there was considerable anxiety among those who had been concerned. Byron wrote to the British *chargé d'affaires*, Dawkins, at Florence. Depositions were made. Byron's coachman, Vincenzo Papi, who had been driving Teresa and Mary, and, inevitably, Tita were put under arrest. As soon as Papi exonerated himself, Antonio Mallucelli was arrested. But Italian legal processes were no more expeditious in 1822 than they are now, and continued for a couple of months. In the meantime the English showed that solidarity and sangfroid which Latin peoples are required to expect of them. On the day after the affray the usual party rode out to Cisanello for pistol-shooting, watched by a noticeably more respectful crowd of Pisans. Among them was Francesco Domenico Guerrazzi, later to achieve fame as a novelist – one of his books treated the story of Beatrice Cenci in a sentimental manner. At this time he was a law student at the University, and he remembered the sensational stories which heralded Byron's arrival in Pisa, 'an evil genius of superhuman intelligence' and all the rest of it. He made a point of seeing him – 'he looked like the Vatican Apollo' – and he read and was deeply influenced by his poems. Now, on this day after the wounding of Masi, 'I saw all the Englishmen who were then living in Pisa,' he wrote, 'whether they were friends of Byron or not, going off with their arms to his palazzo, to defend their great national poet. And then I thought if he had been an Italian, the Italians would have united to stone him. And so I began to understand why the English are a great people.' On the Tuesday, Pietro joined a party of Italians who were discussing the incident. 'Ah! the only pity is,' said one of them, 'that in ten days the affair will be forgotten, and the cursed English will go abroad as secure as ever.' They were already doing so. On Wednesday Shelley, Trelawny and Williams went for a sail on the river; afterwards they went round to see Byron. On Thursday there was the pistol-shooting party again. By Friday they knew that Masi was out of danger, and as Mary told Leigh Hunt, 'to us, ever since the convalescence of the soldier it has been a matter of perfect indifference.' She admitted that Byron did not share this feeling.

Byron was much annoyed by the particularly inglorious part played by Taaffe, whose complaint of jostling by Masi had started off the whole incident. Mary told Maria Gisborne about this:

> You have no notion what a ridiculous figure Taaffe cut in all this – he kept far behind during the danger but the next day he wished to take all the honour to himself, vowed that all Pisa talked of him alone, and coming to Lord Byron said, 'My Lord, if you do not dare ride out today, I will alone.' But the next day he again changed; he was afraid of being turned out of Tuscany, or of being obliged to fight with one of the officers of the sergeant's regiment, of neither of which things there was the slightest danger. So he wrote a declaration to the Governor to

say that he had nothing to do with it; so embroiling himself with Lord Byron, he got between Scylla and Charybdis.

Even Shelley and Williams thought him much to blame. Jane summed up their feelings about this braggart soldier by nick-naming him False Taaffe.

Taaffe got himself into further trouble by telling Lord Bradford, who had come over from Lucca to find out what had happened, 'that he had nothing to do in occasioning the row,' and asking him to publicise this in England. Taaffe also wrote to Dawkins to ask him to keep his name out of the affair. Byron, to prevent misrepresentation in the London papers, asked Mary at the beginning of April to send copies of all their depositions to Hunt, with a request that he should print a correct account in *The Examiner*. On the 12th at Shelley's suggestion, Mary asked Byron for a copy of the report to the Governor which they had both signed together with Trelawny and Hay. If no notice was taken of the affair in other papers, Mary added, Hunt need not do so, 'for there is no great glory attached to such a row'. Taaffe also went to see Masi's commander, Captain Chiesi, without telling any of the rest of the party, to ask him to guarantee the English against reprisals. Chiesi very properly snubbed Taaffe by telling him that it would not consist with the honour of his men to attempt anything of the kind. Eventually, on 3 April, the same day that John Hay left for England, Byron was formally reconciled to Taaffe. But Jane's nickname, which had been too well-merited, stuck; and the comic figure of the Irishman scarcely reappears.

As early as 7 February Shelley and Williams went up to Spezia, to look for houses by the sea where they might spend the summer in the enjoyment of the boat that Roberts was building for them. Dr Vaccà gave them an introduction to a friend of his named Luciardi at Sarzana. In spite of his help and that of local clerics and fishermen, they achieved nothing, and returned to Pisa late on the 11th with no plans settled. The Masi affray did not make it any easier for them. They did nothing further until 23 April when the Williamses, accompanied by Claire, whom Shelley had invited to join them for the summer, went back to Spezia to try to find a house. Two days later they were back still with nothing accomplished. Next day Shelley 'like a torrent hurrying everything in its course' sent off the practical Mary, with Claire and Trelawny, with instructions to find a house at all costs. By the 29th Mary had rented Casa Magni, a small, slightly dilapidated house with an open loggia in front at the edge of the sea just outside San Terenzo. It was not nearly big enough for the two families, together with Claire and their servants, among whom was Tita, just released from prison*; but it was the only one available. Mary and Jane were far from satisfied with the arrangements, or with the cramping proximity to one another. Mrs Mason viewed the prospect with some concern, and told Shelley she wished the Williamses were elsewhere, and that she dreaded Claire's return to Mary's household. So, no doubt, did Mary.

But a new crisis had arisen which made Claire's presence unavoidable. On the day on which Claire and the Williamses left for their fruitless visit to Spezia, but after they had set out, Shelley heard from Byron the news of the death of Allegra, which had taken place on the 20th. He realised that he must get Claire away from Pisa again before he broke the news to her; hence Mary's urgent mission when she took Claire with her. Mary knew of Allegra's death, but Shelley insisted on breaking the news to Claire himself; in the meantime he needed to consult Byron, as well as to make arrangements for their removal to Casa Magni. He joined Mary there on 30 April, and the next day the Williamses moved in too. On 2 May Shelley was discussing with Mary and Jane and Edward Williams how best to break the news, when Claire walked in. There was no need to tell her. By the sudden, embarrassed pause in their conversation, by the look on their faces, she guessed what had happened.

To everyone's surprise Claire accepted her loss with dignity. After her first excessive grief, Mary said, she had grown tranquil, more tranquil than when prophesying disaster. Byron also was deeply distressed at the news, and felt some remorse

* Tita had acted as Shelley's servant before, when he stayed at Ravenna.

at having left Allegra so far away, against the wishes of Shelley as well as of Claire, even though, as the Shelleys acknowledged, she was well looked after at Bagnacavallo, and it was considered a healthy place. The day after Claire had the news Shelley wrote to Byron on her behalf. Claire wished to see the coffin before it was sent to England; Shelley would go with Claire, he suggested to Leghorn rather than Pisa. 'She also wishes you would give her a portrait of Allegra, and if you have it, a lock of her hair, however small.' Shelley offered, if Byron had only one portrait, to have it copied for Claire; he would return the original to Byron. By return Byron sent a portrait and a lock of hair. In thanking Byron for these Shelley said he had dissuaded Claire from visiting the coffin at Leghorn, on its way to England. Byron had enclosed a wild letter which he had received from Claire, no doubt blaming him for the child's death. Shelley did not know that she had written such a letter; if he had, he would have prevented it being sent.

Byron was too upset by Allegra's death to see the priest and his companion who brought her body to Leghorn. He left the practical arrangements for sending it to England to Teresa, and he wrote to Murray about his wishes for the funeral service. She was to be buried at Harrow, in the church, near a monument to Thomas Ryves, which Byron recalled. She was to be commemorated in a marble tablet, inscribed:

In memory of
Allegra,
daughter of G.G. Lord Byron,
who died at Bagnacavallo,
in Italy, April 20th, 1822,
aged five years and three months.
'I shall go to her, but she shall not return to me.'
2[d] Samuel, XII. 23.

But the prudery of parishioners and churchwardens forbade this public acknowledgment of Allegra's illegitimacy, and she was buried in the church porch on 10 September without a memorial.

Shelley's grief for the loss of the little girl to whom he had stood as a father during the first fifteen months of her life, and whom he had loved so much, was intense. On the evening of 6 May he and Williams were walking by the shore, watching the moonlight on the sea. Shelley 'complained of being unusually nervous,' Williams wrote in his diary,

> and stopping short he grasped me violently by the arm and stared steadfastly on the white surf that broke upon the beach under our feet. Observing him sensibly affected, I demanded of him if he was in pain – but he only answered saying, 'There it is again! There!' He recovered after some time, and declared that he saw, as plainly as then he saw me, a naked child rise from the sea, clap its hands as if in joy, and smiling at him. This was a trance that it required some reasoning and philosophy entirely to awaken him from, so forcibly had the vision operated on his mind.

Fortunately there were the practical problems of settling in at Casa Magni to occupy them, and a long summer by the sea to look forward to. The Williamses, as in Pisa, were occupying part of the same house, even if Casa Magni was big enough to allow them only one room, instead of a floor, but Shelley and Williams would be out in their boat all day and every day as soon as she arrived. Roberts had written to Trelawny to say that she would be launched on 21 March. From a later letter it seemed that she should be fitted out by the second week in April. Now, at the beginning of May they were on the look-out for her, expecting her any day.

CHAPTER TEN

The Death of Shelley

MAY–AUGUST 1822: ITALY

BAD weather in the Gulf of Spezia delayed the boat's arrival. Williams' journal records the impatience and the anxiety with which he and Shelley waited for her. On 8 May they heard from Trelawny that she would arrive next day: 'every eye strained in hope of seeing the boat come in.' But on the 9th she did not come, and on the 10th, when there was a heavy swell and the weather was threatening, they heard that she had not risked putting out. Next day was again cloudy and threatening, with distant thunderstorms; Shelley and Williams went into Lerici to see if they could get further news. On the 12th, a Sunday, Williams noted that the weather was once again cloudy and threatening. Maglian, the harbour master at Lerici, called after dinner, and

while walking with him on the terrace, we discovered a strange sail coming round the point of Porto Venere, which proved at length to be Shelley's boat. She had left Genoa on Thursday last [May 9th] but had been driven back by the prevailing bad winds. A Mr Heslop and two English seamen brought her round and they speak most highly of her performance. She does indeed excite my surprise and admiration. Shelley and I walked to Lerici, and made a stretch off the land to try her: and I find she fetches whatever she looks at. In short we have now a perfect plaything for the summer.

Shelley wrote a couple of days later to thank Captain Roberts:

She is a most beautiful boat, and so far surpasses both mine and Williams's expectations that it was with some difficulty that we could persuade ourselves that you had not sent us the *Bolivar* [the boat Roberts was building for Byron] by mistake. I do not know how I can express, much less repay, my obligation to you for having sacrificed so much of your time and attention as must have been requisite to produce anything so complete.

He soon wrote off to Byron and Trelawny to tell them of her arrival, and of his delight in her. 'She serves me at once for a study and a carriage,' he told Byron; and he was looking forward to the arrival of the *Bolivar* in about a fortnight.

Shelley's boat was twenty-four feet in length, with a beam of eight feet, and drawing four feet. She was undecked and Torbay-rigged, fast and light – too light, in fact, for she needed two tons of pig-iron to bring her down to her bearings and even then, said Trelawny, was very crank in a breeze. Two days after she arrived Shelley and Williams, going out in the tail of a south-westerly gale, discovered this defect: 'she required more reefs than we found in her sails,' Shelley told Roberts. They retained the services of one of the sailors who had brought her from Genoa, an English lad named Charles Vivian, to replace Shelley's Italian servant, Domenico, who had helped them in the earlier boat. Shelley was eager to race his boat against the feluccas or other large craft in the bay, he told Trelawny: 'she passes the small ones as a comet might pass the dullest planets of the Heavens.' Experience would teach them what modifications in her sails or gear might be necessary.

In the meantime their enjoyment was unbounded. On 15 May Mary and Jane went for a sail with their husbands to Porto Venere and back: 'the boat sailed like a witch.' The sea was covered with Portuguese men-of-war, brought in by the recent heavy weather. On the 18th Shelley and Williams sailed to what they called the outer island, Isola del Tino, and were delighted to discover beyond it another, Isola del Tinetto, which they named the Syren's rock.

This name was chosen in consequence of hearing at the time we were beating to windward to weather it, a sort of low murmuring, which as if by magic seemed to proceed from all parts of our boat, now on the sea, now here now there. . . . The Syren's island was well named for standing in close to observe it, from a strong current setting towards it the boat was actually attracted so close that we had only time to tack and save ourselves from its alluring voice.

They found, as owners of boats always find, plenty of work to do on the *Don Juan*. They made a light dinghy of canvas and reed, a sort of curragh it seems, to carry with her. Williams discovered he was not very skilful at the job, and after ten days' work dismantled all he had done. Eventually he finished his task on 12 June: she was light enough for the two of them to carry, and she could be stowed on board.

Then there was the problem of the disfigured mainsail to attend to. Shelley had from the first accepted the name which Trelawny proposed for his boat, *Don Juan*. However when she arrived they were all dismayed to see the name painted in large letters on the mainsail. Mary was especially indignant: it made the boat look like a coal-barge, she said. They supposed that Byron had in his vanity asked Roberts to have the name painted on the sail, but even at the risk of offending him, they could not have her beauty marred by these large black letters. (The days of racing yachts with class letters and numbers blatantly inscribed on their sails were not yet.) It was easier said than done, however, and, though they consulted Maglian about erasing the letters, in the end they had to cut them out and have a new piece let in. When that was done they were satisfied with her appearance. Her sailing capacity they looked forward to testing during the summer months that stretched enticingly before them.

When Trelawny came down in June he 'found Shelley in ecstasy with his boat, and Williams as touchy about her reputation as if she had been his wife. They were hardly ever out of her, and talked of the Mediterranean as a lake too confined and tranquil to exhibit her seagoing excellence. They longed to be on the broad Atlantic, scudding under bare poles in a heavy sou'wester, with plenty of sea-room.' Trelawny, writing, it is true, with the benefit of hindsight, was sceptical.

He went out for a sail with them, and was favourably impressed by Williams' seamanship. But Shelley! Shelley had a book in his hand, and claimed that he could read and steer at the same time 'as one was mental, the other mechanical'. He was, needless to say, awkward and clumsy as well as inattentive, and incapable of carrying out Williams' orders. Williams reprimanded him. 'Shelley was, however, so happy and in such high glee, and the nautical terms so tickled his fancy, that he even put his beloved Plato in his pocket, and gave his mind up to fun and frolic.' This was in contrast to Byron who, in spite of his shipwreck in *Don Juan* II, resented the time, toil and trouble which it cost him to get his sea-terms right, and confessed to being a land-lubber. Trelawny was not satisfied. 'You will do no good with Shelley,' he told Williams, 'until you heave his books and papers overboard; shear the wisps of hair that hang over his eyes; and plunge his arms up to the elbow in a tar-bucket.' But for him as for Williams the *Don Juan* was simply a plaything, a relief from the anxious and often sad world ashore; it was of the very essence of Shelley's pleasure in his yacht that he refused to take its demands seriously. Trelawny warned him that if a squall had caught them when they were in the muddle they had just been in they would have had to swim for it. 'Not I,' said Shelley gaily, 'I should have gone down with the rest of the pigs in the bottom of the boat,' that is with the ballast of pig-iron.

Mary, in spite of her misgivings about the *Don Juan*, yet found some pleasure in occasionally sailing with Shelley. She was three months pregnant and suffering 'from languor and hysterical affections' (as Shelley described her condition), and the cramped quarters at Casa Magni which she had to share with Jane and with Claire added to her irritability. Claire fortunately left for Florence before long, on 21 May, but Jane was 'by no means acquiescent,' Shelley observed; 'she pines after her own house and saucepans to which no one can have a claim except herself. – It is a pity that anyone so pretty and amicable should be so selfish.' This was all very well: Shelley and Edward Williams were out in the boat all day and every day, unconcerned with saucepans and the feeding of small children.

But even they had reminders of the less idyllic world. The Masi affray was not yet settled, and on 16 May Shelley wrote to Byron, who, reluctant as ever to move, was still lingering in Pisa, to say he had heard from Lega Zambelli, Byron's secretary, urging him, in incomprehensible Italian legal terms, to prosecute Masi for assault. This he was most unwilling to do, not only because of his natural generosity, but because he did not wish to go on with the tiresome business. But Byron wrote by return urging him to do so: he himself could not, since Masi had not attacked him, but he thought it necessary in order to protect his servants Tita and Antonio Mallucelli, who had been accused of wounding Masi. He assured Shelley that Masi was not in the least likely to be punished. Three weeks later Shelley asked Byron for news of the prosecution, which he must have agreed to undertake.* 'They say that Masi is to be degraded and severely punished. This would be a pity, and I think you would do well, so soon as our own points are gained, to intercede for the poor devil.' At the end of June Byron was still without news of the outcome. Eventually Masi was pensioned off, and for the rest of his days kept a tobacconist's shop where he used to divert English visitors to Pisa with a first-hand account of Lord Byron's life there. He had the tact never to show any resentment against Byron, but the story he had to relate was rewardingly sensational, and Masi was delighted to be told that his portrait was to be seen in London. Such celebrity might even a chance encounter with the most famous man of the age confer.

Early in the year Byron and Shelley had hoped to find houses where they might spend the summer together on the Gulf of Spezia. But when Shelley and Williams went there in February they could find nothing suitable for themselves, much less for Byron and his large household, and, as Mary told the Hunts, they were a colony, 'which moves all together or not at all'. At the beginning of April they had still found nothing. Byron

* See note 11, p. 272.

then decided to rent the Villa Dupuy at Montenero, just south of Leghorn, for six months from 1 May. Shelley had stayed near by at the Villa Valsovano in 1819, and now, in order to be near Byron, he was willing to accept this change of plan. A week later he and Williams went down to Leghorn and along the coast as far as Montenero to look for houses for themselves but they found nothing to suit them. When, a few days after his return, Shelley heard from Byron of the death of Allegra he had to make an immediate decision, before Claire heard the news, and he must have thought that it would be wise, if Claire was to spend the summer with them, not to take a house too near Byron. He therefore decided on Casa Magni on the Gulf of Spezia, which was much too far from the Villa Dupuy to allow of that daily intercourse to which he and Byron had been looking forward. But this separation had been brought about by urgent need, not by deliberate choice.

Had this not been so, Shelley and Williams would hardly have agreed to take so small and inconvenient a house as Casa Magni, and would probably have found something nearer Leghorn. Byron was very pleased with the Villa Dupuy when at last he settled in there. From his balcony he could see in clear weather the islands of Elba and Corsica, and he rejoiced, he said, to have 'my old friend the Mediterranean rolling blue at my feet'. Besides, in the country there was less gossip than in Pisa, and he could have Teresa, with her father and brother, under his own roof.

Shelley's letters to Byron at this time, and Byron's replies, show the candour of close friendship. On 16 May Shelley was looking forward to seeing Byron soon at Leghorn, and to hearing his news, literary and domestic. Byron replied at once: 'the only literary news that I have heard of the plays (contrary to your friendly augury) is that the Edinburgh Review has attacked them all three* as well as it could.' Murray too had written discouragingly. Byron was beginning to discover the public hostility which had always been Shelley's experience, and his further comments show how much detached self-

* *Cain, The Two Foscari, Sardanapalus,* published 19 December 1821.

appraisal he had learnt from Shelley's criticism of his poetry:

You see what it is to throw pearls to swine. As long as I wrote the exaggerated nonsense which has corrupted the public taste, they applauded to the very echo, and now that I have really composed, within these three or four years, some things which should 'not willingly be let die,' the whole herd snort and grumble and return to wallow in their mire. However, it is fit I should pay the penalty of spoiling them, as no man has contributed more than me in my earlier compositions to produce that exaggerated and false taste.

Whether or not Byron knew it (and most probably he did), he was here accepting Shelley's judgment of his achievement. For Shelley saw that the acclaim which had greeted *Childe Harold* and the Tales had given Byron that encouragement which any poet needs, but of which he himself had so long felt the lack; and he supposed that it was because of this that Byron had lately had the power to move on regardless of popular taste to his greatest poetry. Without the success of the earlier poetry not even Byron could have gone on. Inevitably Shelley compared Byron's experience to his own, without jealousy, but in clear-sighted admiration. 'I write little now,' Shelley told John Gisborne in June; 'it is impossible to compose except under the strong excitement of an assurance of finding sympathy in what you write. . . . Lord Byron is in this respect fortunate. He touched a chord to which a million hearts responded, and the coarse music which he produced to please them disciplined him to the perfection to which he now approaches.'

Sometimes the contrast between Byron's success and his own lack of it, between the more fortunate development of Byron's genius and the perhaps too uncompromising conduct of his own, made Shelley despondent. He had abandoned his tragedy of *Charles the First*, at least for the time. 'I feel too little certainty of the future,' he told Gisborne, 'and too little satisfaction with regard to the past, to undertake any subject seriously and deeply. I stand, as it were, upon a precipice, which I have ascended with great, and cannot descend without greater peril.' He could not go back now, to write more popular, more human poetry, such as Mary had so long urged him to attempt; he could not attempt whatever his own equivalent of *The Corsair* and *The Bride of Abydos* and *The Prisoner of Chillon* might have been. It was too late. And to Horace Smith half-humorously he put the dilemma in more personal terms. 'I do not write – I have lived too long near Lord Byron and the sun has extinguished the glowworm.' Not because he had come to feel that Byron's genius was so far beyond his reach that it was not longer worth inviting comparison, but rather because he recognised the truth there had been in Mary's criticism of his poems, in Peacock's, in Byron's; and he could not, yet, see the way down from his metaphysical mountain to the haunts and habitations of men.

Yet his statement that he did not write was untrue. Towards the end of May, only a few days after the comparison of the glowworm and the sun, he told Claire he had been writing during a few recent mornings; and the poem he was writing, though he did not describe it, was nothing trivial, but promised to be among the best he had done. This was *The Triumph of Life*: 'the most mystical of his poems,' Mary called it, perhaps deceived by its incompleteness. She supposed that he had thrown aside *Charles the First* for this new poem, because he found that 'he could not bend his mind away from the broodings and wanderings of thought, divested from human interest, which he best loved.' For once Mary was not being very perceptive. She was far from well during May and June; she disliked their paltry little house; she had her constant forebodings about the *Don Juan* on which Shelley spent so much of his time. Besides, Shelley never discussed his poems with her during composition – *The Cenci* was the one exception – and knowing that he had given up *Charles the First*, which had promised to be another *Cenci*, full of human interest, she assumed that the new poem would be in Shelley's usual vein. Afterwards, naturally, she was unwilling to live again through weeks that in her memory led so inexorably to disaster; she averted her attention likewise from the poem he was then writing.

We cannot blame her, but we need not follow her. For *The Triumph of Life* is not remote, like *The Witch of Atlas* or *Epipsychidion* (which were not at all to Mary's taste), nor even like *Prometheus Unbound* or *Adonais*. It is much more closely concerned with human life as most men know it; also it is more detached and, in that respect, more mature. It shows the strong influence that growing familiarity with Italian poetry was having on him. Petrarch's six *Trionfi* together provide a vision of human life which

> Stains the white radiance of Eternity,

and Shelley took from Petrarch the general conception of his poem, though in detail he owed more to Dante. In *Epipsychidion* Shelley had made some use of Dante, but of Dante the lyrical poet of the *canzoni*. Now he felt that he could learn from Dante of the *Divina Commedia*,

> him who from the lowest depths of hell,
> Through every paradise and through all glory,
> Love led serene, and who returned to tell
> The words of hate and awe; the wondrous story
> How all things are transfigured except Love.

In the previous summer, when Shelley was once again urging Byron to write a great and connected poem, he had hoped that this would stand to their own time as the *Iliad*, the *Divina Commedia*, and *Paradise Lost* had done to theirs: 'not that you will imitate the structure, or borrow from the subjects, of any of these, or in any degree assume them as your models.' Now, with Byron set out once more on *Don Juan*, which Shelley recognised as fulfilling this ambition, might not he too, however diffidently, attempt some new narrative poem on a large scale?

Six years before, when Shelley and Byron made their tour of the Lake of Geneva together, Byron introduced him to the Rousseau of *La Nouvelle Héloïse*. Now Shelley, looking forward to a summer's sailing on the Mediterranean, to be shared in friendly rivalry with Byron, conceived the plan of a

Dantesque poem about the modern world in which Rousseau should take the part played in the *Inferno* by Virgil. This would have been but one episode in the completed poem which, like *Prometheus Unbound*, would no doubt have culminated in a *Paradiso*, where Rousseau could have had no part, but where Love would once again be celebrated as the sole law which should govern the moral world. Shelley had read and greatly admired Byron's *The Prophecy of Dante* published the previous year, and he saw in it something more within reach of his own genius than in the incomparable *Don Juan*. 'The poetry,' he wrote to Byron, while waiting for his arrival in Pisa, 'the poetry . . . is indeed sublime; and if it have not general admiration, you ought still to be contented; because the subject, no less than the style, is addressed to the few.' In this Shelley was writing, without bitterness, of his own experience of addressing the few: it was something unknown to Byron these ten years. Byron saw Dante, as Shelley saw Milton, in his own likeness: 'Dante is the poet of liberty. Persecution, exile, the dread of a foreign grave, could not shake his principles.' For Byron, deeply involved in the Carboneria while he was at Ravenna, Dante was a suitable national hero. He intended his poem for the Italians, and in it foretold, through the mouth and through the metre of Dante, the coming liberty of a united Italy. And he came near to Shelley's view of the liberating power of poetry in describing the poet as 'the new Prometheus of new men'. The poem was a call to action of the kind which he would soon undertake in Greece, for Byron shared the Aristotelian and Renaissance view that all thought is for the purpose of action; but Shelley was coming more and more to accept the Platonic view of the superiority of the life of contemplation, and both *Hellas* and *The Triumph of Life* are thus in contrast with *The Prophecy of Dante*. Byron had already tried his hand, in a translation of the episode of Paolo and Francesca, at *terza rima*, and he used it again with admirable skill for his original *Prophecy*. Shelley had attempted *terza rima*, even before Byron, in *Prince Athanase*, and now wrote his Italianate poem in the metre used by both Dante and Petrarch. By means of frequent quotations from the *Inferno* and *Purgatorio* he constantly suggests Dante's manner, while at the same time retaining the Petrarchan form. So yet once again the interchange of literary ideas with Byron, which had been so valuable in *Julian and Maddalo* and in *Prometheus Unbound*, was inviting Shelley towards one of his finest poems.

Much of the poem, Mary said, was written while he was out sailing with Williams and the boy in his new boat. He could relax in Williams' company; for once he had a friend who would take practical cares off his shoulders, instead of imposing them. And he was in better health than for many years. 'We drive along this delightful bay in the evening wind under the summer moon, until earth appears another world. Jane brings her guitar' – Shelley's gift to her – 'and if the past and the future could be obliterated, the present would content me so well that I could say with Faust to the passing moment, "Remain thou, thou art so beautiful." ' From this idyllic point of vantage he could watch the pageant of worldly life go by, and rejoice in his new-found detachment, content to be withdrawn from participation. In a letter to Horace Smith at the end of June, after referring to the political situation at home in England, he wrote, 'I once thought to study these affairs and write or act in them – I am glad that my good genius said *refrain*.' This was a new mood for Shelley, and it is the mood in which he was writing *The Triumph of Life*. It is very different from Byron's eager involvement in political action, or in political controversy as in the new cantos of *Don Juan* which he was now writing, and of which Trelawny brought news.

There were, inevitably, reminders for Shelley of the imperfection of human existence. There was that irritating inscription on the mainsail of the *Don Juan*. The Shelleys' cook left on 21 May. The same day Shelley's books, which Peacock had sent from England, arrived at La Spezia, but had to be sent back to Genoa for examination. They reached him at last on 29 June. There were more than the usual demands for money from Godwin, against whom judgment had recently been given for £900. There were Jane's squabblings over the domestic arrangements at Casa Magni. Then on 16 June Mary, who had not been well for some time, had an alarming miscarriage. Claire was staying with them again, and Jane was at hand, but, as usual, it was Shelley who took the decisions, and 'by dint of making her sit in ice, I succeeded in checking the haemorrhage and the fainting fits, so that when the physician arrived all danger was over, and he had nothing to do but to applaud me for my boldness.' (For once Shelley allowed himself a little self-congratulation.) Mary recovered slowly, but the experience did nothing to reconcile her to Casa Magni. Two days later Shelley in a letter to Trelawny, asked him to procure for him a small quantity of prussic acid. 'You remember we talked of it the other night, and we both expressed a wish to possess it; my wish was serious, and sprung from the desire of avoiding needless suffering. I need not tell you I have no intention of suicide at present, – but I confess it would be a comfort to me to hold in my possession that golden key to the chamber of perpetual rest.' Was it perhaps the fear of losing Mary that prompted these thoughts? We do not know, for indeed Shelley had never been happier. Long afterwards Mary recalled the tranquillity of soul with which at this time she herself had contemplated death.

Shelley had seen Trelawny on 13 June when he and Captain Roberts brought Byron's boat the *Bolivar* down from Genoa to Lerici. With liberal enthusiasm Byron had decided to name her in honour of the liberator of Venezuela: he had thought of emigrating there in the autumn of 1819. Shelley and Williams were afloat in the *Don Juan* when she came in sight; Trelawny, who had been commissioned by Byron to take charge of his boat, greeted them with a salute of six guns from the brass cannon, embossed with Byron's coronet, which she carried, and Williams set the *Don Juan* to try her paces by the *Bolivar*. The weather was stormy, and it was not until the 18th that Trelawny could take the *Bolivar* on down to Leghorn. When she arrived there Byron was refused permission to keep his boat anywhere but in the harbour, and the officials at Leghorn were instructed to apply the health regulations with the utmost strictness. This meant that he could not take his friends cruising along the coast as and when he wished: it seemed likely that the *Bolivar* would prove to be something of a white elephant. In the meantime Shelley and Williams took advantage of Captain Roberts' presence at Lerici to have some modifications carried out in the *Don Juan.* She was provided with a false stem and stern, to improve the elegance of her line, and with two topmasts which must have increased the instability which Trelawny had already noted in her. They were occupied with this work during the last two weeks of June, and were delighted with the result. In Williams' eyes she looked like a vessel of fifty tons.

While they were busy with the *Don Juan* Shelley heard from Leigh Hunt that he had at last arrived in Italy and was in Genoa. From there he expected to continue his voyage, in the ship which had brought him from England, so as to reach Leghorn about the end of June. Shelley immediately wrote to him a letter of welcome, and promised to come down as soon as he heard that Hunt had left Genoa, to meet him at Leghorn. He was a little apprehensive about the success of the collaboration of Hunt and Byron in the journal, 'this new alliance between the wren and the eagle', and he warned Hunt, who would see Byron before Shelley could join them, that Byron was not at his most genial. He had been much annoyed, Shelley understood, by an anonymous *Memoirs of the Life and Writings of Lord Byron* which had just been published. In fact Byron had not seen the book, though he had heard of it. The author, one John Watkins, had included Shelley and Hunt in his anathema: Byron, he alleged, had collected a literary group in Pisa, 'for the purpose of propagating his principles', which, as was well known, were entirely vicious, and had invited Hunt, 'the proprietor and editor of the most seditious paper in England', to come out to Pisa to edit there a literary journal of comparable disrepute. During recent months various journals in London and Edinburgh had been making similar allegations. A 'Letter from Paddy' in the April issue of Blackwood's

Edinburgh Magazine, after noting Shelley's influence on *Cain*, forecast the coming influence of Hunt on Byron:

Now Leigh Hunt is about to join him, I'll lay a guinea to an apple-paring, that his Lordship sets up an Examiner, or writes a Cockney poem, commencing

> Lack-a-day! but I've grown wiser
> Since Mister Hunt has come to Pisa*r*.

All things considered, it was as well to put Hunt on his guard.

Hunt's arrival at the Villa Dupuy however was in the genre not of satire or invective but of comedy and melodrama.* It was a very hot day, and the salmon-red wash over the villa made it the hottest-looking house Hunt had ever seen. The servants' tempers also were over-heated, and Byron's coachman, Vincenzo Papi, refused an order to fetch water from a spring. (The water-supply was very inadequate, and had already caused Byron to write to his landlord requesting to terminate the lease.) Not only did Papi refuse an order: he had the impudence to declaim against the rich and the aristocracy, and to prate of equality and fraternity and such stuff. The other servants, inevitably, joined in: Byron's cook, Gaetano Forestieri (whom Count Alessandro Guiccioli was using to spy on Teresa), sided with Papi, and the Gambas' servants, who were anyhow disposed to boss Byron's, opposed them. Pietro came in to see what was the matter, and the excited Papi gave him a slight wound in the arm with a knife. At this point Hunt arrived and was greeted by Byron, who had the good manners not to embarrass his guest by noticing that the house was in some confusion, but took him indoors and introduced him to Teresa. She was 'in a state of great agitation. Her face was flushed, her eyes lit up, and her hair (which she wore hanging loose), streaming as if in disorder.' Pietro came in presently, also in a state of agitation, and with his arm in a sling. This lack of restraint on the part of his Italian friends made it necessary for Byron to explain to Hunt that there had been some sort of a row below stairs. Pietro 'was very angry; Madame Guiccioli

* See note 12, p. 272.

was more so, and could not admit the charitable comments of Lord Byron, who was for making light of the matter. They seemed to think the honour of their nation was at stake.' Papi, wearing a red cap like a *sansculotte*, was threatening anyone who dared to leave the house. Hunt looked out of a window, and met his eye 'glaring upwards like a tiger'. Fletcher, who had been sent for the police, had not yet returned, but the hour had come for Byron's evening ride, and he was not to be deflected by a bunch of squabbling Italians.

Byron, 'composed, and endeavouring to compose', went out, accompanied by Hunt and Pietro. The tiger Papi at once threw himself on a bench, burst into tears, and begged for forgiveness. 'To crown all, he requested Lord Byron to kiss him. The noble lord conceived such an excess of charity superfluous,' but readily pardoned Papi, as did Pietro and Teresa. Byron at once dismissed Papi from his service. (If he had not done so the police would have insisted.) The absurd scene quite properly concluded with Shelley. On his way out of Tuscany Papi called on Shelley, 'who was shocked at his appearance, and gave him some money out of his very antipathy; for he thought nobody would help such an ill-looking fellow, if he did not.'

Leigh Hunt, somewhat startled by this introduction to life in Italy – 'I fancied myself pitched into one of the scenes in the *Mysteries of Udolpho*' – went back into Leghorn and took rooms for his family until Shelley came. On 1 July Shelley received news of Hunt's arrival, and that afternoon with Williams and Captain Roberts set off for Leghorn in the *Don Juan*. Mary, who was not well enough to go with them, could hardly endure to see Shelley leave, called him back two or three times, and cried bitterly. But Shelley felt obliged to go, for he realised that it was necessary at once to put *The Liberal* on a sound practical basis, and that without him Byron and Hunt were unlikely to do so. It was half-past nine in the evening when they reached Leghorn, and since the health office shut at sunset they were not allowed ashore. They moored their boat astern of the *Bolivar*, borrowed some cushions off her, and slept on board.

Next morning, even before they went ashore, they heard from the crew of the *Bolivar* that she was about to sail for Genoa, that the Gambas had been exiled from Tuscany, and that Byron would go with them. As soon as they got ashore they met the Counts Gamba coming out of the police office, where they had received an order to leave Tuscany within four days. The reason for this order was not the fracas which had just taken place at the Villa Dupuy, for the order had been signed before that was known, but the government regarded the conduct of the Gambas in the Masi affray as unsatisfactory. However, the real purpose was to force Byron to leave Tuscany without the embarrassment of ordering a distinguished foreigner into exile. Byron suspected as much.

He at once wrote to the Governor of Leghorn to ask for more time in which to arrange his affairs, since, as he said, he intended to accompany the Gambas, having no wish to remain longer in a country which persecuted his friends. He had much to see to. He must give up the lease of the Villa Dupuy; he must make arrangments for his servants; he must decide what to do about the *Bolivar*, whether to sell her – if he did, Mary feared that Shelley would wish to buy her – or to send her to Genoa, or overland to Geneva; for Switzerland, or South America, again seemed to offer havens of peace and liberty. Then there were the arrangments to be made with Hunt about the editorship of *The Liberal* for which he had come out to Italy. When Shelley came ashore on the 2nd, Byron was still intent on immediate departure, but on the following day, when Shelley accompanied the Hunts into Pisa to install them in the rooms that had so long been prepared for them in the Palazzo Lanfranchi, Byron and Teresa meekly followed within a few hours.

Hunt, feckless as ever, had nothing left of the £400 subscribed by Byron and Shelley to bring him and his family to Italy except for £30 providentially withheld by Shelley. The original of Dickens' Mr Skimpole had come to Italy fully prepared to sponge on his friends; he was indeed, as usual, in debt. (Shelley mildly observed to him, 'I relied on your being better off than fortune seems ever to permit a person of generous feelings to be – but we must try to cure fortune of this antipathy.') Shelley told Mary that Byron would have to provide for him for the time being, since he himself had no ready money. Byron had already generously offered Hunt the copyright of *The Vision of Judgment* for the first number of *The Liberal*, and he wrote to Murray on the 3rd, requesting him to hand the corrected proofs over to Leigh Hunt's brother, John. This, as Shelley saw, would be more than enough to set up their new journal. A few days later Byron wrote to Moore to ask him for a contribution, verse or prose, and he wrote again to Murray asking him to give John Hunt the translation from the *Morgante Maggiore* in addition to *The Vision of Judgment*. In the meantime 'everybody is in despair and every thing in confusion': Marianne Hunt was ill, and Dr Vaccà, whom Shelley sent for at once, pronounced her case hopeless; Trelawny was moody and disappointed, after a succession of contradictory orders from Byron about the *Bolivar*; Mary, ill at Lerici, wrote Shelley a letter full of foreboding. In spite of all this, in spite of having to cope, once again, with a variety of practical problems on behalf of his friends, Shelley was in brilliant spirits. So Mrs Mason, on whom he called on Sunday 7 July, told Mary: she remembered his light-hearted mood and his sunburnt face – she had never known him happier.

That same day after taking Hunt to service in the Cathedral, and to see the Leaning Tower, Shelley returned by post-chaise to Leghorn, where he had left Williams in charge of the *Don Juan*. Trelawny went with him. Next morning he went to his banker, Guebhard & Co., to cash a draft for £50 which Byron had lent him. (Nothing could more clearly reveal on what good terms they were at this time, for Shelley had hitherto refused ever to become indebted to Byron.) Then there was some shopping to do before returning to San Terenzo: food, and milk, a gift of wine for Signor Maglian, and so on. The day was hot and sultry, and Captain Roberts suggested that they might do better to wait till next day; but, although Shelley might have stayed, Williams had for days been fretting and fuming to get away, so Shelley, who was anxious to get back to Mary, agreed to sail. About noon they were ready and went on board, Shelley, Williams and Charles Vivian, while Trelawny prepared to accompany them out of harbour in the *Bolivar*. As soon as they were under way the guard-boat came up to look at their papers. Trelawny had not got his port clearance and had to return. Roberts who had seen them on board walked out to the end of the Medicean mole to watch the *Don Juan*, and, at about three o'clock, when he saw a squall coming into the bay, he obtained permission to go up the watch-tower in order to follow her further progress. By then the *Don Juan* was about ten miles out. Through his telescope Roberts saw the crew taking in the topsails; then in the haze of the storm he lost sight of her, and when it cleared could not pick her up again. Trelawny, watching from the deck of the *Bolivar* had lost sight of her some time before: he went down to his cabin to sleep.

He slept for about half an hour and then was called by one of the crew. He went on deck to find a great bustle in the harbour, with the crews of the ships there 'getting down yards and masts, veering out cables, hauling in of hawsers, letting go anchors' to make all safe before the approaching storm. Though it was still quite early, it was almost dark. 'The sea was of the colour, and looked as solid and smooth as a sheet of lead, and covered with an oily scum. Gusts of wind swept over without ruffling it, and big drops of rain fell on its surface, rebounding as if they could not penetrate it. There was a commotion in the air, made up of many threatening sounds, coming upon us from the sea.' Everywhere he could see small craft and fishing-boats seeking shelter in the harbour. Suddenly the sounds of human activity were overwhelmed by the crash of thunder, and the noise of wind and rain. In twenty minutes the storm was over, but Trelawny, looking everywhere among the sheltering boats for the *Don Juan*, could see no sign of her. He sent the mate of the *Bolivar* to inquire for news among the boats which had just come in, but there was none. Next day, and the next, he made further inquiries, but in vain.

On the morning of 11 July Trelawny rode into Pisa, hoping to find a letter from Shelley to tell of his safe arrival. There was no letter. He went to the Palazzo Lanfranchi, where he saw Hunt and told him of his fears for the safety of the *Don Juan.* He went on upstairs to Byron: 'When I told him, his lip quivered, and his voice faltered as he questioned me.' He then rode on towards Viareggio; when he got there he learnt that Williams' home-made dinghy had been washed up, together with a water-keg and some bottles which he also recognised as having been on Shelley's boat.

Mary and Jane, waiting at Casa Magni, were becoming anxious. On the Monday Jane had a letter from Edward, written on the Saturday, in which he said that he would wait for Shelley two more days, but that if he was still not ready, he himself would come up in a felucca: she might expect him on Tuesday evening at the latest. On Wednesday several feluccas came in from Leghorn, but Williams was not on board; they brought news that the *Don Juan* had sailed on the Monday, but it had been such a stormy day at Lerici that neither Mary nor Jane believed that this could be true. When on Thursday there was still no sign of the *Don Juan* they supposed that Shelley or Williams might have been detained by illness. However, Jane decided to go down to Leghorn next day to discover the truth. On Friday a heavy sea was running, and no boat could put out. At midday the post came, bringing a letter from Hunt to Shelley, written before Trelawny saw him: 'Pray write to tell us how you got home, for they say that you had bad weather after you sailed Monday, and we are anxious.' Mary dropped the letter, trembling uncontrollably. Jane picked it up and read it. 'Then it is all over!' Jane cried. Mary, calm and self-possessed even now, said, 'No, my dear Jane, it is not all over, but this suspense is dreadful. Come with me, we will go to Leghorn, we will post to be swift and learn our fate.' They set out immediately. At Lerici people tried to encourage them by saying there had been no report of a wreck, which must have been known had one occurred. Mary knew that Hunt was at the Palazzo Lanfranchi, from where he had written to Shelley; she thought Byron was still at Leghorn.

Mary took charge, and decided that they would go first to

the Palazzo Lanfranchi, before going on to Leghorn, and that when they got there she would get out and ask Hunt, 'Do you know anything of Shelley?' She rehearsed the scene as they drove to Pisa, but when they entered the city Mary's courage almost failed at the thought of having to ask Hunt such a question on seeing him for the first time in four years. It was nearly midnight when they stopped at the Palazzo Lanfranchi. A servant called out the usual inquiry, '*Chi è?*' Mary recognised the voice: it was Teresa's maid. So Byron after all was in Pisa. Hunt, Mary learnt, had gone to bed; she was to see Byron instead. This was a great relief to her, for she had been seeing him frequently these last eight months, and there was none of the embarrassment she had feared at the thought of meeting Hunt in such circumstances. 'I staggered upstairs,' Mary wrote, 'the Guiccioli came to meet me smiling, while I could hardly say – "Where is he? Sapete alcuna cosa di Shelley?" They knew nothing.' Byron did not distress her further by telling her of Trelawny's visit the day before: as he knew, she had just been seriously ill; she had been travelling for hours; and her anxieties were great enough. She looked like a ghost, light seemed to emanate from her features, her face was as white as marble – so Byron and Teresa told her later. They tried to make her rest till morning, but she refused, and went on with Jane to Leghorn where they arrived after two o'clock. Their coachman put them down at the wrong inn, but they were so exhausted that they lay down fully dressed and slept for a few hours.

At daylight they went off in search of Trelawny and Captain Roberts. Trelawny was at Viareggio, but they found Roberts. 'He came down to us with a face which seemed to tell us that the worst was true.' He told them all he could, without trying to hide his fears, but also without suggesting there was no hope. They might have been driven across to Corsica, and, since they did not know the coast, they might have reached some remote place from which communication would be difficult. There was nothing more for Mary and Jane to do in Leghorn, except to arrange for a courier to go north along the coast to inquire at every watch-tower if anything of the *Don Juan* had been seen or found. They set out for Lerici again at nine, stopped a moment in Pisa to leave a note from Roberts asking Byron for permission to take the *Bolivar* up the coast to search, and went on to Viareggio. Here they had the first news of disaster, learning what Trelawny had already heard, that Williams' dinghy and a water-cask had been washed up. Here too they found Trelawny, who went back with them to Casa Magni. They did the last stretch of their journey, from Lerici home, by boat. In San Terenzo there was a festa. 'What a scene!' Mary wrote a month later, 'the roaring sea, the scirocco wind, the lights of the town towards which we rowed, and our own desolate hearts that covered all with a shroud.' The wild villagers dancing on the sands close to their door, running into the sea and back up the sands again, all the time screaming some hateful song, the noise of the wind and the sea, intensified their misery. There was nothing to be done, but to wait for more news, to wait while hope waned as each day passed.

Trelawny stayed with them at Casa Magni for a few days, but on the Thursday morning, 18 July, he returned to Leghorn to see if he could get any news. He told Claire to open any letters addressed to him, and the day after he left one came from Roberts, with the information that two bodies had been washed up. Claire did not tell the others of this, but wrote off at once to Leigh Hunt begging him to come to break the news, for she could not. Somehow, she managed to keep it to herself throughout the long day.

As soon as Trelawny reached Leghorn he heard that two bodies had come ashore, one near the tower of Migliarino, close to the mouth of the Serchio, the other nearer Viareggio. He went off at once to get whatever information he could. The description given him by the health authorities, who had buried the corpses in quicklime where they came ashore, left him in little doubt of their identity. Byron wrote to Roberts a day or two later: 'Shelley's body has been completely identified by a book in his pocket, which was found by the Health Officers upon him, in his jacket.' He was then less certain of the other corpse being Williams'. Trelawny, who was disposed to be somewhat possessive towards Shelley, especially after his death, implied in later accounts that he had seen the two bodies as they lay unburied on the shore, but clearly he had not. However, there was no longer any doubt in his mind that his friends were dead.

Now that he knew, Trelawny realised that he must inform Mary and Jane, and he rode back to Casa Magni as fast as he could, to tell them before they heard from some stranger. When he reached the house – it was about seven o'clock on the Friday evening – he paused a moment to compose himself before going in. As he waited there his mind went back to his parting from Shelley and Williams a month before, when he took the *Bolivar* down to Leghorn. An hour or so earlier Mary, believing that no news is good news, said to Jane that as Trelawny had not come back, she still had some hope. The children's nurse, Caterina, passing across the hall, saw a man's figure in the doorway and uttered a shriek of alarm. Trelawny spoke to her, and then went upstairs unannounced to where Mary and Jane were waiting. 'I neither spoke, nor did they question me. Mrs. Shelley's large grey eyes were fixed on my face. I turned away. Unable to bear this horrid silence, with a convulsive effort she exclaimed – "Is there no hope?" I did not answer, but left the room and sent the servant with the children to them.' So Trelawny recalled the scene long after. But Mary remembered with gratitude how, instead of attempting to console her, 'he launched forth into as it were an overflowing and eloquent praise of my divine Shelley – until I was almost happy that I was thus unhappy, to be fed by the praise of him, and to dwell on the eulogy that his loss thus drew from his friend.'

In the days that followed Mary's midnight call at the Palazzo Lanfranchi Byron also had joined in the search along the coast. On the 17th he received a letter from Roberts informing him that two bodies had been thrown ashore three or four miles from Viareggio. He believed they were Shelley's and Charles Vivian's. He at once set out with Hunt to investigate, and learnt that a body had been buried at the mouth of the Serchio.

They were certain it was not Shelley's, and thought it was not Williams' either. When they got back home Hunt wrote to Trelawny at Casa Magni to inform him of this, but Trelawny did not receive the letter until he got back on the evening of the 19th. Hunt also said that Byron wished to invite Mary and Jane to come back to Pisa, to the Palazzo Lanfranchi if they would, or, if they preferred, to the rooms where they had been living till April. Trelawny urged them to accept the suggestion and next day took them back with him to Pisa. They went to their old quarters in the Tre Palazzi.

A month later Mary wrote a long letter to Maria Gisborne about the disaster. 'And here we are still,' she wrote, 'days pass away, one after another, and we live thus.' They saw the Hunts occasionally. 'Lord Byron is very kind to me and comes with the Guiccioli to see me often.' They had both loved Shelley. In the first extant letter in which Byron refers to his death, written to John Murray on 3 August, he says: 'You were all brutally mistaken about Shelley, who was without exception, the *best* and least selfish man I ever knew. I never knew one who was not a beast in comparison.' Murray perhaps demurred, for he had been one of Shelley's denigrators in the past, and in December Byron again told him they were all mistaken about Shelley. 'You do not know how mild, how tolerant, how good he was in society; and as perfect a gentleman as ever crossed a drawing-room, when he liked, and where he liked.' This had also been Teresa's immediate judgment of Shelley when she first met him. Now they could help Mary by the sincerity with which they shared her grief, by keeping her company, and talking with her.

Byron could help Mary too in some of the practical matters which are inescapable at such times: there was Shelley's will to be executed; there were the financial arrangements to be made with Sir Timothy for the support of Mary and her son; then, where was she to live? where were Shelley's remains to be given decent interment? Besides, Byron would wish to consult Mary about the Hunts, and about the future of *The Liberal*: was she willing to let some of Shelley's poems appear? Would she herself contribute? And Mary would seek Byron's advice about the publication of Shelley's uncollected and unfinished poems. In the meantime Byron gave her some of his own poems to transcribe, as she had done before when in distress at the loss of Clara; among them were the new cantos of *Don Juan* which Shelley had known of, but not seen. How closely, in these last months in Pisa, their two lives had been interwoven!

The most urgent matter was to arrange for exhumation and reinterment of Shelley's body. Mary decided that he should be buried beside their son William in the Protestant Cemetery in Rome. Dawkins, who had been trying, on Byron's behalf, to get permission for the Gambas to remain in Lucca, also undertook to get permits from the Tuscan and Lucchese authorities to cremate the bodies of Williams and Shelley and then to remove the ashes. This took time, and it was more than three weeks before everything was ready. Cremation, on which the Health officials insisted, needed improvisation in a Roman Catholic country: Trelawny had a furnace made in Leghorn, 'about four feet and a half long by 18 or 20 inches broad with a rim of three or four inches'. It stood on four iron legs. This, with a supply of fuel, and with wine, oil and spices to provide Shelley a truly Hellenic pyre, Trelawny loaded on to the *Bolivar* on 13 August, and set out accompanied by a friend, Captain Shenley, then visiting Leghorn, for Migliarino.

The next day was taken up with seeing the officer in charge, who promised Trelawny all assistance, and in carrying the furnace to the spot where Williams was buried. It had been marked by the gnarled root of a pine-tree. Trelawny sent a messenger to Pisa to tell Byron and Hunt that the grave would be opened next morning; about noon they arrived in Byron's carriage, bringing with them the lead-lined oak coffin which Trelawny had ordered. It was very hot, and Byron and Hunt remained in the carriage until the body was uncovered. Byron then got out to look at the jaw. 'I can recognise any one by the teeth, with whom I have talked,' he said. 'I always watch the lips and mouth: they tell what the tongue and eyes try to conceal.' He had no doubt it was Williams. Trelawny had brought a boot belonging to Williams with him: it matched one on the body. Byron pointed to a black silk kerchief about the neck of the body which he recognised as one that Williams wore: 'See, an old rag retains its form longer. What a degrading reflection!' The sandy shore here is always littered with driftwood and the dry stems of reed piled together in a prickly tangle: these the soldiers who had been sent to protect the party against interference gathered together, and they brought wood from the edge of the pine forest; when all was ready Trelawny's furnace was lifted on to the pyre, which was then set alight. Byron and Hunt, Trelawny and Shenley threw incense, salt, sugar and wine on to the flames.

Byron then proposed a swim while the pyre was burning, and he, Trelawny and Shenley stripped and plunged into the sea. Byron swam out about a mile, and was then violently sick, but he would not return until the fire was dying down. Then Trelawny doused his furnace in the sea, removed the ashes and placed them (except for the jawbone, which he kept as a memento) in the coffin. This Byron took back with him into Pisa to deliver to Jane.

On the following day, 16 August, they went through the same ghastly procedure for the cremation of Shelley. Trelawny took his furnace to the place where Shelley lay, and Byron and Hunt joined him. Hunt could not face seeing the exhumation of his friend of friends, and remained in Byron's carriage. Shelley's grave had not been clearly marked, and there was some delay in finding the body. Byron, lacking patience to watch, walked away, and again went for a swim, out to the *Bolivar* which was anchored a mile or so off shore. In doing so he got badly sunburnt, so that a few days later all his skin peeled off. Trelawny stayed by the pyre until the body was consumed. He had hoped to save some relic of Shelley from the flames, if possible the volume of Keats' *Lamia, Isabella, The Eve of St Agnes and other Poems*, which Shelley had borrowed from Hunt that last day in Pisa, and which had been found, doubled back open, in his pocket. But nothing of it remained except the binding, and this was left to burn. When he carried the furnace down to the water to cool it off Trelawny noticed the heart still unburnt, and snatched it out, burning his hand as he did so. He preserved it in spirits of wine. The rest of the ashes he placed in the coffin prepared for them, and carried it on board the *Bolivar*.

Then Byron and Hunt drove off to Viareggio where they dined together before returning to Pisa. The strain of the last two days, of watching while the disintegrating and putrescent remains of their friends were exhumed, the dramatic effect of the two funeral pyres on the desolate shore, between mountains and sea, the sense of emptiness now that Shelley was gone, made the two men almost hysterical as they drove home through the pine forest. 'We sang, we laughed, we shouted,' Hunt remembered. 'I even felt a gaiety the more shocking because it was real and a relief. . . . I wish to have no such waking dream again. It was worthy of a German ballad.'

While the men were busy about the cremations Mary was writing to Maria Gisborne:

Today, this day, the sun shining in the sky, they are gone to the desolate sea coast to perform the last offices to their earthly remains – Hunt, L. B. and Trelawny. The quarantine laws would not permit us to remove them sooner, and now only on condition that we burn them to ashes. That I do not dislike. His rest shall be at Rome, beside my child, where one day I also shall join them. . . . I have seen the spot where he now lies, the sticks that mark the spot where the sands cover him. He shall not be burned there, it is too near Viareggio. They are now about this fearful office, and I live!

CHAPTER ELEVEN

From the Death of Shelley to the Death of Byron

THE Pisan circle – Shelley himself had used the term – centred upon Shelley. He and Mary had found that they could settle there more happily than anywhere else; he had invited his cousin Tom Medwin to visit them; Medwin's account of Shelley had brought his friends Edward and Jane Williams there early in 1821, Trelawny a year later. Shelley's presence in Pisa had decided Byron to find there the refuge for himself and Teresa and her family after her father and brother had been exiled from Ravenna. Finally Shelley had brought Leigh Hunt to Pisa from England to edit there a literary journal which had long been one of Byron's projects. Now Shelley was dead there was nothing to keep the company together. Or, as Trelawny put it, 'the fine spirit that had animated and held us together was gone. Left to our own devices, we degenerated apace.'

There were, indeed, reasons why, even if Shelley had lived, Byron would have had to remove from Pisa. Counts Ruggero and Pietro Gamba were in Lucca, where they arrived on 8 July, the very day on which Shelley and Williams were lost. Through Dawkins Byron tried to get permission for them to reside there: if it were granted, he would remove there with Teresa. But Dawkins was unable to obtain permission for them to remain except from day to day, and before long they went off to Genoa. Teresa, in spite of her brother's warning that Count Guiccioli would cause trouble if she lived in Byron's house instead of in her father's, and against Byron's advice, refused to move from the Palazzo Lanfranchi. It was only a year since she had left Ravenna ahead of Byron; she remembered all too vividly the heartache that had followed, and then she had had Shelley to plead with Byron on her behalf. No wonder she stayed with him now. As usual, he took his time over moving, and it was not until the end of September that they left Pisa.

Teresa's father and brother had now left; Medwin had left some months before; Shelley and Williams were dead. Of the men who formed the Pisan circle (and it was essentially a masculine company) only Byron and Trelawny and Hunt remained. Hunt provided little solace to Mary: he had arrived only a few days before Shelley's death and, not having seen him for more than four years, had not known the mature Shelley who had written his greatest poetry during these years in Italy. He had, Mary said, 'the same want of tact which he ever had', which showed itself in asserting his claim to Shelley's heart against hers. Trelawny had saved it from the cremation, and Hunt wrote to Mary, the very next day, to say that his love for Shelley had been such that 'no ordinary appearance of rights, even yours, can affect me'. Byron naturally took Mary's part – 'What does Hunt want with the heart?' he said. 'He'll only put it in a glass case and make sonnets to it.' – but he could not persuade a man who mistook sentimentality for sensibility. 'Lord Byron has no right to bestow the heart,' Hunt wrote to Mary, 'and I am sure pretends to none. If he told you that you should have it, it could only have been from his thinking I could more easily part with it than I can. . . . I have my moments of impatience as well as you.' In the end, after Jane had intervened, Hunt grudgingly surrendered the relic to Mary. She preserved it to her dying day, wrapped up in the sheets of *Adonais*, which she regarded as Shelley's elegy upon himself.

Byron, in contrast to Hunt, did all he could to help Mary. He gave her the new cantos of *Don Juan* to transcribe. He and Teresa visited her twice a week while she remained in Pisa. She constantly refers in her letters to his kindness and thoughtfulness. Besides, he reminded her most of Shelley, in spite of the difference between their minds. She had always seen them together, had heard them talking together, and his voice had a distinctive quality of its own which carried her mind back to that happy summer in Switzerland when she had seen him almost every day. 'I do not think that any person's voice has the same power of awakening melancholy in me as Albe's,' she wrote in her journal when she took it up again in October. 'I have been accustomed, when hearing it, to listen and to speak little; another voice, not mine, ever replied.' Others, Hunt and Trelawny, Peacock and Hogg, she had often heard speak when Shelley was not present; their voices did not bring the inescapable reminder of Shelley's that Byron's must. 'Since incapacity and timidity always prevented my mingling in the nightly conversations of Diodati, they were, as it were, entirely tête-à-tête between my Shelley and Albe; and thus, as I have said, when Albe speaks and Shelley does not answer, it is as thunder without rain – the form of the sun without heat and light – as any familiar object might be, shorn of its dearest and best attribute; and I listen with an unspeakable melancholy that yet is not all pain.' Byron could help Mary in practical matters too. He believed that Shelley might have appointed him an executor, but inevitably there was delay in receiving confirmation of this. In the meantime he invited Mary to regard him as her banker, and he wrote to his own bankers in Leghorn promising to see that Shelley's creditors were duly paid. When news of the contents of Shelley's will came, in September, Byron was indeed an executor, and Peacock was the other.* Shelley had left Byron £2,000; but this, conscious of the unpaid wager of £1,000 due from his own inheritance from Lady Noel, he declined to accept. Mary thought that perhaps she should go to England to see about an allowance for her son from Sir Timothy Shelley's estate, but Byron advised her against doing this; her presence in England could make no difference. He suggested that Mary should get her father to call on John Hanson, who acted for Byron, to discuss the matter with him. He had mentioned him to Shelley as a

* Shelley had made a later will at Pisa, in which he named T. J. Hogg as one executor in place of Byron, but this was never found.

capable lawyer some time before. In October, after Mary had had a letter from Peacock, at her request he wrote to ask Hanson to apply to Sir Timothy's solicitor, William Whitton, on behalf of Mary and her son. He told his bankers that it would do no harm for them to write to Sir Timothy, if they were concerned about Shelley's debts, to ask him to meet them; it would probably do no good either. 'They were not upon good terms,' he wrote, 'and I have observed that even the tenderest parents are somewhat tenacious on the score of similar disbursements.'

Fortunately there was no urgency, for Mary had enough to live on in Italy. Early in September Roberts salvaged the *Don Juan* and among other things found the money which he knew was on board and which he handed to Byron. Of this part belonged to Jane – it was in Williams' trunk – but Mary received ninety-odd crowns. At Byron's suggestion the boat was sold at auction in Viareggio, and half the proceeds went to the salvors, and the other half to Mary. Roberts himself bought her, and refitted her. Mary also received £36 for Shelley's and her own contributions to the first two numbers of *The Liberal.* In September she could look forward to many long months of peace as to money affairs; in January she told Trelawny she was very well off and had no need to accept the frequent offers of money which Byron had made to her; in March she was again thanking Byron for offers of help, but did not think she would need to accept unless she decided to go back to England. In January Byron wrote direct to Sir Timothy Shelley to appeal to him to make provision for Mary and his grandson. Sir Timothy's letter reached Byron on 24 February. In it he refused to have any dealings with Mary. 'As to the child, I am inclined to afford the means of a suitable protection and care of him in this country, if he shall be placed with a person I shall approve.' Mary refused to accept what she rightly called an 'insolent and hard-hearted proposition', and to surrender her son to the care of a guardian appointed by Sir Timothy. She did not know what was best to do, but now began to think she must go to England, and by April she had taken her decision. Byron was very kind, she told Maria Gisborne in writing to tell her that they would soon meet in England. 'He promises that I shall make my journey at my ease, which on Percy's account I am glad of.' But she could not leave until after Marianne Hunt's confinement, which Dr Vaccà had predicted might be fatal to her. After eleven months in the country this stupid and commonplace woman could not speak a word of Italian, and needed Mary's help.

In the September after Shelley's death Byron asked Mary to try to find him a suitable house in Genoa, as a year before she had found the Palazzo Lanfranchi for him. She was happy to undertake this for him, and the thought that she could be useful to the man whose friendship had meant so much to Shelley in these last six years, helped to restore her confidence in herself. Only a fortnight before she had written: 'I am now on the eve of completing my five and twentieth year – how drearily young for one so lost as I! How young in years for one who lives ages each day in sorrow.' It was good to have a practical task to undertake for someone else, and on 11 September she and Jane went off to Genoa. There she found a suitable house for Byron, Casa Saluzzo, in the suburb of Albaro, large enough for his own household and the Gambas. On the 27th Byron and Teresa left Pisa. For two or three weeks Mary was alone with her child in the large house, Casa Negroto, which she took for herself and the Hunts in Albaro. Claire, who had gone to Florence when Mary left Pisa, now went to Vienna to join her brother there. The Hunts were to travel north with Byron. Jane, with her two children, left for England on the 17th. Later that day Mary wrote to Maria Gisborne. 'After Jane left me I again went to rest and thought of Pugnano, its halls, its cypresses – the perfume of its mountains and the gaiety of our life beneath their shadow. Then I dozed awhile and in my dream saw dear Edward most visibly; he came, he said, to pass a few hours with us, but could not stay long. Then I woke and the day began.' And she wrote of the constant feeling of despair that shadowed her.

When Byron and the Hunts arrived she was soon busy. There

were more cantos of *Don Juan* to copy – she finished Canto x by 15 October, and Canto xi a week later. Byron had completed Canto x on the 6th shortly after reaching Genoa and Canto xi on the 17th: he was finding consolation for the loss of Shelley in continuing at a galloping pace the poem which Shelley had so much admired. He had resumed work on the poem, after the lifting of Teresa's ban, in April; by the end of June he had written Cantos vi and vii; since Shelley's death he had already added four more. Before he left for Greece he had begun Canto xvii. Mary, copying the latest of them now, was delighted with Byron's reference to Landor, who

Has taken for a swan rogue Southey's gander,

for she realised that Southey had influenced Landor to refuse to meet Shelley in Pisa. She was pleased with the stanza on Keats, for all its scepticism about Shelley's theory that he had been 'snuff'd out by an article' in the *Quarterly*. And the stanzas

Where is the world of eight years past?

had a particular poignancy for her, since she and Shelley had been together just eight years. With a bitter reference to *Epipsychidion* she ended her letter to Byron, 'There might be something sunny about me then, now I am truly cold moonshine.'

Hunt had taken upon himself to accuse Mary of coldness towards Shelley – later he tried to put the blame for this on Jane – and added to her unhappiness during the autumn and winter. It was unfortunate that Mary had to share a house with the Hunts, all the more so because the stove in Mary's room smoked so much that she could not sit there, and had to share the Hunts' sitting-room with them, which proved, as she told Claire, 'the annihilation of study, and even of pleasure to a great degree'. In spite of these difficult relations Mary loyally did her best to compose the inevitable misunderstandings that arose (as Shelley had foreseen) between Hunt and Byron. For, in spite of his admiration for Hunt's courage and integrity, Byron found his presence, and, still more, the presence of his large and disorderly family, insufferable.

As soon as Byron got to Genoa, Mary asked him for a sofa which he had. She had mistaken the piece, which Byron had in fact bought after she left Pisa. In sending her another in its stead, he told her, 'I have a particular dislike to anything of Shelley's being within the same walls with Mrs. Hunt's children. They are dirtier and more mischievous than Yahoos. What they can't destroy with their filth they will with their fingers.' He had had words with Mrs Hunt on this subject when they were still in the Palazzo Lanfranchi. She recorded her view of the incident in her diary. 'Can anything be more absurd than a peer of the realm – and a *poet* – making such a fuss about three or four children disfiguring the walls of a few rooms. The very children would blush for him. Fye Lord B. – fye.' Hunt, naturally, had had to speak to Byron on the matter. Byron relied on Tiger, his bulldog, to keep the Hunt children from coming upstairs to his apartments. When Trelawny called on him, as he left, Byron patted the dog on the head, with 'Don't let any Cockneys pass this way.' He could well sympathise with Mary's plight, sharing a house with them at Genoa.

In November word got back to Hunt, through the indiscretion of Murray, of some comments Byron had made in a letter to his publisher a month before, where he expressed doubts about the prospects for *The Liberal*.

I have done all I can for Leigh Hunt since he came here [he had written], but it is almost useless: his wife is ill, his six children not very tractable, and in the affairs of this world he himself is a child. The death of Shelley left them totally aground; and I could not see them in such a state without using the common feelings of humanity, and what means were in my power, to set them afloat again.

This was all true, but not the more palatable for that. Mary calmed Hunt down, and wrote to Byron to smooth things over: 'Consider that however Moore may laugh at Rimini-pimini, that Hunt is a very good man. Shelley was greatly attached to him on account of his integrity, and that really your letter *does* place him in an awkward situation. The journal is now a work of charity – a kind of subscription for Hunt's family – this must hurt the work.' This was good sense, such as Byron could appreciate. He was not now going to acknowledge that Moore and his other London friends had been right to warn him against the partnership with Shelley and Hunt; he respected Hunt's character, as Shelley had done; and besides what right had Murray to circulate the contents of his letters? He reprimanded Murray and pointed out that by such injudicious rudeness he and his friends, so far from breaking the association with Hunt, were likely to confirm it. And he made his apologies to Hunt.

But the trouble lay deeper, as both Mary and Byron very well knew. In his reply to Mary's letter Byron referred to the scrupulous delicacy with which he had always treated Hunt: 'I have forborne intruding advice which I thought might be disagreeable, lest he should impute it to what is called "taking advantage of a man's situation".' This was just the point, Mary replied. In Byron's relations with Shelley there had never been any need for that 'delicacy' which he mentioned; but for Hunt there was always the inhibiting awareness of the difference in social position: 'He talks about you being a *Lord*;' said Mary, 'he is quite in the wrong – it is *rimini-pimini* and *follage*,* and all that, which makes you dislike entering into the journal, although his talents of another kind have caused you to enter into it.' Such misunderstandings Shelley would have prevented or overcome, as Byron knew, even though the Hampstead intelligentsia was no more congenial to Shelley than to him. 'I do not know what world Hunt has lived in,' Byron admitted in a letter to Murray; 'I have lived in three or four, and none of them like his Keats and Kangaroo *terra incognita*. Alas! poor Shelley! how he would have laughed had he lived, and how we used to laugh now and then at various things which are grave in the suburbs.'

Trelawny, even if at first it had been difficult to take him quite seriously, was much more congenial company for both Mary and Byron. Mary was deeply grateful to him for the way

* Hunt's *The Story of Rimini*, 1816, and *Foliage*, 1818.

he had broken the news of Shelley's death to her, and remembered the sincerity of his eulogy of Shelley that evening at Casa Magni. Since then he had arranged for the cremation of Shelley's body, and had undertaken to supervise the burial of his ashes in Rome. In the event they were buried on 21 January 1823, but when Trelawny got to Rome a month later he bought a new plot against the old wall of Rome for his own grave, and had Shelley's ashes interred next to it. For the stone that marked Shelley's grave he chose the lines from Ariel's song in *The Tempest*,

> Nothing of him that doth fade
> But doth suffer a sea-change
> Into something rich and strange.

This was marvellously apt in its allusion to the manner of Shelley's death and to his genius, and also, as Mary reminded Trelawny in a letter thanking him for what he had done, because the lines had pleasing associations for her. One afternoon in the previous spring Trelawny had come into their house in Pisa in high spirits, bringing news of the progress of the *Don Juan*. 'Oh we must all embark, all live aboard,' he had exclaimed; 'we will all suffer a sea-change.' Shelley had been delighted with the quotation, and said he would take it for the motto of his boat when it was delivered. And he was prompted to use the name Ariel for himself.

Trelawny was generous and impulsive, and his devotion to Shelley was as unselfish as it was sincere. He had snatched Shelley's heart from the pyre, but had not claimed it for himself; he had dug his own grave in Rome next to Shelley's, 'so that when I die, there is only to lift up my coverlet and roll me into it,' as he told Mary; and he added, 'You may lie on the other side, or I will share my narrow bed with you, if you like. It is a lovely spot.' Shelley had thought so too when he first visited Rome. Mary understood Trelawny, and accepted him on his own terms; she could not forget how much she had been attracted to him when he first came to Pisa. 'You found me so full of spirits and life,' she wrote to him, 'that methinks when you first saw me you must have thought me even a little wild.' Now, a year later, though all was changed, Mary could open her heart to Trelawny more than to any other survivor of the Pisan circle; and for Trelawny, friendship with her, so he told Claire, had been almost unmingled pleasure.

In September Byron persuaded Mary to stay on in Italy after Jane and Claire had left, and Trelawny strongly approved. He offered to share his income with her if she would stay in Italy – he had about £500 a year – but this was not needed, for, at least until she decided that she must return to England, she had enough to live on. By that time Byron was thinking how he might best help the Greeks in their War of Independence, in whose hopeful beginnings he and Shelley had together taken a lively interest. In April he received a visit from Edward Blaquiere, representing the recently formed London Greek Committee, and Andreas Luriottis, a delegate from the provisional Greek government. He promised what help he could with money, medical supplies, and so on; but soon Blaquiere and Luriottis, knowing that nothing could more certainly draw the world's attention to the Greek cause, were urging Byron himself to go to Greece. Encouraged by Pietro Gamba (who had been chafing for action ever since the failure of the Carbonari, and his exile from the Romagna) and impatient of a literary life without the stimulus of Shelley's company, he decided to go. His mind turned to Trelawny, with his knowledge of ships and his experience of active service; would he go too? He asked Mary to write to him in Rome to suggest this. Trelawny's response was immediate and enthusiastic. Mary wrote to tell Byron:

I have had a letter from Trelawny today which I must answer by return of post. He expresses the greatest willingness to accompany your Lordship to Greece, and anxiety lest you should change your resolution, which resolution he says has excited great praise and admiration everywhere. Is your vessel hired? and is your going more certain than when I last saw you? Trelawny says that he is willing to stake his all on the Grecian cause.

A few days later Byron himself received a similar letter from Trelawny.

In the meantime Byron was busy, trying to sort out his financial affairs and to obtain funds from Kinnaird for the Greek expedition which he was fitting out, and which was likely to be an expensive affair. Trelawny did not reach Genoa until the end of June, and unfortunately Hunt thought it his duty to try to obtain from Byron the money which he had promised Mary for her journey to England. He carried on the negotiations with that lack of tact which Mary had long known to be characteristic of him. Among other things, Hunt told Byron that he owed Mary the £1000 of the wager with Shelley. Byron realised that Hunt could have heard of this only from Mary, and was naturally piqued that she had been discussing his behaviour in this way, especially since no mention was made of Shelley's guarantee of the money which Byron advanced to Hunt in February 1822, 'with unsuspecting goodness', Shelley had said. Mary made matters worse by sending a note to Byron in which she said she would not now accept money from him, because of their 'estrangement', as she called it. Byron retained his good temper, and suggested that Hunt should say that he had raised a loan for her on his own account: if he had any scruples about such a fib, 'give me a scrap of paper as your note in hand, thus she will be spared any fancied humiliation.'

Byron's good-natured tact was no match for Hunt's lack of either quality. Teresa was most upset by this unnecessary estrangement between Byron and Mary. 'I don't know what to say to you, my dear,' she wrote to Mary, 'for I can't do anything. I feel that I can be of little use, that L.B. will not take advice, that he is very much irritated.' Mary replied a little too haughtily to this affectionate letter. 'I thank you warmly for your offer, but if I am to understand that you wish to be a peace-maker between me and Lord Byron, you will not succeed. . . . Lord Byron having said that it would be disagreeable to him to see me, I cannot have the pleasure of calling on you, but I shall be delighted to see you here.' Teresa tried again, but Mary, in spite of knowing very well that Byron, and not only Byron, might in a moment of irritation say wounding things which he would at once regret, could not unbend. '*From a friend* I would accept anything,' she wrote to Teresa, 'and if he will show me the least sign of friendship and will again be *glad* to help me, I will feel a renewed obligation to him and be grateful.' Teresa tried yet again, for she could not endure the thought that Byron should set off for Greece with this breach of friendship unhealed. Mary at last had the grace to admit that she might have been a little to blame: 'If Lord Byron will forget anything painful that he may have endured from me and on account of me, if he will recognise what Shelley deserves, it will be with real pleasure that I shall wish him by word of mouth what I now wish him by letter – a good voyage and all the success that I feel sure his plans will have in Greece.'

Byron's preparations for departure went on rapidly, and they were to sail in mid-July, on the brig *Hercules*, Captain John Scott. On the 13th Mary wrote to thank Byron for a message transmitted through Teresa. 'I did not wish to spare myself the pain of taking leave. We understood from Conte Pietro today that you did not embark till tomorrow evening or mid-day at the earliest. I intended therefore to settle this pecuniary matter first by letter, there being better subjects for discourse in this world; and then to come down and bid you farewell, which I will do accordingly, if you please, tomorrow morning.' But there was some uncertainty in Mary's mind about what Byron had arranged, and he seems not to have replied to her request that he would do her the favour to state in whose hands he had left this matter or what was its precise nature. There was indeed no time for a reply, for Pietro had misinformed Mary, and Byron went on board at five o'clock that same evening, the 13th, in defiance of superstition. He said, as Shelley had once said, that he thought a bad beginning a favourable omen for success. He sent Mary a note only to ask her if she would be kind enough to go up to Casa Saluzzo to keep Teresa company and to comfort her. Besides, he could not bear any more partings – he had even asked Hunt to excuse him from saying goodbye – and so Mary did not see him to say farewell. A few days later she wrote to tell Jane of his departure. 'His unconquerable avarice prevented his supplying me with money, and a remnant of shame caused him to avoid me.' In this she was being less than just. But she went up, as he had asked her to do, to be with Teresa. From the house they looked down over the harbour to where the *Hercules* rode at anchor, waiting to carry Byron away over the waters where, a year before, Shelley had been drowned.

With him went Teresa's brother Pietro, and Trelawny. Whatever Mary's feelings for Byron were that summer evening, for Trelawny she had an affectionate admiration and gratitude. When she would not accept money from Byron she asked Trelawny to help her. He replied on 12 July that he would be glad to help her if she would let him know her wants. 'You are sure of me, so let us use no more words about it.' Mary knew this was so. But here there is uncertainty about what happened. Could Byron have promised Trelawny the money for Mary, with firm instructions not to disclose its source? He had told her that he had left this financial matter, that had caused so much misunderstanding, in someone else's hands. He would scarcely have trusted Hunt further, but he thought that he could rely on Trelawny's discretion; Trelawny, in his impulsive way, is likely to have raised the subject, since Mary had applied to him the day before. Scornful of Byron's avarice as he became, he does not suggest that it ever injured Mary, and on the voyage out to Greece Byron attempted to reimburse him. Trelawny refused to accept the money, or so he said. But, as Byron once remarked, Trelawny could not tell the truth to save his life. Teresa, who must have known the truth, and who had been so distressed by the misunderstanding between Mary and Byron, believed that in the end Byron assisted her as he had always promised.

On the day after Byron embarked for Greece Teresa left for the Romagna with her father, the order for whose exile would be withdrawn if he returned and brought Teresa with him. Mary remained at Albaro a week more, and then set off on her journey to England. The Hunts – Marianne had been safely delivered of her seventh child early in June – remained in Italy until the autumn of 1825.

Almost exactly a year after she left Italy Mary wrote a long letter to Trelawny, in reply to one she had recently received from him from Greece:

So, dear Trelawny, you remember still poor Mary Shelley – thank you for your remembrance and a thousand thanks for your kind letter. It is delightful to feel that absence does not diminish your affection, excellent, warm-hearted friend, remnant of our happy days, of my vagabond life in beloved Italy, our companion in prosperity, our comforter in sorrow! You will not wonder that the late loss of L.B. makes me cling with greater zeal to those dear friends who remain to me. He could hardly be called a friend, but connected with him in a thousand ways, admiring his talents and with all his faults feeling affection for him, it went to my heart when the other day* the hearse that contained his lifeless form, a form of beauty which in life I often delighted to behold, passed my window going up Highgate Hill.

A day or two before she had been to the house in Great George Street where Byron's body lay in state. She had seen there his faithful valet Fletcher, and his secretary Lega Zambelli. Fletcher, who had been with Byron from his earliest travels and was with him when he died at Missolonghi in April, promised to call on Mary after the funeral. This took place on 16 July when his remains were interred in the family vault in Hucknall Torkard church.

Byron could hardly be called a friend, Mary said. That was to Trelawny. In the privacy of her journal, when she heard the news of Byron's death, she had been less restrained. There she recalled the progress of their friendship from that first summer together by the Lake of Geneva to the months after Shelley's death when he had been so attentive and consoling. 'Albè – the dear, capricious, fascinating Albè – has left this desert world! . . . God grant I may die young!' But to Trelawny, who

* 12 July 1824.

would remember those last difficult days before he and Byron sailed for Greece, she must be more reticent, and she could not cry out, as she felt, that with Byron's death all her old friends were gone. Once Byron had told her that friendship was a propensity in which his genius was very limited: 'I did not even feel it for Shelley, however much I admired and esteemed him.' He acknowledged friendship for only one man, he then said, the friend of his school days, Lord Clare; perhaps also for Tom Moore. But, as Mary thought at the time, this was giving too restricted a meaning to the word. In another mood he would have agreed with her. That last spring in Genoa he made one of his candid self-appraisals to Lady Blessington, who was staying in the city.

> People take for gospel all I say [he observed], and go away continually with false impressions. . . . Now, if I know myself, I should say that I have no character at all . . . I am so changeable, being everything by turns and nothing long, – I am such a strange mélange of good and evil, that it would be difficult to describe me. There are but two sentiments to which I am constant, – a strong love of liberty, and a detestation of cant, and neither is calculated to gain me friends.

These sentiments, above all else, formed the basis of the friendship between Byron and Shelley. When they first met by the Lake of Geneva they can hardly have expected to become friends. Of Shelley Byron knew nothing but what Claire had told him and what he had read in *Queen Mab*: from this he could have deduced a love of liberty comparable to his own, but Claire's account of her Otaheite philosopher cannot have been reassuring as to Shelley's freedom from cant. Of Byron Shelley knew what everyone knew: that he had been accorded, as he deserved, chief place among contemporary poets, and that after four years as a celebrity in London society, he had been driven into exile by a scandal of which that society whispered, but which it never declared. Byron was a public figure about whose personality and about whose poetry everyone was arguing; Shelley was unknown and his poetry unnoticed. Besides, the fact that both men were poets was no reason why they should become friends; rather the reverse for, as Dr Johnson observes, 'the reciprocal civility of authors is one of the most risible scenes in the farce of life.'

They were both, it is true, from the same governing class in English society, so that they were immediately at ease with one another as Keats never was with Shelley, nor Leigh Hunt with Byron. If they had not been men of genius, Byron would have continued to make occasional speeches in the House of Lords, and would in the end, like his friend Hobhouse, have held a post of no great importance in a Victorian cabinet; and Shelley would have followed his father in the House of Commons, from time to time producing well-argued pamphlets which his back-bench colleagues would have consistently ignored. Something of this sort was the destiny to which the heirs to peerages and baronetcies in Regency England were born, and for which they were educated. Byron had very much enjoyed his schooldays at Harrow, and at Cambridge he had led the gay and irreverent and slightly dissipated life which Rowlandson depicts. Shelley, on the other hand, had not enjoyed Eton, and had soon been sent down from Oxford for refusing to disavow the untimely scepticism of *The Necessity of Atheism* or to acknowledge that he was its author.

They never seem to have talked together of their days at school or university, yet their schooling had developed minds that were naturally inquiring, and had given them both the ability to read Greek and Latin, and to read whatever they read with critical attention. They were for ever discussing books together, introducing each other to new or neglected works, and so enlarging an experience of literature far greater than most men's. In their first month together Byron introduced Shelley to *La Nouvelle Héloïse*, and Shelley responded by dosing Byron with Wordsworth. Later, Byron persuaded Shelley to return to Pope, and Shelley convinced Byron that *Hyperion*, at least, gave Keats claim to respect. They had many favourites in common, where neither needed persuading: Aeschylus and Spenser and Milton, Dante and Ariosto and Tasso; among their own contemporaries, Walter Scott and

Coleridge; and also the great English dramatists of Queen Elizabeth's time. Byron in London had been concerned with the management of Drury Lane Theatre, and was a constant theatre-goer; probably that experience made him doubt the value of the Elizabethans as models for modern dramatists, and to prefer to seek fresh inspiration in neo-classic drama. Shelley preferred the opera, especially the opera of Mozart, but he wished to write for the theatre and chose to rely on Shakespeare and Webster instead of trying to introduce something new.

When they first met, Byron, uprooted from the London society which had so enthusiastically acclaimed his poetry since *Childe Harold* I and II had brought him fame overnight, needed to find new sources for his poetry, and a new manner. It was not likely to be easy. He could not suddenly reject the success of *Childe Harold* and the Tales, which was beyond what any other poet had ever known; he was always extremely sensitive to other men's opinion of him, and he saw little reason for deriding their judgment of his poetry. Even if he had never written another line after leaving England, he would still be remembered as a poet of considerable achievement. Besides, when his public condemned him as a man, there was an ironic pleasure in observing that they continued to applaud him as a poet. He did not, at the time, foresee that he would never return to England, and his contact with old friends during that summer at Geneva, with Madame de Staël, with Monk Lewis, Hobhouse, Scrope Davies,* prevented him realising that the break with the old life was final.

Shelley was anchored by no weight of fame. He could, and did, reject *Queen Mab* and *Alastor*, and was eager to move on to the greater poetry which he knew he would some day write. He was indifferent to what anyone thought of him, and even if he had not been, hardly anyone yet gave him or his poetry a thought. He was not self-exiled from England, and returned there after an absence of only four months. He took back with

* In January he dedicated *The Siege of Corinth* to Hobhouse and *Parisina* to Davies; the two latest of his Tales.

him two poems of finer accomplishment than any he had written before; but the poems which he took to Murray for Byron, the third Canto of *Childe Harold*, *The Prisoner of Chillon*, the first passage written for *Manfred*, *Darkness*, *Prometheus*, were of far greater significance. In all of them Shelley's influence on Byron during their three months together can be seen, as Byron, by giving Shelley authority to make certain revisions, acknowledged. Shelley had achieved more this summer by beginning to free Byron's imagination from the habits of his years of fame than by anything he had himself written.

Byron was still continuing with *Childe Harold*, and would not shift over to *Don Juan* until he met Shelley in 1818; but he was continuing it in a manner very different from that of the first two cantos. He also continued the series of Tales, with *The Prisoner of Chillon*, but this is more mature than its predecessors, and Bonivard's character is developed with greater insight than before: he is not just a repetition of the 'Byronic' hero, reckless, wicked and histrionic; he is a recognisable human being. The Prometheus myth would eventually mean more to Shelley than to Byron, though Byron often alludes to it, but the concern of the two poets with it now at their first meeting found its first expression in Byron's poem. Prometheus was a nobler romantic hero than the Giaour or the Corsair, for his defiance of Zeus was not mere defiance, but was prompted by the Shelleyan ideal of service to mankind. Byron's recollection of Aeschylus' play also gave a firmer control to his diction in the poem of *Prometheus*.

Manfred, mostly written after Shelley had returned to England, describes a hero tortured by remorse, something incomprehensible to Shelley whose lack of a consciousness of sin was far removed from Byron's obsessive sense of guilt – 'Why do you indulge this despondency?' he asked Byron. A hero who had rejected his youthful hope to be 'the enlightener of nations', and who now sought nothing but forgetfulness of inexpiable crime, is not Promethean, but he is not the defiant outlaw either; if he is not idealistic, he is not untouched by idealism; incapable of self-sacrifice for others, he has at least thought of its possibility. He is a Byronic hero modified by rediscovery of the Prometheus myth which Shelley taught him to look at afresh. Shelley had also made Byron more sensitive to the splendour of Alpine scenery than he would have been without the physic of Wordsworth; but Byron soon realised that his proclamation that to him high mountains were a feeling was too extravagant. That was what Shelley had made him wish to feel, rather than what in fact he had felt, and in *Manfred*, with his usual honesty, he admits this. *Manfred*, therefore, begun while Shelley was with him, and continued after Monk Lewis had translated Goethe's *Faust* to him, denotes the stage in his poetic development which Byron had then reached: he had been made aware by Shelley of new possibilities of human experience, but his own self-knowledge had brought him to realise, however regretfully, that they were not for him. In form also the play is Shelleyan, rather than Aeschylean, lyrical drama, and owes nothing to Byron's practical experience of the theatre. It is a precursor of *Prometheus Unbound*, where, in turn, Shelley is often indebted to Byron; but the relation between the two works is too complex for brief discussion.

The poetry of that first summer together, and of the ensuing autumn, illustrates the contrast between the characters of the two men. Byron, always immediately responsive to those he was with, had at once shown the influence of Shelley on his poetry; when Shelley had gone, and he made a tour to the Bernese Alps with Hobhouse and Scrope Davies, friends from earlier days, the reaction came. In intellectual content *Manfred* shows Byron returning towards his earlier mood, after the experiment with Shelleyan idealism in *Childe Harold* III and *Prometheus*: 'It is too much in my old style,' he wrote to Murray. 'I certainly am a devil of a mannerist, and must leave off.' Mary recognised Byron's responsiveness as characteristic of his behaviour generally: when she and Shelley were trying to decide whether or not to take Allegra out to him in the autumn of 1817 Mary wrote, 'Promises with Albe! the first object that engaged his attention would put them all out of his head!' This instability of character was the price to be paid for that extraordinary responsiveness which distinguishes his best poetry. Byron knew it was so, and could not avoid the cost; his friends were those who recognised it, and were willing to go on paying for the sake of his company, like Hobhouse, or like Shelley, for the sake also of his poetry.

Shelley was not easily influenced, either in his poetry or in his conduct. He lived much more in the world of intellectual ideas than in the world of the senses, and his best poetry is the product of coherent thinking more often than of an immediate response to experience. That too could inspire such poems as the *Ode to the West Wind*, *To a Skylark*, *Julian and Maddalo*, or the poems to Jane; and in *Mont Blanc*, written that summer in Switzerland, we may perhaps see the first influence upon him of Byron's habit of mind. But Shelley had a strong will, and a power of decision, which were quite unlike Byron. 'I go on until I am stopped,' he once said of himself, 'and I never am stopped.' Byron applied to himself Dryden's line on Buckingham, who

Was every thing by starts, and nothing long.

At least they were alike in the candour of their self-knowledge, a good foundation for friendship. When they met again in Venice the wit and subtlety of Byron's talk helped Shelley, he said, to know himself. The complementary qualities of Shelley's mind, the clarity of vision, the power of argument, similarly affected Byron.

Until that time each was disposed to continue writing in his own earlier manner. During his eighteen months in England Shelley wrote *The Revolt of Islam*, which, though far removed from the juvenile tub-thumping of *Queen Mab*, still makes its design upon the reader too palpable. He began, and laid aside, two other poems, *Prince Athanase*, which, as Mary Shelley observed, was modelled on *Alastor*; and *Rosalind and Helen*, a more human story which Mary persuaded him to finish in Italy during the summer of 1818 when he was unable to begin anything new. In Shelley's opinion it was of little importance: 'it is in no degree calculated to excite profound meditation,' he wrote in the Advertisement, with the implication that such must be the purpose of the greatest poetry. *Rosalind and Helen* was therefore a diversion from his true progress as a poet.

Byron continued *Childe Harold* with a fourth canto which, without showing a return to the manner of the first two, is yet free of the 'metaphysics' imposed by Shelley on Canto III. He wrote *The Lament of Tasso* after a visit to Tasso's cell at Ferrara in the spring of 1817, interrupting *Childe Harold* IV to do so; its closest analogy is with *The Prisoner of Chillon*, written after the visit to the Castle where Bonivard was imprisoned. That had interrupted the previous canto of *Childe Harold*, and had been a similar attempt to imagine the sufferings of a victim of tyranny. So far Byron had not found the means to escape, as he realised that he must, from the 'old style' which had established his fame. But in the summer he read a newly published poem, *Prospectus and Specimen of an intended National Work* by William and Robert Whistlecraft – he at once guessed the identity of the brothers with his old friend John Hookham Frere – and this poem, with its hilarious, colloquial *ottava rima* stanzas, provided the key to a new freedom. In September he wrote *Beppo* in the manner of Whistlecraft, based on an anecdote which the husband of his latest Venetian mistress, Marianna Segati, told to him and Hobhouse a few days before. In the spring he had been complaining to Tom Moore about his reputation for gloom and misanthropy: 'I suppose now I shall never be able to shake off my sables in public imagination.' Now he had found the means, and though *Beppo* was no more than an experiment, he would soon be able to shake off his sables, and to reveal in *Don Juan* every side of a personality so various that he seems to be not one, but all mankind's epitome.

Yet nearly a year passed before Byron could transfer from *Childe Harold* to *Don Juan*, and it was not until he saw Shelley again that he began the new poem on which he was to work intermittently until he left for Greece. Frere had shown him the means to his greatest poetry, but he needed Shelley's unshakeable confidence in his power to write a poem that would be the *Iliad*, the *Divina Commedia*, the *Paradise Lost* of their day before he could set out on his task. Shelley in turn needed the stimulus of Byron's talk again before he could free himself from the uncertainties which had prevented him writing for six months; but then with *Julian and Maddalo* and the first act of *Prometheus Unbound* he too began the work that sets him beside Byron among the greatest of English poets.

Tom Moore, who knew Byron so well, and who, though to his regret he never met Shelley, had heard Byron talk of him, summed up the effect of the two men on one another:

The conversation of Mr. Shelley [he said], was of a nature strongly to arrest and interest the attention of Lord Byron. . . . As far as contrast, indeed, is an enlivening ingredient of such intercourse, it would be difficult to find two persons more formed to whet each other's faculties by discussion, as on few points of common interest between them did their opinions agree; and that this difference had its root deep in the conformation of their respective minds needs but a glance through the rich, glittering labyrinth of Mr. Shelley's pages to assure us.

The complementary nature of their minds, thus apparent in their poetry, was not less so to those who knew them; it was this that made their friendship so rewarding, above all by increasing in each that self-knowledge which is the evidence of maturity.

Those who knew both Byron and Shelley – Trelawny, Leigh Hunt, Medwin – found it impossible when writing their recollections, to remain impartial. Shelley's simple goodness and the tragic waste of his death invited an adulation which they could not accord to the far more complex Byron, whose death at Missolonghi assured the eventual liberty of Greece. They wished to portray Shelley as they saw him, and so to correct the only published accounts of him in the vindictive travesties of the reviews. There was no need to add to the portrayal of one whom Goethe had already proclaimed to be the greatest genius of the nineteenth century, and whose friends were all hurrying into print with their *Lives* and *Memoirs* and *Conversations*.

Mary Shelley, forbidden by her father-in-law to write a memoir of Shelley, had made a vow she told Murray, never to make money out of her acquaintance with Byron. 'His ghost would certainly come and taunt me if I did.' But she helped Moore with reminiscences of Byron in Switzerland and Italy. 'Very gentle and feminine,' he noted in his diary on first meeting her in July 1824, and they remained on friendly terms. She was very pleased with Moore's *Life* when it came out.

The great charm of the work to me, and it will have the same to you [she wrote to Murray], is that the Lord Byron I find there is our Lord Byron – the fascinating, faulty, childish, philosophical being, daring the world, docile to a private circle, impetuous and indolent, gloomy and yet more gay than any other. I live with him again in these pages, getting reconciled (as I used in his life time) to these waywardnesses which annoyed me when he was away, through the delightful and buoyant tone of his conversation and manners.

This was the Byron whom she portrayed as Raymond in *The Last Man*, a novel that owed something to the poem *Darkness* which he wrote when they were first together in Switzerland, the Byron whose charm of manner and whose manly beauty were irresistible. 'The usual expression of his eyes was soft, though at times he could make them even glare with ferocity; his complexion was colourless; and every trait spoke predominate self-will; his smile was pleasing, though disdain too often curled his lips – lips which to female eyes were the very throne of beauty and love.' In that same novel Mary gave her fullest portrait of Shelley, as Adrian. (She herself is represented by Lionel.) *The Last Man* derived in part from her feeling that when Byron died, of that once happy circle of friends, she was sole survivor, 'the last relic of a beloved race'.

Not only Mary used fiction to portray the two poets; Peacock had done so some years before in *Nightmare Abbey* though without suggesting any particular friendship between Mr Cypress and Scythrop Glowry. And others followed. H. A.

Driver in 1835 published *Harold de Burun a semi-dramatic poem*, in which Harold is Byron, Percy Shelley, and Teresa Teresa; it is of minimal interest. Two years later Disraeli, whose father had known Byron, and who had grown up, like most of his generation, fascinated by the Byronic myth, attempted a portrait of him as the young Plantagenet, Lord Cadurcis, in *Venetia*. He also introduced Shelley into the novel, as Marmion Herbert, but, perhaps because he realised that great poets cannot be confined to the role of characters in a work of fiction, he converted him into a successful American general in the War of Independence. The result was unconvincing.

Since then, by the often more sober methods of biography, many have explored the life of Byron or the life of Shelley, for no two lives could better illustrate the Romantic theme of the uniqueness of the individual. The friendship between them was of more significance than any other relationship of their lives, both for the development of their personal qualities and for the expression of these in their poetry. This was so because of their candour in recognising, and their generosity in respecting, the contrast between them, so that each helped the other to be more completely himself. That is not to say that this friendship brought them greater happiness, that it more constantly occupied their thoughts, or more deeply influenced their personal conduct than any other; yet, in that both were poets, the friendship begun that May evening by the Lake of Geneva was not limited to their hazardous, brief lives, but continues to reveal itself in the great poetry which from that time on Byron and Shelley knew that they had the power to write, and in the record of two personalities whose fascination is as enduring as their poetic fame.

Notes

1. There were living in Geneva at this time two men of the name of Pictet, Marc-Auguste Pictet (1752–1825) and Jean Marc Jules Pictet de Sergy (1768–1828). Polidori unhelpfully describes Byron's visitor as 'an oldish man, about forty-six'. Marc-Auguste in 1816 was about sixty-four, not forty-six, and it seems likely that Polidori simply transposed the digits. C.-E. Engel prefers Marc-Auguste and I have followed her.

2. In a letter to Coleridge of 18 October 1815 (printed in *Byron: A Self-Portrait*) Byron wrote:

> Last spring I saw Wr. Scott. He repeated to me a considerable portion of an unpublished poem of yours – the wildest and finest I ever heard in that kind of composition. The title he did not mention, but I think the heroine's name was Geraldine. At all events, the 'toothless mastiff bitch' and the 'witch Lady', the description of the hall, the lamp suspended from the image, and more particularly of the girl herself as she went forth in the evening – all took a hold on my imagination which I never shall wish to shake off.

He plagiarised *Christabel* from his recollection of Scott's recitation in *The Siege of Corinth*, as he realised when Coleridge sent him a manuscript copy of *Christabel.* He added a note about this to his own poem when it was published early in 1816.

3. Shelley described the tour of the lake in a letter to Peacock of 12 July, and he seems to have dated it incorrectly. He says that they left on 23 June and returned on 30 June, that is that they were away only one week. Mary's journal is unfortunately lost for this time, but Polidori says that they left on 22 June, and this date is confirmed by Byron's dating a letter from Evian 23 June. Polidori says that they returned on 1 July. Since he was writing at the time and Shelley ten days or so later Polidori is more likely to be correct.

4. That *Frankenstein* was published in January, not March, 1818 is proved by Shelley's letter to Sir Walter Scott of 2

January, with which he enclosed a copy, and by a letter from Claire to Byron of 12 January, in which she says: 'Mary has just published her first work, a novel called Frankenstein or the Modern Prometheus. It is a most wonderful performance full of genius and the fiction is of so continued and extraordinary a kind as no one would imagine could have been written by so young a person.' She gives no hint that she knew that the story derived from Byron's proposal that they should each attempt to write a ghost story; Claire had not been present on that occasion, and apparently neither Mary nor Shelley ever told her of it.

5. So Teresa in her unpublished 'Vie de Lord Byron' quoted by Iris Origo in *The Last Attachment*. Coleridge once observed to H. F. Cary, the translator of Dante, that Byron's eyes were like 'the Gates of Heaven: they bewitched one in his favour'. Teresa, recollecting the passage, transferred it to Byron's smile rather than confining it to his eyes.

6. I cannot accept F. L. Jones's opinion (Shelley, *Letters* II 197n) that Shelley's letter to Byron refers to the letter which arrived on 19 May, as recorded by Claire in her diary. For, first, Shelley did not leave Pisa till 22 May, and he told Byron that he found his letter *on his return*, on the 25th; and, second, he refers to 'your letter *about* Claire', not '*to* Claire'; and, third, if the letter had been addressed to Claire, Shelley would hardly have said 'of necessity she was obliged to read it', since Byron presumably expected her to read letters addressed to her. A letter from Byron addressed to Shelley must have come while he was away at Casciano, beteeen 22 and 25 May; since it has not been preserved we can deduce its contents only from Shelley's reply.

7. The vexed question whether or not Byron forwarded Mary's letter to Mrs Hoppner seems to me to have been settled by John Murray in *Lord Byron's Correspondence* II 191–4. The letter addressed only 'A Madame/Mme. Hoppner' was enclosed by Mary to Shelley *unsealed*. Shelley then read it to Byron and sealed it himself. But his seal is broken, and can only have been broken by Mrs Hoppner, who then returned it to Byron.

8. A letter in Lord Abinger's MSS. which Medwin wrote to Jane on 25 February 1823 probably refers to Johnson. 'A circumstance has occurred here [Paris] with which it is necessary you and Mrs Cleveland should be acquainted. The wretch who has been the bane of your existence is about to pay the forfeit of his crimes with his life or at least will be condemned to the gallies for life.' From Medwin's letter it appears that this man had turned up at Genoa, after Williams' death, of which he had presumably received news, where he had posed as the British Consul. He had subsequently been accused of forgery and theft, and had been recognised by a friend of Medwin, Captain Bergher of the 16th Dragoons, who had exposed him. If in fact this man was Jane's legal husband, he may have heard that Jane was (or had been) at Genoa, and hoped to indulge in a little blackmail at her expense. He may even have been the occasion of Jane's hasty departure from Genoa in September 1822. But since Medwin does not name the man, we cannot be certain, though no other bane of Jane's existence is known, and the fact that he was recognised by an officer whom Medwin had known, presumably in India, makes it probable that Johnson is meant.

9. A quotation from Dante, *Inferno* xxxiii 30. Shelley quoted the line in a letter to Hogg of 22 October 1821. In a letter to Mary of 9 February 1822 Maria Gisborne quotes this same line, and adds that Dante mentions the Lanfranchi (in fact, two lines later). The passage must have had many associations for the Pisan circle and their friends.

10. F. L. Jones in his edition of Mary's *Journal* has unfortunately conflated her entries for 23 and 24 March, under the date of 23 March, with the implication that Mary made no entry on the 24th. In fact she wrote in her journal on both days, as follows:

> Saturday 23rd. Translate Italian – walk with Jane – S and W go to Leghorn – ride with TG. The W and T . . .y in the evening.
> Sunday 24th. Translate Italian; read Homer – walk with Jane – ride with TG. A *Zuffa*, and the evening tutto sotto sopra.

She used the same word, *zuffa* (scrimmage, brawl) in a letter to Byron written early in April: 'I understand that your Lordship wishes that Hunt should have a detailed account of your *Zuffa* . . . '. This was in response to Byron's request that she would make copies of the depositions to send to Hunt (see p. 215). Byron probably used this disparaging word in order to make light of the affair to Teresa.

11. Shelley's letter to Byron numbered 704 in F. L. Jones's edition is incorrectly dated and out of sequence. The postmark is '12 Giugno', not, as given by Jones, 'Mag. 17' and '20 Maggio'. In fact he has attributed the postmark of letter 703 to 706, of 704 to 703, and of 706 to 704. (All three are addressed to Byron.) He has also confused the addresses. And letter 703 is clearly dated by Shelley 'May 8', not 'May 9'. In any event the date of letter 704 is clear enough from its contents. In the first sentence Shelley says that he has heard of Hunt's 'third embarkation on the 13th of May' – the day *after* Jones's dating of the letter! (And the news must have come from England.) Byron in his letter to Shelley of 20 May, printed by Jones in a note on p. 421, says: 'Of Hunt I hear nothing – nor you. I suppose that he has embarked then.' This letter is in reply to Shelley's of 16 May. In the same letter Byron says: 'The American Commodore has invited me on board his Frigate, and I go to see her and him tomorrow', that is, on 21 May. To this Shelley makes a humorous reference in his letter 704. Then Shelley says that he hears nothing of the arrival of the *Bolivar*, but that Williams is on the look-out for her. But in his letter of 16 May, which he dated, Shelley says that the *Bolivar* is expected 'in about a fortnight'. The whole letter confirms the date suggested by the postmark, and must have been written about 10 or 11 June.

12. The date of Hunt's arrival at the Villa Dupuy is open to some doubt. In *Lord Byron and Some of his Contemporaries* he says that he sailed from Genoa on 28 June. The police records of the fracas at the Villa are also dated 28 June, and this led Mrs Angeli, in *Shelley and his Friends in Italy*, to question Hunt's dating. Shelley heard of Hunt's arrival in Leghorn in time to leave in the afternoon of 1 July with Williams. Papi must have called on him before he left for Leghorn and therefore probably on the 30th; he may even have brought Shelley the first news of Hunt's arrival. If Papi was dismissed on the 28th in the late afternoon it is likely that he would have been given until next morning to leave, and he could hardly have reached Casa Magni before the afternoon of the 30th at earliest. It seems more likely that Hunt's recollection was wrong than that the police records, made at the time, were so. Therefore I am inclined to date Hunt's arrival at the Villa Dupuy 28 June.

Bibliography

The primary sources for our knowledge of the lives of Byron and Shelley are the letters and journals of both men, and of those most closely associated with them; their poems and prose writings; reminiscences and biographies written by those who knew them personally; and occasional references in the letters or journals of chance acquaintances and observers. To these may be added reviews of their published writings in contemporary journals.

I have here listed first those sources which are relevant throughout, followed by minor sources of which I have made use occasionally.

I

BYRON

LETTERS

There is no complete collection of Byron's known letters, of which many remain unpublished. Published letters for the years 1816–24 are to be found in the following collections:

The Works of Lord Byron, Letters and Journals, ed. Rowland E. Prothero, vols. III–VI, 1899–1901.

Lord Byron's Correspondence, ed. John Murray, vol. II, 1922.

Byron: A Self-Portrait, ed. Peter Quennell, 2 vols., 1950.

Others will be found in the following works:

Earl of Lovelace: *Astarte*, ed. Countess of Lovelace, 1921.

Iris Origo: *The Last Attachment*, 1949.

L. A. Marchand: 'Byron and Count Alborghetti', *PMLA* lxiv, 1949.

C. L. Cline: *Byron, Shelley and their Pisan Circle*, 1952.

L. A. Marchand: *Byron, a Biography,* 3 vols., 1957, the standard biography.

POEMS

The Works of Lord Byron: Poetry, ed. Ernest Hartley Coleridge, 7 vols., 1898–1901.

RECOLLECTIONS, ETC.

Medwin's Conversations of Lord Byron (1824), ed. Ernest J. Lovell Jr, Princeton, N.J., 1966.

Thomas Moore: *Letters and Journals of Lord Byron, with Notices of his Life*, 2 vols., 1830.

John Galt: *The Life of Lord Byron*, 1830.

James Kennedy: *Conversations on Religion with Lord Byron*, 1830.

Conversations of Lord Byron with the Countess of Blessington, 1834.

Countess Teresa Guiccioli: *My Recollections of Lord Byron* (*Lord Byron jugé par les témoins de sa Vie*, translated by H. E. H. Jerningham), 2 vols., 1869.

Lord Broughton: *Recollections of a Long Life*, ed. Lady Dorchester, 6 vols., 1909–11.

His Very Self and Voice. Collected Conversations of Lord Byron, ed. Ernest J. Lovell Jr, New York, 1954.

SHELLEY

LETTERS

There is no complete collection of Shelley's known letters, owing to the refusal by the Pforzheimer library in New York of access to the letters which they claim to possess. The fullest edition, which supersedes all others, is *The Letters of Percy Bysshe Shelley*, ed. F. L. Jones, 2 vols., Oxford, 1964. The privately printed *Shelley and Mary*, ed. Lady Shelley, 4 vols., 1882, is indispensable for correspondence addressed to Shelley.

POEMS AND PROSE

The Complete Works of Percy Bysshe Shelley, ed. Roger Ingpen and Walter E. Peck, 10 vols. (The Julian edition), 1926–30.

The Complete Poetical Works of Percy Bysshe Shelley, ed. Thomas Hutchinson, 1905.

Verse and Prose, from the Manuscripts of Percy Bysshe Shelley, ed. Sir John Shelley-Rolls, Bart, and Roger Ingpen, 1934.

Plato's Banquet, translated from the Greek etc., by Percy Bysshe Shelley, ed. Roger Ingpen, 1931.

RECOLLECTIONS, ETC.

Mary Shelley: Notes to *Poetical Works of Percy Bysshe Shelley*, 4 vols., 1839 (reprinted by Hutchinson, and by Ingpen and Peck).

Thomas Medwin: *The Life of Percy Bysshe Shelley*, a new edition etc. ed. H. Buxton Forman ('Medwin's Revised Life of Shelley'), 1913.

T. L. Peacock: 'Memoirs of Shelley' in *The Life of Shelley*, ed. Humbert Wolfe, vol. II, 1933.

E. J. Trelawny: *Recollections of the Last Days of Shelley and Byron*, 1858 (reprinted in *The Life of Shelley*, ed. Humbert Wolfe, vol. II, 1933). Preferable to the revised *Records of Byron, Shelley, and the Author*, 1878.

Thornton Hunt: 'Shelley, by One who Knew him', *Atlantic Monthly*, 1863 (reprinted in *Shelley and Keats as they Struck their Contemporaries*, ed. Edmund Blunden, 1925).

Also:

Newman Ivey White (ed.): *The Unextinguished Hearth*, Shelley and his Contemporary Critics, Durham, N.C., 1938.

Newman Ivey White: *Shelley*, 2 vols., 1947, the standard biography.

Still valuable are:

Edward Dowden: *The Life of Percy Bysshe Shelley*, 2 vols., 1886, reprinted in 1 vol. 1966.

Helen Rossetti Angeli: *Shelley and his Friends in Italy*, 1911.

MARY SHELLEY

LETTERS AND JOURNAL

There is no complete edition of her known letters. The fullest collection is:

The Letters of Mary W. Shelley, ed. F. L. Jones, 2 vols., Norman, Okla., 1944.

Others will be found in the following:

Samuel Smiles: *A Publisher and his Friends*, 2 vols., 1891.

F. L. Jones: 'Mary Shelley to Maria Gisborne. New Letters, 1818–22', *Studies in Philology*, lii, 1952.

Mary Shelley's Journal, ed. F. L. Jones, Norman, Okla., 1947.

WORKS

History of a Six Weeks' Tour, 1817 (in collaboration with Shelley).

Rambles in Germany and Italy in 1840, 1842, and 1843, 2 vols., 1844.

Frankenstein, or The Modern Prometheus, 1818, 1831 (frequently reprinted, e.g. in Everyman's Library).

Valperga, or The Life and Adventures of Castruccio Prince of Lucca, 3 vols., 1823.

The Last Man, 3 vols., 1826 (reprinted 1954).

Mathilda, ed. Elizabeth Nitchie, Chapel Hill, N.C., 1959.

The Choice, A Poem on Shelley's Death, ed. H. Buxton Forman, 1876. See also: R. Glynn Grylls: *Mary Shelley*, 1938. Appendix D.

CLAIRE CLAIRMONT

Neither her letters nor her journal have ever been published *in toto*. A number of her letters to Byron are included in Appendix VII to vol. III of Byron's *Letters and Journals*, 1899. Others will be found in George Paston and Peter Quennell: *To Lord Byron, Feminine Profiles based upon Unpublished Letters, 1807–24*, 1939.

See also:

R. Glynn Grylls: *Claire Clairmont, The Mother of Byron's Allegra*, 1939.

CONTESSA TERESA GUICCIOLI

Her *Vie de Lord Byron en Italie* remains unpublished, but was extensively used by the Marchesa Iris Origo in *The Last Attachment*. For the English version of her earlier work, *Lord Byron jugé par les témoins de sa Vie*, see under 'BYRON'.

LEIGH HUNT

LETTERS

There is no complete edition of his known letters.

The Correspondence of Leigh Hunt, edited by his Eldest Son [Thornton Hunt], 2 vols., 1862.

L. A. Brewer: *My Leigh Hunt Library*, vol. II, The Holograph Letters, Iowa City, Iowa, 1938.

Also:

Shelley–Leigh Hunt: How Friendship made History, ed. R. Brimley Johnson, 1928.

WORKS

Autobiography, ed. J. E. Morpurgo (from text of 1859), 1949. This is much to be preferred to the malicious and mean earlier work, *Lord Byron and Some of his Contemporaries*, 1828.

E. J. TRELAWNY

LETTERS

There is no complete edition of his known letters.

The Letters of Edward John Trelawny, ed. H. Buxton Forman, 1910.

See also above, under 'SHELLEY'.

II

Figures in brackets indicate the chapters to which each entry is especially relevant.

M. Baron-Wilson: *The Life and Correspondence of M. G. Lewis*, 1839 (*2*).

A. H. Beavan: *James and Horace Smith*, 1899 (*3*).

Gavin de Beer, 'The Atheist, an Incident at Chamonix' in *On Shelley*, Oxford, 1938 (*2*).

William Benbow: *A Scourge for the Laureate*, 1825 (*6*).

Countess of Blessington: *The Idler in Italy*, 2 vols., 1839 (*2*).

Edmund Blunden: 'The Family of Edward Williams', *Keats–Shelley Memorial Bulletin* iv 49–51, 1952 (*7*).

Karl Viktor von Bonstetten: *Briefe . . . an Friederika Brun*, ed. Friedrich von Matthisson, Frankfurt-am-Main, 1829 (*1*).

C. P. Brand: *Torquato Tasso, a Study of the Poet and his Contribution to English Literature*, Cambridge, 1965 (*4*).

Kenneth N. Cameron: 'Shelley vs. Southey, New Light on an old Quarrel', *PMLA* lxvii 489–512, 1952 (*8*).

H. Cary: *Memoir of the Rev. H. F. Cary*, 2 vols., 1847 (*5*).

Charles and Mary Cowden Clarke: *Recollections of Writers*, 1878 (*3*).

John Dix: *Pen and Ink Sketches of Poets, Preachers, and Politicians*, 1846 (*3*).

Sylvester Douglas (Lord Glenbervie): *The Diaries*, ed. Francis Bickley, 2 vols., 1928 (*1*, *4*).

Rev. Alexander Dyce: *Recollections of the Table Talk of Samuel Rogers*, ed. Oliver Morchard Bishop, 1952 (*3*).

C. E. Engel: *Byron et Shelley en Suisse et en Savoie, Mai-Octobre 1816*, Chambéry, 1930 (*1–3*).

George Finlay: *A History of Greece from its Conquest by the Romans to the Present Time, 146 B.C. to A.D. 1864*, new edition ed. H. F. Tozer, vol. VI, The Greek Revolution, Part I, A.D. 1821–27, Oxford, 1877 (*7–8*).

John Forster: *The Life of Walter Savage Landor*, 1869 (*6*).

[James Gallatin]: *A Great Peace-Maker, the Diary of James Gallatin*, ed. Count Gallatin, 1914 (*1*).

Maria Gisborne and Edward Williams, Shelley's Friends: Their Journals and Letters, ed. F. L. Jones, Norman, Okla., 1951 (*6–10*).

F. D. Guerrazzi: *Memorie*, Leghorn, 1848 (*9*).

H. W. Häusermann: *The Genevese Background*, 1952 (*1–2*).

Anne Hill: 'Trelawny's Family Background and Naval Career', *Keats–Shelley Journal* v 11–32, 1956 (*8*).

Marianne Hunt: 'Unpublished Diary', *Keats–Shelley Memorial Bulletin* ii 69–77, 1913 (*11*).

F. L. Jones: 'Shelley's Revised Will', *MLN* 542–44, 1944 (*11*).

John Keats: *The Letters* (*1814–21*), ed. H. E. Rollins, 2 vols., Cambridge, 1958 (*3, 6*).

L. H. Kendall: 'Leigh Hunt on Shelley's Missing Will', *Keats–Shelley Journal* xv 6–7, 1966 (*11*).

[W. S. Landor]: *Idyllia Heroica Decem . . . edit Savagius Landor*, Pisa, 1820 (*7*).

W. S. Landor: *Imaginary Conversations* iii (Florentine, English Visitor and Landor), 1828 (in *Works*, ed. T. Earle Welby, 1927, ix, 127–28) (*6*).

E. C. McAleer: *The Sensitive Plant*, a Life of Lady Mount Cashell, 1958, University of North Carolina (*6–10*).

L. A. Marchand: 'Trelawny on the Death of Shelley', *Keats–Shelley Memorial Bulletin* iv 9–34, 1952 (*10*).

L. A. Marchand: 'A Note on the Burning of Shelley's Body', *Keats–Shelley Memorial Bulletin* vi 1–3, 1955 (*10*).

William H. Marshall: *Byron, Shelley, Hunt, and 'The Liberal'*, Philadelphia, 1960 (*8–9*).

Richard Monckton Milnes (Lord Houghton): *The Life, Letters, and Literary Remains of John Keats*, 1848 (*3*).

Thomas Moore: *The Letters*, ed. Wilfred S. Dowden, 2 vols., Oxford, 1964 (*8, 9*).

Elizabeth Nitchie: *The Reverend Colonel Finch*, New York, 1940 (*5–6*).

Iris Origo: *A Measure of Love*, 1957 (Allegra, *3–9*, The Lady in the Gondola, *4*).

C. Kegan Paul: *William Godwin, his Friends and Contemporaries*, 1876 (*3*).

John William Polidori: *The Diary* (1816), ed. W. M. Rossetti, 1911 (*1–3*).

J. J. F. Poujolat: *Toscane et Rome, Correspondance d'Italie*, Paris, 1840 (*10*).

Henry Crabb Robinson: *The Correspondence . . . with the Wordsworth Circle* (*1808–66*), ed. Edith Morley, 2 vols., 1927 (*7*).

Jean-Jacques Rousseau: *Julia, or The New Eloisa*, translated from the French, Edinburgh, 1794 (*1*).

Robert Southey: *The Correspondence . . . with Caroline Bowles*, ed. E. Dowden, 1881 (*6*).

Terence Spencer: *Fair Greece Sad Relic, Literary Philhellenism from Shakespeare to Byron*, 1954 (*7*).

Harriet Beecher Stowe: *Lady Byron Vindicated*, 1870 (*4*).

John Taaffe: *A Comment on the Divine Comedy of Dante Alighieri*, 1822 (*8*).

Felice Tribolati: *Saggi Critici e Biografici* ('Lord Byron a Pisa'; 'Un Processo civile di Lord Byron'; 'Lord Byron a Livorno'), Pisa, 1891 (*10*).

E. Viviani della Robbia: *Vita di una Donna*, Florence, 1936 (*7*).

[John Watkins]: *Memoirs of the Life and Writings of Lord Byron*, 1822 (*10*).

Index